Praise for
Origins of the Specious

"Accessible, conversational and commonsensical, full of witty and clever turns of phrase and historical insight. Wordplay abounds on every page. . . . O'Conner and Kellerman clearly are having fun."
—*The Washington Post*

"*Origins of the Specious* adeptly demolishes plausible but insupportable etymologies . . . and other obliquely derived phrases and words. . . . O'Conner [offers] characteristically good advice."
—*The New York Times Book Review*

"Bestselling word maven O'Conner (*Woe Is I*) is that rare grammarian who values clear, natural expression over the mindless application of rules. In her latest compendium, she debunks the hoariest of false strictures. . . . Writers will appreciate O'Conner's liberating, common-sense approach to the language, and readers the entertaining sprightliness of her prose."
—*Publishers Weekly*

"This wide-ranging exercise in debunkery . . . would be a revelation to your favorite new graduate, and it should offer even a well-informed wordie something new to disbelieve."
—*The Boston Globe*

"The authors assault illusions about language with such élan that the who. muses. . . . Besides opening up a lexical treasury, the authors teach substantive linguistic lessons. . . . No one has ever coaxed more fun out of dictionaries."   —*Booklist*

"One of those rare books that hits the sweet spot, combining a light-hearted and easy style with rigorous research and useful notes. Any language lover should put this one near the top of their must-read list."   —Wordorigins.org

"An educational, trivia filled book about the English language. A lighthearted, fun-filled discussion of our fickle, capricious language."   —*Writers' Journal*

"Informative and entertaining."   —*Columbia Journalism Review*

"*Origins of the Specious* is a great read, even for grammar gurus. It's cleverly written and answers those burning questions we all have about the English Language."
                              —*The Post and Courier* (Charleston, S.C.)

"Amusing, surprising, delightful, lively . . . For those who love words and language, *Origins of the Specious* is a great read. . . . To the horror of purists and traditionalists, [the authors] delve into language as a living, changing thing."
                              —*The Free Lance-Star* (Fredericksburg, Va.)

"*Origins* is a must read for any language lover or trivia buff."
                              —Examiner.com

"You're likely to find *Origins of the Specious* shelved with the grammar books, but it might just as easily be stowed with the humor. . . . O'Conner and Kellerman are wonderful, straightforward prose writers who excel at turns of the phrase which keep the reading light but memorable. This is the sort of book that you'll keep consulting long after you finish it."

—bookotron.com

"It's right there on page 54: 'It's better to be understood than to be correct'—pull that out the next time someone corrects your grandma. This tour de force of our beautifully corrupted language is both. And dull it ain't. If you're planning to buy just one book of etymology this year, you've got it right in your hand."

—GARRISON KEILLOR

"Every bartender in the land should have a copy of this vastly amusing and highly informative book. Then when some tipsy bore declares that 'posh' derives from 'port out, starboard home,' or that you must never say 'disinterested' when you mean 'uninterested,' he can bring it out from behind the jar of cocktail cherries and smack him on the head with it."

—SIMON WINCHESTER, author of The Professor and the Madman

"A delightful romp through the minefields of the English language. With common sense and uncommon wit, O'Conner and Kellerman solve more mysteries than all the *Law & Order* series combined. *Origins of the Specious* will teach you why it is OK to bravely split an infinitive, why using 'ain't' ain't so bad, and why ending a sentence with a preposition is where it's at."

—DAVID FELDMAN, author of the "Imponderables" book series

"A witty and informative guide to the perplexities of the English language."

—STEPHEN MILLER, author of The Peculiar Life of Sundays

"[A] stunning success . . . [O'Conner] is a knowledgeable linguist who is also a wise human being."

—Sewanee Review

Origins
OF THE
Specious

Origins

OF THE

Specious

Myths and Misconceptions

of the English Language

Patricia T. O'Conner
and Stewart Kellerman

RANDOM HOUSE TRADE PAPERBACKS

NEW YORK

2010 Random House Trade Paperback Edition

Published in the United States by Random House Trade Paperbacks, an imprint of The Random House Publishing Group, a division of Random House, Inc., New York.

RANDOM HOUSE and colophon are registered trademarks of Random House, Inc.

Originally published in hardcover in the United States by Random House, an imprint of The Random House Publishing Group, a division of Random House, Inc., in 2009.

Grateful acknowledgment is made to the following for permission to reprint previously published material:

The Michael Barson Collection: Excerpt from *Flywheel, Shyster, and Flywheel* by Michael Barson (New York: Pantheon Books, 1988), copyright © 1988 by Michael Barson. Reprinted by permission of The Michael Barson Collection.
Campbell Thomson & McLaughlin Ltd.: Excerpt from a limerick by Stanley J. Sharpless, © Stanley J. Sharpless. Reprinted by permission of Campbell Thomson & McLaughlin Ltd on behalf of the copyright owner.
HarperCollins Publishers: Eight lines of verse from page 30 of *The Notebooks of Raymond Chandler* by Raymond Chandler, copyright © 1976 by Helga Greene for the Estate of Raymond Chandler. Reprinted by permission of HarperCollins Publishers.
Scribner, a division of Simon & Schuster, Inc., and A. P. Watt Ltd.: Four lines from "When You Are Old" from *The Collected Works of W. B. Yeats, Vol. 1: The Poems, Revised,* edited by Richard J. Finneran (New York: Scribner, 1997). Rights outside of the United States are controlled by A. P. Watt Ltd. Reprinted by permission of Scribner, a division of Simon & Schuster, Inc., and A. P. Watt Ltd. on behalf of Gráinne Yeats.

LIBRARY OF CONGRESS CATALOGING-IN-PUBLICATION DATA

O'Conner, Patricia T.
Origins of the specious: myths and misconceptions of the English language/
Patricia T. O'Conner and Stewart Kellerman.
p. cm.
Includes bibliographical references and index.
ISBN 978-0-8129-7810-0
eBook ISBN 978-1-5883-6856-0

1. English language—Etymology. 2. English language—Variation.
3. English language—Usage. I. Kellerman, Stewart. II. Title.
PE1574.O36 2009
422—dc22
2008036277

Printed in the United States of America

www.atrandom.com

2 4 6 8 9 7 5 3 1

Book design by Christopher M. Zucker

For Dan Green

Contents

Authors' Note

Two people wrote this book, but it's been our experience that two people can't talk at the same time—at
least not on the page. So we've chosen to write *Origins
of the Specious* in one voice and from Pat's point of view.

Introduction

My family was the first on our block to get a television set—a mahogany Philco console with rabbit ears protruding at odd angles from somewhere in the back. It was an imposing piece of furniture that occupied a place of honor in the living room. This was the early 1950s, and I was about two years old.

My TV watching was rationed, more out of necessity than principle, since it required an adult to turn on the set, fiddle with the knobs, and adjust the rabbit ears for maximum reception. To a toddler, the whole undertaking seemed very grown-up—like reading, or driving a car—and was invested with a certain solemnity.

Over time, a few programs became weekly events: *Our Miss Brooks, Your Hit Parade,* and *What's My Line?* Two of the panelists, Dorothy Kilgallen and Arlene Francis, were the most dazzling creatures I'd ever seen. But the shows that made the deepest impression on me were the specials that were broadcast from the Metropolitan Opera and the NBC Opera Theater. My mother never missed them.

It wasn't the music that made them so memorable—it was my child's-eye view of history. Until I was six or seven years old, I thought that ordinary speech must have been a recent invention, because in the olden days (the days of *Carmen* and *The Magic Flute*), people apparently didn't know how to talk. It seemed that they had to sing whatever they wanted to say. This was my first major misconception about language. (The second was that my mother had invented "scrumptious," a word I regarded as too silly to be real.)

All of us, I'm convinced, have similar misconceptions. When we grow up, our mistakes get more sophisticated—that's all.

Shortly after my first book, *Woe Is I,* came out in 1996, people started sending me their questions, observations, and grievances about language. When I began appearing regularly on WNYC, a public radio station in New York, the comments multiplied. And they multiplied again when I started a language blog. My in-box was overflowing. To my surprise, every other message seemed to involve a myth, misunderstanding, or mystery about English. If the emailer wasn't misinformed, then it was his daughter-in-law or her boss or a golf partner or even the word maven herself.

And so an idea was born. I had a ready-made source of information: all that correspondence from readers and listeners. Why not write a book to save them from themselves? No one, especially a language junkie, wants to sound like a fool and risk public humiliation. (I know this from personal experience. I once embarrassed myself on the radio by misleading listeners about the origin of the word "jeep.") Besides, it would be fun to collect and correct the more amusing, mystifying, and startling misuses of our language.

No subject was safe. Many people insisted that "no room to swing a cat" referred to the cat-o'-nine-tails once used on British warships. Quite a few, I found, were puzzled by what they took to be "in high dungeon"; one even imagined a dungeon on stilts. Still others thought the word "crap" could be traced to a man named Thomas Crapper, the supposed inventor of the flush toilet. Some believed that "posh" was an acronym for "port out, starboard home." Would-be sticklers scolded me whenever I split an infinitive on the air or (gasp!) ended a sentence with a preposition. Yet all those are misconceptions, even that business about what not to end a sentence with. Where do these ideas come from, and why do the persistent ones persist?

In some cases, we imagine interesting acronyms for words with ambiguous or prosaic roots. The origin of "posh," for instance, has never been pinned down. In other cases, our ears play tricks on us, especially when unfamiliar words resemble more familiar ones. "Dudgeon," a case in point, is frequently misheard as "dungeon."

Other mistakes have more complicated histories. Mr. Crapper, for instance, did exist and did sell flush toilets. But he didn't invent them, and the word "crap" was in use when he himself was barely potty trained. As for those bogus "rules" against splitting an infinitive and ending a sentence with a preposition, blame a gang of eighteenth- and nineteenth-century Latinists who stubbornly and snobbishly tried to make English more like their favorite language.

In fact, we've been bungling the mother tongue since the days of *Beowulf*. A medieval scribe once miscopied a single letter in a list of kitchen terms and transformed a cooking utensil into a ferocious hunting dog. He wrote *hrodhhund* (Old English for a mastiff or hunting hound) instead of *brodhhund* (believed to be a metal rack for simmering pots of broth). That one had scholars scratching their heads for many a year.

Sometimes, a centuries-old blunder can lead to a modern one. A fifteenth-century mistranslation by the Dutch scholar Erasmus is responsible for the expression "call a spade a spade." (The original Greek meant, roughly, "call a trough a trough.") Today, many people who don't know the etymology—that is, the history—of this phrase unjustly condemn it as racist. Thus a myth is born.

Even language experts aren't immune to these boo-boos. None other than Samuel Johnson, who wrote the great-grandmother of all dictionaries, is responsible for one of them. He suggested that the word "nincompoop" was derived from *non compos mentis,* Latin for "mentally incompetent." Sorry, Dr. Johnson. The precise origin is unknown, but "nincompoop" is probably related, like "ninny," to the word "innocent."

Perhaps the biggest myth of all is that English never changes, that it's immutable, like the multiplication tables or the boiling point of H_2O. But its ability to renew itself is what has kept English alive and kicking—especially kicking. Words evolve over time, and legitimately so. A "wife," for instance, was once simply a woman. The word didn't mean a married woman until 150 years after it first appeared. And "flair" once meant an odor or the sense of smell; a dog with keen "flair" had a good nose. But today the original definition exists only in old dictionaries, those repositories of linguistic fossils. Not every fossil is dead, though. The spelling of "fiery"—which many people think makes no sense whatever—is a living fossil, a leftover from the thirteenth century, when "fire" was spelled "fier."

The truth is that English is all about change. It's as absorbent as a sponge, as flexible as a rubber band, and it simply won't stand still—no matter where it's spoken. I'm sometimes asked, "When did we Americans lose our British accent?" Answer: We didn't lose it. The British once spoke pretty much as we do. What we think of as the plummy British accent is a fairly recent happening in a language that welcomes happenings. Fortunately, there's no English equivalent of the French Academy (though the idea was floated a time or two). That's all we need—

a lot of officious bureaucrats telling us what's English and what's not. Besides, it wouldn't work in a million years. English is too ungovernable and too, well, democratic. Rival words and usages are allowed to fight it out.

Change may be our language's greatest strength, but it's also the source of a lot of unnecessary angst. Many card-carrying sticklers dig in their heels about the supposed misuse of a word that has in fact taken on a new meaning ("data") or pronunciation ("flaccid") or usage ("hopefully"). Others complain about words like "synergy" and "doable" that look like brash newcomers but are actually venerable old warhorses newly revived. Sometimes outright errors (like pronouncing "niche" as NEESH) get so entrenched that they not only become acceptable but virtually drive out the original.

People often ask me who decides what's right. The answer is we all do. Everybody has a vote. The "rules" are simply what educated speakers generally accept as right or wrong at a given time. When enough of us decide that "cool" can mean "hot," change happens. Those who object (as I often do) get dragged along, gnashing their teeth. Like it or not, correctness is determined by common practice, even when a new usage collides with an old established rule. If enough people break it, the rule is dumped. As more and more people misused "agenda," for example, it was transformed from a plural word for the items on a list to a singular word for the list itself. And in recent years it's taken on an additional personality: "agenda" has become a loaded word for an underlying scheme or purpose or ideology. This is how today's blunder in spelling or meaning may become tomorrow's standard usage.

A slip of the tongue can lead to a new usage too. So many Americans mangled "lingerie" that now the most common pronunciation (lawn-zhuh-RAY) is a Frenchified mélange unrecognizable to a Parisian. And so many people mistakenly stuck an *n* into "restaurateur" that dictionaries now list "restauranteur" as an acceptable spelling. I'm still kicking and screaming about that one, but a lot of good it does me.

You may kick and scream too, when you find that many of your most cherished beliefs about English are as phony as a three-dollar bill. Hey, I know the feeling! I was startled more than a few times myself while tracking down popular misconceptions for this book. Here you'll find myths about grammar, etymology, usage, political correctness, fractured French, British superiority, gutter language, and plain old bloopers.

Keep an open mind and expect the unexpected. Feel free to grumble too. Democracy can be exasperating when you're on the losing side. But English is a work in progress and always will be, especially now that it's not just British or American or Canadian or Australian or . . . you get the idea. English is a global language—*the* global language—and it's being reinvented every day all over the world. It's never finished, and that's its greatest strength. We owe much of the language we have today to the liberties we've taken in the past. And we're still taking liberties. As English reinvents itself, we'll have winners and losers. May the best words win.

Origins
OF THE
Specious

Chapter 1

Stiff Upper Lips

Why Can't the British Be More Like Us?

Winston Churchill gave the folks at Bartlett's plenty of fodder for their books of *Familiar Quotations:* "so much owed by so many to so few" . . . "blood, toil, tears, and sweat" . . . "this was their finest hour" . . . and more. But he didn't describe England and America as "two nations divided by a common language," though thousands of websites say so. What he did, though, was pass along a great story about how the two nations were indeed divided by their two Englishes at a meeting of Allied leaders during World War II.

"The enjoyment of a common language was of course a supreme advantage in all British and American discussions," Churchill wrote in *The Second World War.* No interpreters were needed, for one thing, but there were "differences of expression, which in the early days led to an amusing incident." The British wanted to raise an urgent matter, he said, and told the Americans they wished to "table it" (that is, bring it to the table). But to the Americans, tabling something meant putting it aside. "A long and even acrimonious argument ensued," Churchill wrote, "before both parties realised that they were agreed on the merits and wanted the same thing."

I'm no mind reader, but I'll bet the Brits at the table felt their English was the real thing, while the Yanks felt apologetic about theirs. If there's one thing our two peoples agree on, it's that British English is purer than its American offshoot. My in-box gets pinged every week or two by a Brit with his knickers in a twist or an American with an inferiority complex. A typical comment: "Why do you refer to 'American English' and 'British English'? Surely it should be 'American English' and 'proper English.'" Ouch! Is their English really more proper—that is, purer—than ours? Which one is more like the English spoken in the 1600s when the Colonies and the mother country began diverging linguistically?

First of all, "American English" and "British English" are how authorities refer to the two major branches of English, and reflect the changes in the language since the Colonies separated themselves linguistically from England. The differences are many, but they're minor from a grammarian's point of view. Most have to do with spelling, pronunciation, and usage. English grammar is English grammar no matter where you live, despite a few exceptions here and there.

The truth is that neither English is more proper. In some respects American English is purer than British English: We've preserved some usages and spellings and pronunciations that have changed over time in Britain. But the reverse is also true. The British have preserved much that has changed on our side of the Atlantic. In many cases, it's nearly impossible to tell which branch has history on its side. Take "table," the word that gave those Allied leaders such grief. In the eighteenth century, the phrase "to lay on the table" could mean either to bring up or to defer. By the nineteenth century, the Brits had preserved one of those meanings and the Yanks the other. So the verb "table" meant one thing there and quite another here.

In case you're wondering who should get the credit for that crack about "two nations divided by a common language," the answer is nobody exactly. George Bernard Shaw was quoted in 1942 as saying, "England and America are two countries separated by the same language." But nobody is certain where or when he said it. What we do know is that Oscar Wilde said the same thing in different words in 1887: "We have really everything in common with America nowadays, except, of course, language."

Sound Bites

We've all seen *My Fair Lady,* on stage or screen or iPod or whatever, and we all have our favorite scenes. One of mine is the bit where Henry Higgins, the arrogant professor of phonetics, first encounters the flower girl Eliza Doolittle at Covent Garden and is appalled by her Cockney accent. Higgins belittles her for turning the language of Shakespeare and Milton into "such disgusting and depressing noise," and she screeches, "Ah-ah-aw-aw-oo-oo." Fed up with her "detestable boo-hooing," he sings, "Why can't the English learn to speak?"

So what would a real Professor Higgins make of the way Americans speak? We don't have to look hard to find the answer, and many apologetic Americans may be surprised to hear it. Professor William A. Read, a distinguished linguist, put it this way in a journal of philology: "The pronunciation of educated Americans is in many respects more archaic than that of educated Englishmen." This should be no surprise, he said, since "the phonetic basis of American pronunciation rests chiefly on the speech of Englishmen of the seventeenth and eighteenth centuries." And those Englishmen sounded much like the Americans of today. The "English accent" that we now associate with educated British speech is a relatively new phenomenon and didn't develop until after the American Revolution.

Look at the way the letter *r* is pronounced (or not pronounced), perhaps the most important difference in the speech of educated people in the US and the UK. Since Anglo-Saxon days, the English had pronounced the *r* in words like "far," "mother," "world," "church," and "mourn." English speakers on both sides of the Atlantic pronounced the *r*'s in these words when the Colonies broke away from England. Most Americans still do. But educated people in Britain began dropping their *r*'s in the late eighteenth and early nineteenth centuries. The Americans most likely to drop their *r*'s were those, like New Englanders, who had strong commercial and social ties with the mother country.

This dropping of *r*'s in Britain didn't happen all of a sudden, and the sticklers of the day didn't take it lying down. "The perception that the language was 'losing a letter' was a cause of profound upset to some writers," the linguist David Crystal has written. The poet Keats, for example, was cruelly upbraided by critics for rhyming "thoughts" with "sorts," and "thorns" with "fawns." Lord Byron blamed a critical article for hastening Keats's death in 1821: "'Tis strange the mind, that very fiery particle, / Should let itself be snuffed out by an Article." But by the time Keats died, the dropped *r* was a standard feature of educated British pronunciation.

The other letter that's a dead giveaway in telling a Brit from a Yank is the *a* in a word like "past." We all know how an American would say it—with an *a* like the one in "cat." And as anyone who's watched *Masterpiece Theatre* can tell you, the standard

British pronunciation is PAHST. But it wasn't always so. The Brits used to say it the same way Americans do now. Here again, the Americans stuck with an old way of speaking, one the British abandoned about the same time they dropped their *r*'s.

The *a,* like the *r,* has ping-ponged in British pronunciation. Until the 1500s, the English did indeed pronounce words like "bath" and "laugh" and "dance" with an "ah." But in the sixteenth century they began pronouncing the *a* in what we now consider the American way (as in "cat"). So things remained for the next two or three hundred years. This is the *a* that went to America on the *Mayflower* in 1620. And this is the *a* that both the Redcoats and the Colonists used during the Revolutionary War. Not until the 1780s did Londoners begin pronouncing their *a*'s like "ahs" again, and for a few decades the broad *a* and the short *a* battled it out. But by the early 1800s, educated Britain was saying BAHTH and LAHF and DAHNCE.

That's also about when literate Britons started pronouncing the *h* in "herb." Before the nineteenth century, both the English and Americans pronounced it ERB. In fact, the word was usually spelled "erbe" for the first few hundred years after it was borrowed from the Old French *erbe* in the 1200s. The *h* was added later as a nod to the Latin original (*herba,* or grass), but the letter was silent. Today, Americans pronounce "herb" the way Shakespeare did, with a silent *h,* while the Bard wouldn't recognize the word in the mouths of the English.

Speaking of aitches, some British speakers, especially on the telly, use "an" before words like "historic" or "hotel," and some Anglophiles over here are slavishly imitating them. For shame! Usage manuals on both sides of the Atlantic say the article to use is "a," not "an." The rule is that we use "a" before a word that begins with an *h* that's pronounced and "an" before a word that starts with a silent *h.* And dictionaries in both Britain and the

United States say the *h* should be pronounced in "historic" and "hotel" as well as "heroic," "habitual," "hypothesis," "horrendous," and some other problem h-words.

When the British aren't adding or subtracting an *h*, stretching out an *a*, or dropping an *r*, they're chopping off whole syllables from words like "secretary," "necessary," "military," "extraordinary," "satisfactory," "literary," and others. "Secretary," for example, is shortened to SEC-ruh-tree, cutting off the next-to-last syllable. Americans, on the other hand, pronounce all four syllables (SEC-ruh-teh-ree), as the British did until the eighteenth century. We know this because British textbooks of the time recommended pronouncing all the syllables. But by 1780, the British educator Thomas Sheridan was complaining about people who spoke too quickly and dropped syllables, leading to "indistinct articulation." In *A General Dictionary of the English Language,* Sheridan suggested that the guilty parties "pronounce the unaccented syllables more fully than necessary, till they are cured of it." The cure didn't work. If it had, the British would be saying "necessary" today as Americans do, instead of NESS-uh-sree. No doubt Sheridan would have found that satisfactory.

Back to the Future

Prince Charles's mom may be the queen of England, but he has a lot to learn about the Queen's English. In 1995, the prince complained that Americans were corrupting the English language. In a speech to the British Council, an institution that promotes British culture and the English language, Charles said Americans "tend to invent all sorts of nouns and verbs and make words that shouldn't be." If the English don't protect their language, he said, "the whole thing can get rather a mess."

"We must act now to insure that English—and that, to my mind, means English English—maintains its position as the world language well into the next century," he said.

Balderdash. And no, we didn't invent that one. Both Britons and Americans have invented all sorts of words since the two languages went their own ways a few hundred years ago. (We rub out mistakes with an "eraser" while they use a "rubber"; we stow a spare "tire" in the "trunk" and they keep a "tyre" in the "boot"; we take the "elevator" and they use the "lift.") But many of the words that Anglo-purists like Prince Charles condemn us for are actually words that we've preserved from the English spoken in the 1600s and 1700s, before the Great Divide.

Let's look at the two English words for the season when leaves turn, wheat is harvested, and the days get shorter. Americans call it "fall" or "autumn." The British call it "autumn" and think "fall" is a Yankee eccentricity. The truth is that we all once had two words, but the British lost one along the way while Americans preserved them both. Interestingly, the Brits discarded the Anglo-Saxon one and kept the one they got from the French. The word "fall" has been part of English since the reign of King Alfred the Great in the ninth century, though it wasn't used for the season until the sixteenth century. It made its eloquent debut in a 1545 book on archery: "Spring tyme, Somer, faule of the leafe, and winter." The word "autumn," on the other hand, was borrowed in the fourteenth century from Old French, which got it from the Latin *autumnus*.

To the Londoner who lives in a "flat," the word "apartment" sounds like an Americanism, and a clunky one at that. But "apartment" was the usual word for a suite of rooms in seventeenth-century England, and that's the word the Colonists brought with them. The British didn't start using "flat" for a dwelling until the 1820s or so. By the end of the nineteenth century, the lease was up on "apartment."

Another so-called Americanism is the use of "mad" to mean angry. To the British "mad" means insane, and any other usage is crazy. But this is one more example of Yankee preservation. The word "mad" had been used in Britain since the fourteenth century to mean both insane and angry. Americans kept both meanings, but British usage guides dropped one in the late eighteenth century.

Americans have saved many, many other words that the English have lost. We both used "druggist" in the 1600s. Americans still do (as do the Scots), but the English began switching to "chemist" in the eighteenth century. Both of us once walked on a "sidewalk" or a "pavement," but Americans now tread on one and the British on the other.

We all used to cook on a "stove" or a "range," and Americans still do, but the British decided in the nineteenth century to make their bangers and mash on a "cooker." And at one time, we both used a "skillet" as well as a "frying pan." We kept the two of them, but the British threw out the "skillet." Is your head spinning? Then how about this one: Our kids take rides on a "merry-go-round," while theirs go on a "roundabout." Which is older? The newer one is just a roundabout way of saying "merry-go-round."

Noah and the Flood

Why does an ill-*humored* American hypochondriac eat lots of *fiber* and *dramatize* his aches and pains, while (or, rather, *whilst*) his ill-*humoured* British counterpart wolfs down the *fibre* and *dramatises*? We can largely blame two cranky old men—Noah Webster and Samuel Johnson—for this state of affairs.

Many of the words that are now spelled one way here and another there had multiple spellings once upon a time. When the two lexicographers wrote their influential dictionaries, Webster chose one and Johnson another. But the story isn't as simple as that. Johnson adopted many Frenchified spellings that had been introduced in Britain in the eighteenth century. But Webster often stuck with older spellings, the ones the Colonists had brought from England in the seventeenth century.

Webster wanted, among other things, to purge English of words "clothed with the French livery" and rid spelling of the "egregious corruptions" imposed by Francophiles. He considered the eleventh-century conquest of Britain by French-speaking Norman princes the "dark ages of English." Johnson, on the other hand, wanted to preserve the spelling of his day, even if "it is in itself inaccurate, and tolerated rather than chosen." He was well aware of the Gallic corruptions but chose not to fiddle with them "without a reason sufficient to balance the inconvenience of change." In other words, if it ain't broke, don't fix it. And Johnson wasn't big on fixing: "All change is of itself an evil, which ought not to be hazarded but for evident advantage." Excuse me if I mix a few metaphors here, but English was a fine kettle of fish in those days, and these were two very complicated curmudgeons with more opinions than you could shake a stick at. So here comes an abridged version of the many differences between British and American orthography (the art of proper spelling, from the Greek *orthos* for "straight" and *graphein* for "write").

The story of "color/colour," "honor/honour," "labor/labour," "vigor/vigour," and similar words is anything but straight. The spellings have zigged and zagged over the years between the Latin ending -*or* and the Norman French -*our*. In fact, Shakespeare flip-flopped on this, using "honor" and "honour," "humor" and "humour," and so on. The two endings were common on both sides of the Atlantic in the 1700s and 1800s, when our great lexicographers decided to tidy up this messy situation. Johnson usually picked the *-our* endings for his British dictionary of 1755, and Webster generally went with the simpler *-or* ones for his American dictionary of 1828.

It was a similarly messy story with "center/centre," "fiber/fibre," "luster/lustre," "theater/theatre," etc. The spellings went this way and that over the years, but *-er* endings were common for many of these words when the early Colonists took their English with them to the New World. The pendulum had swung back to French-influenced *-re* endings in Britain when Johnson was putting his dictionary together, so he went with those. Webster, for his part, considered "centre" and company "outlaws in orthography" that had strayed from proper English, so he stuck with *-er* endings.

You've undoubtedly noticed that verbs ending in *-ize* over here usually end with *-ise* over there. Which English is more Englishy? The *-ize* ending is the traditional one and the only proper one, according to the *Oxford English Dictionary,* which ought to know. The first of these words to enter English, "baptize," appeared in the thirteenth century with its *z* intact, and was later joined by "authorize" (fourteenth century), "organize" (fifteenth), "characterize" (sixteenth), "civilize" (seventeenth), and many others. The *-ise* spellings, for the most part, weren't used much until the eighteenth century or later, and we can't pin those on Johnson. The culprits were Francophiles enamored of French verbs like *civiliser, dramatiser, organiser,* and so on. But, as the *OED* says, "there is no reason why in English the special French spelling should be followed." So if an Englishman complains about the *z*'s in your verbs, throw the book at him.

As for "whilst," it's rarely heard in the United States, and for good reason. Although it's common in British English, it means exactly the same thing as "while." And though "whilst" has an air of antiquity about it, "while" is actually the older word. "While" goes back to about the year 1000 (spelled "hwile"), according to the *OED,* and "whilst" dates from the late 1300s. The same is true for "amongst" and "amidst." They too are commonly used in Britain, while Americans use "among" and "amid." Here again, the American preference happens to be for the older word. "Among" dates to about 1000, and "amongst" to 1250; "amid" is from circa 975, and "amidst" from about 1300. Johnson and Webster, who didn't enter this fray, accepted both versions of these words.

I sometimes wonder what the two old lexicographers would make of today's English, with verbs like "google," adjectives like "phat," nouns like "earbud," and phrases like "erectile dysfunction." Not to mention slang, which is different wherever English is spoken. The immovable Dr. Johnson would probably harrumph and return to the grave. Webster, a forward-looking reformer at heart, would want to stick around and see what happens next. "It is quite impossible," he once wrote, "to stop the progress of language—it is like the course of the Mississippi, the motion of which, at times, is scarcely perceptible; yet even then it possesses a momentum quite irresistible. Words and expressions will be forced into use, in spite of all the exertions of all the writers in the world."

Past Perfect

In 1724, Hugh Jones, an Englishman teaching at the College of William and Mary in Virginia, observed that "the *Planters,* and even the *Native Negroes,*" spoke English as well as anyone in the English-speaking world. Lord Adam Gordon, a Scottish nobleman visiting Philadelphia in the 1760s, said "the propriety of

Language here surprized me much, the English tongue being spoken by all ranks, in a degree of purity and perfection surpassing any, but the polite part of London."

These were not isolated opinions. William Eddis, a British customs official in Annapolis, Maryland, confessed that he was "totally at a loss" to explain why the "strange intermixture" of people in the Colonies hadn't corrupted the language. "The language of the immediate descendants of such a promiscuous ancestry is perfectly uniform, and unadulterated," he wrote in a 1770 letter. And Nicholas Cresswell, a young Englishman who was visiting the Colonies when the Revolution broke out, was startled at how well the Americans spoke English. "Though the inhabitants of this Country are composed of different Nations and different languages, yet it is very remarkable that they in general speak better English than the English do," he wrote in his diary.

As the years passed, though, the British strayed from the English spoken in the eighteenth century, and derided as "Americanisms" some of the fine old examples that we kept alive. That's the thanks we get for preserving some of the language the Brits once praised for its "purity and perfection"!

Perhaps no alleged Americanism gets an Englishman's goat more than the word "gotten." In Britain, the only acceptable past participle of the verb "get" is "got"; in the United States we use "gotten" in some cases and "got" in others, depending on our meaning. At one time, English routinely used both past participles. But after the two branches of English split and began developing in different directions, Americans retained both forms while the British abandoned "gotten." (The old form survives in Britain in the expression "ill-gotten gains.") The result is that Americans have a nuance of meaning the British have lost. When we say, "Fiona has got a sequined bustier," we mean she owns one. When we say, "Fiona has gotten a sequined bustier," we mean she's recently acquired one. There's a difference.

I often mention "gotten" as an example of old grammar that we've preserved and the British have lost. The truth is that "gotten" sticks out only because the grammatical differences between us are so few and so piddling. For one thing, we tend to use regular—and often older—past tenses ("burned," "learned," "spoiled," "smelled"), while the British like irregular—and often newer—endings ("burnt," "learnt," "spoilt," "smelt"). For another, we say things like "he's in the hospital," and "she went on a holiday," while they use the more modern, article-free "he's in hospital," and "she went on holiday."

What's more, we say "the government is divided," while the British are more likely to say "the government are divided"— a more recent treatment of collective nouns. We also use the subjunctive a bit more than the Brits do. We say, "I insist he *get* a job," for example, but the British prefer "I insist he *gets* a job." We also have more ways to refer to the recent past. We say, "I just had lunch" or "I've just had lunch," while the British prefer the latter. Punctuation, anyone? We always put periods and commas inside quotation marks, the way the British once did, but now they sometimes put them in and sometimes put them out (never mind the details).

Pretty small stuff. And getting smaller still. "There never has been any major linguistic difference between British English and American English," the linguist Jonathan Culpeper wrote in his *History of English*. "Moreover, the last hundred years or so have seen increasing similarity between British and American English. This has partly been due to ever-improving communication systems, but also to the impact of American culture, notably through television and film."

This is not a one-way street, though. We influence them and

they influence us. We seem to be using the subjunctive less these days, for instance, while they're becoming more flexible about the recent past. We've adopted their expression "gone missing," and they've accepted our use of "I guess" to mean "I suppose" or "I'm kind of sure." At one time, the British had sneered at this casual use of "guess" as an Americanism, insisting that "guess" should strictly mean to judge, estimate, or theorize. But no more. Besides, it wasn't an Americanism in the first place. An example from Shakespeare's *Henry VI:* "Not all together; better far, I guess, / That we do make our entrance several ways." But here's an Americanism for you: the expression "stiff upper lip." Yup, it was coined by Phoebe Cary, a nineteenth-century poet from Cincinnati.

Don't get me wrong. I'm not suggesting that American English is purer than British English. We've both preserved some of the old, and we've both contributed some of the new. We share a common language, but both branches are still evolving. They couldn't possibly have remained identical, since the people who determine common usage are separated (and have been for quite some time) by a rather wide ocean.

Chapter 2

Grammar Moses

Forget These Commandments

A few years ago, I got a call from an editor at *The New York Times*. He had a news flash from Oxford University Press, which publishes the venerable *Oxford English Dictionary* and scores of smaller upstarts: Two new Oxford dictionaries, one in the United States and one in Britain, were saying it was OK to freely split infinitives!

Newspapers on both sides of the Atlantic were abuzz. (It was a slow news week.) Would I write an analysis of this ground-breaking development in the world of language? Sure, I said, I'd be willing to write about it—for the umpteenth time. It's never been wrong to "split" an infinitive. That bogus rule is the most infamous member of a gang of myths that grammarians have been trying to rub out for a century and a half: Don't end a sentence with a preposition! Don't begin one with a conjunction! Don't use a double negative! Don't use "none" as a plural!

Many of these don'ts were concocted in the eighteenth and nineteenth centuries by overzealous Latinists in a misguided attempt to force English to play by the rules of Latin. This makes about as much sense as having the Chicago Cubs play by the same rules as the Green Bay Packers. English is a Germanic language, like Dutch, Swedish, Norwegian, Danish, and of course German. It's not a Romance language like French, Spanish, Italian, and Portuguese, all derived from Latin. As you may imagine, a Germanic language like English and a Romance language like Spanish are put together very differently. Two of the most obvious differences involve word order (American presidents live in the White House, while Argentine presidents live in the Casa Rosada) and verb patterns (both I and we "speak" English, while *yo* "*hablo*" and *nosotros* "*hablamos*" *español*).

But back to the split infinitive. It's a nonissue, so why all the fuss about those two new dictionaries? The editors at Oxford were just as surprised as I was. In fact, the latest dictionary comments on the subject weren't all that different from those in previous Oxford reference books. It turns out that Oxford's publicity department went overboard in its sales pitch. "Infinitives should be split" shouted a press release introducing the British dictionary. The breathless headline hyped an issue that wasn't news and mangled the dictionary's advice besides. Not surprisingly, the news media ate it up.

"You'd think we were splitting the atom or something," an Oxford editor told me.

In short, many of our most beloved ideas about English are bunkum. So let's debunk 'em.

Splitting Headache

If you like Raymond Chandler, you'll like this story. It was back in the 1940s and he was writing an article about Hollywood for *The Atlantic Monthly.* Margaret Mutch, a copy editor and proofreader at the magazine, presumed to "correct" his hardboiled prose. Not a good move. Chandler fired off a letter to her boss: "When I split an infinitive, God damn it, I split it so it will remain split." And so it remained.

Chandler is in good company. Writers have been happily "splitting" infinitives since the 1200s, including such biggies as Shakespeare, Milton, Donne, and Wordsworth. This was considered perfectly acceptable until the mid-nineteenth century, when misguided Latin scholars called it a felony. What was the charge? Knowingly and willfully inserting an adverb (like "presumptuously") between "to" and an infinitive (like "correct"). As in, "Miss Mutch was ill advised to presumptuously correct Chandler's prose."

Henry Alford, a classical scholar and dean of Canterbury Cathedral, was the man most responsible for criminalizing sentences like that one. In a widely popular grammar book, *A Plea for the Queen's English* (1864), he mistakenly declared that "to" was part of the infinitive and that the parts were inseparable. He was probably influenced by the fact that the infinitive, the simplest form of a verb, is one word in Latin and thus can't be split. But Alford was apparently unaware that the infinitive is just one word in English too. You can't split it, since "to" is just a prepositional marker and not part of the infinitive. In fact, sometimes it's not needed at all. In a sentence like "Miss Mutch thought she was helping him to write proper English," the "to" could easily be dropped.

Wiser grammarians began challenging Alford almost immediately. The first volley was fired in 1868, and it's never let up. By the early twentieth century, the most respected authorities on English (the linguist Otto Jespersen, the lexicographer Henry Fowler, the grammarian George O. Curme, and so on) were taking aim at the split-infinitive myth. Since then, grammarians have argued until they were apoplectic that "splitting" is not only acceptable but often preferable. There's a difference, for example, between "Miss Mutch learned to quickly edit" and "She learned quickly to edit." The third possibility, "She learned to edit quickly," could be read either way.

But against all reason, the most notorious myth of English grammar lives on—in the public imagination if nowhere else. Why can't we forget it? Perhaps because it's so easy to remember. To this day, many thoughtful, educated people will turn a sentence inside out to avoid a split infinitive. If there's a lesson to be learned here, it's this: Any rule that leads to clumsy English probably isn't legit. You can't graft the principles of Latin onto a Germanic language like English and expect the tree to grow straight.

As for Miss Mutch, she didn't get her way about that split infinitive, but she got something better in the end. Chandler wrote her a lighthearted poem attacking grammar taboos, "Lines to a Lady with an Unsplit Infinitive." Herewith, a few lines:

> *A lot of my style (so-called) is vile,*
> *For I learned to write in a bar.*
> *The marriage of thought to words was wrought*
> *With many a strong sidecar.*
> *A lot of my stuff is extremely rough,*
> *For I had no maiden aunts.*
> *O dear Miss Mutch, leave go your clutch*
> *On Noah Webster's pants!*

A Modest Preposition

Next time you're in a roomful of linguaholics, mention the old taboo against ending a sentence with a preposition (a positioning word, like "to" or "with" or "up"). Someone is sure to bring up Winston Churchill and the quip "This is the sort of English up with which I will not put." Sir Winston, you'll be told, scribbled the remark alongside a sentence that some pedant had stood on its head to avoid a preposition at the end. In certain circles, the quote is almost as famous as Churchill's wartime speech about "blood, toil, tears, and sweat." It's a great story. Alas, it's probably as apocryphal as the preposition rule itself.

If the split-infinitive prohibition is the number-one myth of English grammar, the final-preposition bugaboo runs a very close second. And we have another Englishman to thank for it: the poet, playwright, and critic John Dryden.

In a 1672 essay, Dryden boasted that the writing of his day was better than that of the previous generation, which included such turkeys as Shakespeare and Ben Jonson. He said the Bard's plays were either "grounded on impossibilities" or "so meanly written" that the comedy wasn't comic and the drama wasn't dramatic. "He writes, in many places, below the dullest writer of ours, or any precedent age." So there!

As for Jonson, Dryden sneered at the "false construction," "ill syntax," and "meanness of expression" in his plays. As if that wasn't bad enough, Jonson was guilty of putting "the Preposition in the end of the sentence: a common fault with him." Dryden was so bugged by this that he went back over his own writings and relocated all the straggling prepositions.

The bee in Dryden's bonnet later took up residence in the miter of an eighteenth-century Anglican bishop, Robert Lowth, who wrote the first popular grammar book to claim that a preposition didn't belong at the end of a sentence in formal writing. Never mind that great literature from Chaucer to Milton to Shakespeare to the King James version of the Bible was full of so-called terminal prepositions.

The bishop's affectation proved popular with Latin-educated schoolmasters—maybe the word "preposition," from the Latin for "position before," suggested to pedagogues that a preposition must never come last. In Latin, sentences don't end in prepositions. But in Germanic languages like English, they do. In fact, it's perfectly natural to put a preposition at the end of an English sentence, and it has been since Anglo-Saxon times.

Nevertheless, the myth lives on, though every major grammarian for more than a century has tried to debunk it. (You might say it's the sort of English "rule" up with which modern grammarians will not put.) But why has it hung on? Perhaps because this rule, like the one about the split infinitive, is so easy to remember, and the "misdemeanor" is so easy to spot. Besides, it's the perfect "gotcha!" There's something self-congratulatory, even smug, about thinking your English is better than the other guy's. Ironically, this is a case where the guy who's never heard of a preposition is more likely to be right.

Which brings us back to Sir Winston and that famous witticism. Famous it is, but Churchill's it probably isn't. Over the years, numerous versions of the quote and the incident that provoked it have circulated on both sides of the Atlantic, all of them claiming to be the genuine article. In various incarnations of the story, Churchill blusters not only at "the sort of English," but also at the "stilted English," "arrant pedantry," "errant pedantry," "errant criticism," "offensive impertinence," "insubordination," "bloody nonsense," "tedious nonsense," "pedantic nonsense," and . . . you get the idea. As for the end of the quote, it can be "up with which I will not put," "up with which I shall not put," "with which I will not put up," or "which I will not put up with."

The provocation that supposedly got Churchill so worked up? It's sometimes a government document clumsily written by someone else, and at other times it's clumsy editing of the great man's own writing—here a book, there a speech, perhaps a memo or whatever. With so many genuine articles to choose from, it would take a linguistic anthropologist to track down the real story. Fortunately, one has. Benjamin G. Zimmer has traced the quotation to a 1942 article in *The Wall Street Journal,* citing an earlier mention in *The Strand Magazine.* The "offensive impertinence" version of the quote is there, but (surprise!) Churchill is missing. The witticism is attributed to an unnamed writer in "a certain Government department."

It wasn't until two years later that the quote (this time it's the "tedious nonsense" version) was pinned on Churchill. On February 27, 1944, the *Chicago Tribune,* the *Los Angeles Times,* and *The New York Times* all ran brief items from London saying Churchill had scrawled the remark on a "long, rambling" government document—and that he'd done it only the week before.

When Sir Ernest Gowers mentioned the anecdote in his book *Plain Words* (1948), he was wise enough to hedge his bets: "It is said that Mr. Winston Churchill once made this marginal comment." Believe what you want. I'll believe it when I see the document, complete with Churchillian scribbles.

The Right Connections

I don't know if this anecdote is true or not, but how often do you get a chance to say something funny about conjunctions?

Back in the days of vaudeville, the story goes, Eddie Cantor and George Jessel were on the same bill. When Jessel got to town, he saw the billing and chewed out his manager, Irving Mansfield.

"What kind of conjunction is that—Eddie Cantor *with* Georgie Jessel?"

Mansfield promised to fix it, and fix it he did—this time with a proper conjunction.

The next day the marquee read: "Eddie Cantor *but* Georgie Jessel."

If you don't believe the story, blame the comedian Joey Adams, who gets the credit (or discredit) for it in *The Friars Club Encyclopedia of Jokes*. I don't know whether his conjunction shtick is mythological, but the old taboo against beginning a sentence with a conjunction definitely is.

A conjunction ("and," "but," "or," etc.) is a connecting word. It's found at the "junction" where words or phrases or clauses or sentences are joined. That's right—sentences, too!

Some English teachers have insisted that "and," "but," and other conjunctions should be used only to join parts of a sentence, not to join one sentence with another. And if you're one of them, listen up. It's been common to begin sentences with conjunctions since at least the tenth century. Just pick up a Shakespeare play or a Dickens novel and flip through a few pages. Before long, you'll find a sentence that begins with "and" or "but." To save you the trouble, here's Hamlet's friend Horatio, speaking about the Ghost: "And then it started like a guilty thing / Upon a fearful summons."

Grammarians have long dismissed the so-called rule against starting a sentence with a conjunction. Henry Fowler called it an "ungrammatical piece of nonsense." You can't even blame this one on Latinists, since a sentence can also begin with a conjunction in Latin (*Et tu, Brute?*).

God only knows where this myth comes from. But the linguist Arnold Zwicky may be on to something. In a posting to the Language Log, an Internet discussion group, he speculates that well-intentioned English teachers could have imposed the "rule" to break students of an annoying habit—starting every other sentence with a conjunction, usually "and." Zwicky notes that "and" is most often the first word children use to link sentences together. Not surprisingly, they use it to death. As an example of chronic conjunctionitis among the young, he cites a Coasters song from the late fifties, "Along Came Jones," with its steady beat of "and then . . . and then . . . and then," capped off by the refrain, "And then along came Jones." Teachers were rightly bugged by all the "ands," "buts," and so on, Zwicky says, but they may have overreacted. He imagines a frustrated teacher concluding, "If they do it too much, they should be told not to do it at all." And thus, a "rule" is born!

"Any fool with a claim to authority and either students or a publisher can get a rule ON the books," Zwicky says, "but there is absolutely no mechanism for getting rules OFF."

Tell me about it.

None So Blind

Every couple of months, I get an email from someone who's shocked or disheartened or puzzled or peeved by seeing "none" as a plural in *The New York Times*.

Here's a confession. I felt the same way when I went to work for the *Times* as a staff editor in the early 1980s and learned that the paper treated "none" as plural in most cases. Like many people, I thought that "none" meant "not one," and that it should always be singular. But I gritted my teeth and followed the *Times* stylebook, apologizing to writers whenever I had to replace a "none is" with a "none are." Sometime later, I sat down with a pot of tea and Volume X (*moul* to *ovum*) of the *Oxford English Dictionary* to explore the etymological roots of "none." What I found gave me new respect for my employer. It seems that "none" has been both singular and plural since Anglo-Saxon days. Alfred the Great used it as a plural back in the ninth century, when he translated a work by the Roman philosopher Boethius.

Although the *OED* lists numerous examples of both singular and plural "nones" since Alfred's day, it says plurals have been more common, especially in modern times. How's that for an eye-opener? As they say, "None are so blind as those who will not see." It's true that "none" is a descendant of the Old English *nan,* which indeed is a combination of *ne* ("not") plus *an* ("one"). But "any" is also descended from the Old English *an,* and historically "none" has always been closer in meaning to "not any."

As we know, "any" can be either singular (any of one thing, like vodka) or plural (any of many things, like martinis). Likewise, "none" is sometimes singular ("none of the vodka is chilled") and sometimes plural ("none of the martinis are left"). All modern grammar books and usage guides agree on this point. Nevertheless, the misconception that "none" means "not one" is among the most widely believed myths of English grammar, right up there with the old split-infinitive nonsense.

Where does all this come from? Why have generations of schoolchildren been hoodwinked into thinking that "none" is always singular because it means "not one"?

The guy responsible for this one may be Lindley Murray, a bestselling grammarian in the late eighteenth and early nineteenth centuries. In his *English Grammar* (1795), Murray says (correctly) that "none" can be either singular or plural. But he also notes that "as it literally signifies *not one* or *no one,* it was formerly confined to the singular." Wrong. It was never "confined to the singular," but Murray's overly literal interpretation apparently captured the hearts and minds of English teachers.

By the late nineteenth century, the spurious belief that "none" meant "not one" had been elevated to the status of a "rule," flying in the face of nearly a thousand years of English usage. Why? Perhaps because simpleminded edicts are simple to remember— and to teach.

My experience has been that when you really do mean "not one," you should say "not one." You'll be singularly clear. Never underestimate the lessons of experience. Henry Fielding had this to say about them in *Tom Jones:* "None are more ignorant of them than those learned pedants whose lives have been entirely consumed in colleges and among books."

Accentuating the Negative

Sidney Morgenbesser was a biggie in twentieth-century philosophy, but he's better known among language junkies for an immortal wisecrack he made in the 1950s during a lecture by an eminent British scholar.

J. L. Austin, a philosopher of language, had just remarked that in some languages two negatives make a positive, but in no language do two positives make a negative.

"Yeah, yeah," Morgenbesser muttered from the audience.

I wonder what he would have said about the old "rule" that a double negative is never right. Never say never?

The biggest problem with this taboo is that not all double negatives are incorrect. That one, for example. There's nothing wrong with using two negatives together to say something positive ("I can't not buy these Ferragamos") or to straddle the fence ("He's not unintelligent"). So anybody who says all double negatives are bad is badly informed. The only double negative that's a no-no is one that uses two negatives to say something negative ("I didn't see nothing!"). Modern grammarians regard this usage as substandard, insisting on only one negative element in a simple negative statement ("I didn't see anything" or "I saw noth-ing").

But why outlaw any kind of double negative? What's wrong with "I didn't see nothing"? I'm glad you asked. It would be cor-rect in French, Italian, Spanish, Polish, Russian, and other lan-guages. And it used to be commonplace in English, too, as a way to accentuate the negative. Chaucer uses double, triple, and even quadruple negatives in *The Canterbury Tales*. Here's how he de-scribes the Friar: "Ther nas no man no-wher so vertuous," or as one would say today, "There wasn't no man nowhere so virtu-ous."

It wasn't until the eighteenth century that a sentence like "I didn't see nothing" was pronounced a crime against English. Guess who's responsible for this one. Yes, Robert Lowth, same guy who condemned the preposition at the end of a sentence. "Two Negatives in English destroy one another," the Anglican bishop declared, "or are equivalent to an Affirmative." In other words, don't use double negatives.

If ever a prohibition had staying power, this one did. By the time Dickens came along, only a poorly educated person, like Peggotty in *David Copperfield*, would say, "Nobody never went and hinted no such a thing." Many linguists argue that there's nothing wrong with speaking like Peggotty today. But I don't hear no linguists saying nothing like that. Why? Because no PhD wants to sound like a high school dropout.

So what's an educated person to do? Don't use two negatives to say something negative ("You never take me nowhere"), but go ahead when you want to be emphatic ("We can't not go home for Thanksgiving") or wishy-washy ("Mom's mince pie is not un-appetizing").

As a former philosophy major (who always went home for Thanksgiving), I can't end this item and not mention my favorite Sidney Morgenbesser anecdote. It doesn't deal with double negatives, but it's not unrelated.

In the 1970s, a radical student asked the philosopher whether he disagreed with Chairman Mao's view that a proposition can be both true and false at the same time.

"I do and I don't," Morgenbesser replied.

There are several versions of this story. It may be true, it may be false, or it may be true and false at the same time.

User Friendly

While driving along I-10 to visit a friend in the Texas Hill Country a few years ago, I was amused by all the road signs reading DRIVE FRIENDLY. Hmm, I thought, those signs must drive the grammar police crazy.

Later I learned that a lot of self-appointed language cops had indeed pounced on the "Drive Friendly" slogan. The charge: incorrectly using an adjective instead of an adverb to modify a verb. "Grammatically incorrect hick speak," one Internet critic sneered. Another, a college professor, insisted in his online grammar guide that the signs should read "Drive Friendlily."

Well, the professor gets an F. The wordsmiths at the Texas Department of Transportation had it right. "Friendly" has been both an adverb and an adjective since the Middle Ages. In fact, "friendlily" is the klutzy latecomer—it didn't arrive on the scene until the seventeenth century. For most of us, it never really did arrive.

We shouldn't be too hard on that professor, though. Lots of people have goofy ideas about adverbs, and "friendly" is a goofy word. It has the telltale mark of most adverbs—an -*ly* ending— but it's widely considered just an adjective.

Much as I enjoyed that fuss about "friendly," another road sign represents the real misconception about adverbs. I hear almost every day from people who get bent out of shape when they see a GO SLOW sign on a suburban street.

"What's happening to adverbs?" the chorus shouts. "Why is everybody using adjectives instead? Is the -*ly* disappearing from English?"

The handwringers apparently believe that an adverb, a word that modifies a verb, has to end with -*ly*. Oh, they'll go along with a few flaky exceptions, like "well" and "soon." But to them, the default adverb comes with a tail. As far as they're concerned, "slow" is an adjective, "slowly" is an adverb, and never the twain shall meet.

The truth is that adverbs can come with or without tails. The ones without -*ly* (they're called simple or flat adverbs) were seen more often in the past, though they may be making a revival now, if my mail is any indication. Many adverbs, like "slow" and "slowly," exist in both forms. In such cases, usage experts generally recommend the -*ly* version for formal writing, but there are lots of exceptions.

No one would insist, for instance, on "lately" in a sentence like "The plane arrived late and we missed our connection." ("Lately," as we know, means recently, not tardily.) The most respected writers use phrases like "sit tight," "go straight," "turn right," "work hard," "rest easy," "look sharp," "aim high," "dive deep," "play fair," and "think fast." Yes, "straight," "right," "hard," and the rest are bona-fide adverbs, and they've been adverbs since the Middle Ages. So why the persistent myth that a legitimate adverb must end in -*ly*?

Here's some history. We've had adverbs with and without the -*ly* (or archaic versions of it) for more than a thousand years. In

Old English, adverbs were often formed by adding -*e* or -*lice* to the end of adjectives. Over the years, the adverbs with a final *e* lost their endings and the -*lice* adverbs evolved into the modern -*ly* ones. Take the word "deep." The Old English adjective *diop* had two different adverbs: *diope* and *dioplice,* which eventually became the modern adverbs "deep" and "deeply."

Sounds simple, right? So how did things get confusing? You guessed it—the Latinists strike again. In the seventeenth and eighteenth centuries, they insisted that adjectives and adverbs should have different endings in English, just as they do in Latin. So these busybodies began tacking -*ly* onto perfectly legitimate flat adverbs, and preferring -*ly* versions where both kinds existed.

The lesson? Next time you start to pounce on someone for using an adverb without -*ly,* go slow. And go to the dictionary.

The Incredible Shrinking Word

One of the weirder movies of the 1950s (and there were a lot of them) was *The Incredible Shrinking Man,* the story of a guy who is sprayed by bug killer and gets smaller and smaller. Before long, he's living in a dollhouse and fighting for his life against the family cat. I was watching it on cable the other day, and it reminded me of contractions, the incredible shrinking words that have had to fight for their lives over the years.

When I got my first computer in the eighties, the word processor used to scold me for using "can't," "don't," "isn't," and so on. But contractions have made a comeback. The Miss Grundy in my latest computer doesn't raise an eyebrow. No, I'm not a big fan of grammar checkers, but the techies who programmed the software got it right this time. A lot of people, though, still seem to think that contractions are not quite . . . *quite*. If you do too, you're quite wrong.

Writers have been shrinking English since Anglo-Saxon days, forming Old English contractions like *nis* from *ne is* ("is not"); *naes* from *ne waes* ("was not"); *nolde* from *ne wolde* ("would not"); *naefde* from *ne haefde* ("did not have"); and *nat* from *ne wat* ("does not know"). And such shortenings were an accepted part of the language for hundreds of years. In Elizabethan times, for instance, Shakespeare didn't spare contractions. He used them in dialogue ("But he's an arrant knave"—*Hamlet*), in titles (*All's Well That Ends Well*), and in sonnets ("That's for thyself to breed another thee"). In fact, there were many more contractions in olden days than there are now, including such quaint old dears as "ha'n't," "sha'n't," "'tis," "'twere," "'twill," "'twon't," "'twouldn't," and "a'n't," the father of "ain't."

Throughout the seventeenth and much of the eighteenth centuries, contractions were normal in speech and respectable in writing, even scholarly prose. 'Twasn't till the early 1700s that anybody thought to question these miracles of compactness. Addison, Swift, Pope, and others began raising questions about their suitability in print, even though educated people routinely used them in conversation. By the late eighteenth century, contractions were in disgrace, tolerated in speech but an embarrassment in writing.

Samuel Johnson, for example, freely used "I'm," "don't," "'tis," "I'd," "we're," and other contractions in his speech, and his biographer, Boswell, faithfully wrote them down that way in his notes. But when Boswell's *Journal of a Tour to the Hebrides* (an account of a trip taken with Johnson) was published in 1785, Boswell and his editor tidied up Johnson's speech for the printed page, removing what they called "informal syntax and inelegant phraseology." Many of Johnson's contractions were expanded into the longer "I am," "it is," "I would," "we are," and so on.

Who put the hoodoo on contractions? How did they become second-class citizens? Blame the opinion makers of the day. In the minds of many book reviewers, drama critics, editors, grammarians, and social commentators, contractions were harsh-sounding, vulgar, low class, ill mannered, or overly familiar. But not all contractions were all bad to all critics. One might sneer at "wasn't," "didn't," "shouldn't," and "couldn't," while another might denounce "don't," "won't," and "we're." This scorn was sometimes carried to ridiculous lengths.

In 1770, an article in the *Monthly Review,* a British journal, went so far as to condemn the use of contractions in the transcript of a notorious adultery trial. Never mind that Lord Grosvenor was accusing the duke of Cumberland, King George's brother, of fooling around with Lady Grosvenor in barns, country inns, and the back rooms of shops. The writer's nose was out of joint because either the judge, Lord Mansfield, or the court reporter quoting him had dared to use the "vile contraction *don't* for *do not,"* which "would be rather expected from the mouth of a hairdresser, or a milliner's apprentice." *Quelle horreur!* That's like pouncing on a superfluous comma in a sensational account of Charles and Diana's breakup.

Contractions were in the doghouse until well into the twentieth century, when opinion makers started coming to their senses. In the 1920s, Henry Fowler used contractions without comment in his famous usage guide, indicating he saw nothing wrong with them. In the '40s, the writing guru Rudolf Flesch went further, calling them "the handiest and most conspicuous device" for helping a writer sound natural. By the end of the century, the legal writer and lexicographer Bryan A. Garner offered this simple test: "If you would say it as a contraction, write it that way.

If you wouldn't, then don't." I might add here that a contraction or the lack of one gives us a handy way to convey our attitude. To the first telemarketer of the evening: "I'm not interested." To the third: "I am NOT interested!"

Most writing handbooks now recommend contractions, but there are still lots of traditionalists out there who haven't gotten the word. Numerous websites, for example, still advise writers to avoid contractions like the plague, especially in formal writing. My advice is to avoid those websites. I'm not saying that every contraction you'll come across is legit. Contractions of all kinds are natural in speech, but most usage guides say some don't belong in writing. These clunkers can look ridiculously awkward ("she'd've," "there're," "this's"), and some ("could've," "should've," "would've") often morph into lousy grammar ("could of," "should of," "would of"). Here are some other clumsy contractions that I avoid in my own writing: "how'd," "how'll," "how're," "it'd," "might've," "must've," "that'd," "that'll," "that're," "that've," "there'd," "there'll," "there've," "this'd," "this'll," "what'd," "what've," "when'll," "when're," "when's," "where'd," "where'll," "where're," "why'd," "why're," "why's."

I also stay away from the unfortunate "who're," which looks too much like "whore." And I don't recommend "ain't" either, though it wasn't always misbehavin' (see pages 48–49).

As You Like It

Back in the 1950s, when millions of us liked Ike and tuned in to *Your Hit Parade* on Saturday night, cigarettes were as American as apple pie and just as wholesome. Or so we were told. "More doctors smoke Camels than any other cigarette!" announced radio, TV, and magazine ads. Rosalind Russell and Barbara Stanwyck assured smokers that L&Ms were "just what the doctor or-dered." Viceroy promised "double-barreled health protection," while Arthur Godfrey and Ed Sullivan cited "scientific evidence" for the benefits of Chesterfield.

Pretty outrageous, right? But hardly anybody seemed to mind. Even the *Journal of the American Medical Association* was ac-cepting cigarette ads. What raised people's blood pressure and gave their smoke-filled lungs a workout was an ad that said, "Winston tastes good like a cigarette should." While all the cig-arette brands were getting away with murder, Winston was being flogged over a point of grammar.

The crime? The rule here is that you use a conjunction ("and," "but," "as," etc.) to join clauses ("Winston tastes good" . . . "a cigarette should"). So the ad, said critics, should have read, "Winston tastes good as a cigarette should." The word "like" is a lot of things—an adjective, a preposition, a verb, and so on—but sticklers insist that it can't be a conjunction. That's been the rule for the last couple hundred years, though the ground is shifting. In casual usage, "like" is gaining steadily on "as."

But wait a minute. Who decided that "like" couldn't be a con-junction? I smell a rat! The truth is that writers have been using both "as" and "like" as conjunctions since the fourteenth century. Chaucer liked "like." Shakespeare, too. So did Keats, Emily Brontë, Thackeray, George Eliot, Dickens, Kipling, Shaw, and on and on. It wasn't until the nineteenth century that anybody was bugged by the use of "like" as a conjunction. The objection was apparently that too many people were likely to do it. In other words, it had become too common for the language snobs of the day. Before you knew it, a "rule" was born, and sticklers were jumping on anyone who broke it. Tennyson went so far as to chew out Queen Victoria's husband for the felony.

"It's a modern vulgarism that I have seen grow up within the last thirty years; and when Prince Albert used it in my drawing room, I pulled him up for it, in the presence of the Queen, and told him he never ought to use it again," Lord Tennyson told the philologist Frederick J. Furnivall.

The sticklers were still at it a century later, when the Winston ad began offending delicate ears. "We hope Sir Winston Churchill, impeccable, old-school grammarian that he is, hasn't chanced to hear American radio or television commercials recently," sniffed *The New Yorker* in 1956. "It would pain him dreadfully, we're sure, to listen to the obnoxious and ubiquitous couplet 'Winston tastes good, like a cigarette should.' That pesky 'like' is a problem for us Americans to solve, we guess, and anyway Sir Winston has his own problems."

That *New Yorker* writer, we guess, hadn't read Sir Winston's wartime letters. Here's an excerpt from one in which he objects to setting up yet another special committee: "We are overrun by them, like the Australians were by the rabbits." Sir Winston may have had his problems, but not, we see, with using "like" as a conjunction.

As for Winston the cigarette, all the free publicity may have helped make it the bestselling brand in the country. R. J. Reynolds delightedly countered with a new ad, tweaking the fuddy-duddies with this playful comeback: "What do you want—good grammar or good taste?"

Now let's fast-forward to today. What's the word on "like"? Is it OK or not? Dictionaries generally accept "like" as a conjunction now, but many style and usage manuals still condemn the practice. Who's right? I'm on the side of the dictionaries, sort of. In theory, I see nothing wrong with using "like" as a conjunction. But in practice, I don't do it. This makes me a coward, I admit. But let's face facts—or, rather, myths. Anyone who uses "like" as a conjunction, especially in formal writing, risks being accused of illiteracy. So this is my advice. When you want your English to be above reproach, think of the old cigarette commercial—and do the opposite.

Words of Passage

English can be sneaky. Take the word "snuck," which has sneaked into common usage and even into dictionaries. Is it legit? Not if you believe the Associated Press stylebook, which bluntly tells its reporters and editors: "Do not use the colloquial *snuck*."

Traditionally, of course, we "sneak," we "sneaked," and we "have sneaked." But "snuck" slipped into English in nineteenth-century America, making an 1887 appearance in *The Lantern,* a New Orleans weekly: "He grubbed ten dollars from de bums an den snuck home."

Since its slangy debut, "snuck" has gotten so popular that US dictionaries now accept it without comment (that is, without calling it slang or nonstandard or colloquial or whatever). Writers on grammar and usage, who are stricter than lexicographers, don't go quite so far, but some (including yours truly) have nothing against "snuck" in casual conversation or informal writing.

For now, "snuck" is more prevalent in the United States and Canada than in Britain. In fact, it's about as common as "sneaked" in North America, according to *Merriam-Webster's Dictionary of English Usage,* and it "stands a good chance to become the dominant form." We don't know why this usage came about, but it may simply be because "snuck" is easier to pronounce than "sneaked."

Another word that has sneaked (or snuck) into common usage, but not into the AP stylebook, is "dove" as an alternative to "dived." Here's the AP's succinct "dive" entry: "Not *dove* for the past tense." You don't say! This is another once-colloquial word that's changed its spots. It showed up in the nineteenth century as a new formation, but it's an echo of an archaic one, the Old English past participle *dofen*. Longfellow introduced "dove" in his 1855 poem *The Song of Hiawatha:* "Plunged as if he were an otter, / Dove as if he were a beaver." (But Longfellow must have had second thoughts, since he changed "dove" to "dived" in later editions. Coward!) Today, "dove" is accepted by American dictionaries as standard English, though the usage hasn't caught on in Britain. Some American usage writers still have reservations, but I rather like "dove." To my ears, it has a familiar Anglo-Saxon ring, along the lines of "drive/drove," "stick/stuck," "weave/wove," "speak/spoke," and similar verbs from Old English.

Who knows? Someday we may find that "dove" has snuck into the AP stylebook.

Who's That?

If you've seen the 1954 version of *A Star Is Born,* you'll remember the smoky nightclub scene in which Judy Garland sings "The Man That Got Away." I'll bet many language-arts teachers would give Ira Gershwin an F for the lyrics of that song, which he wrote with Harold Arlen. A person is a "who," these sticklers insist, and a thing is a "that." And that's that.

Despite what many people believe, though, a person can be either a "that" or a "who." Writers have been using "that" for people as well as things since Anglo-Saxon times, according to the *Oxford English Dictionary.* You can find examples in Chaucer, Shakespeare, and the first complete English Bible. Here's a line from *Hamlet:* "By heaven, I'll make a ghost of him that lets me!"

A thing, on the other hand, is always a "that." As for pets, they aren't people, but they aren't quite things either. A few style guides have pondered this burning issue. Here's my opinion. If an animal is anonymous, it's a "that." But if it has a name, it can be either a "that" or a "who." ("I'm looking for a dog that can act. Lassie is a dog who could direct her own movie.")

Getting back to human beings, there may be a "politeness" issue here. Some people seem to think using "that" in place of "who" or "whom" demeans or objectifies a person. Maybe so. But there's no grammatical reason for such a rule, even though many books on style persist in spreading the misconception. Where did this idea come from? In the eighteenth century, misguided language pundits decided to put "that" and "who" in separate compartments. The anonymous author of *Observations Upon the English Language* (1752), for example, condemned the use of "that" for people, and insisted "who" was "the only proper Word to be used." The linguist Otto Jespersen has speculated that Latinism may be responsible here, too, since this English use of "that" (it's of Germanic origin) has no exact Latin equivalent. Be that as it may, the myth caught on. "It may be that some carryover from the eighteenth-century general dislike of *that* produced the apparently common, yet unfounded, notion that *that* may be used to refer only to things," says *Merriam-Webster's Dictionary of English Usage.*

Personal Pronouncements

Time for a pop quiz. Which is correct—"Madonna loves bustiers more than I" or "Madonna loves bustiers more than me"? You don't have to bust your butt over this one. They're both right, depending on what you mean. The first one means "Madonna loves bustiers more than I do." The second means "Madonna loves bustiers more than she loves me." But a lot of people find the phrase "more than I" too stuffy and use "more than me" for all occasions. That's cheating. If you might be misunderstood and you don't want to sound like a stuffed shirt, simply fill in the blanks: "Madonna loves bustiers more than I do."

Most of the time, though, there's no chance of being misunderstood when we use "than" to compare things, say Madonna's measurements and ours. In such a case, what's wrong with saying, "Madonna is bustier than me"? Nothing at all, though some pedants will bust your chops for doing it. They insist that "than" is strictly a conjunction, and that it can link a clause only to another clause. So "than" has to connect a clause like "Madonna is bustier" with another one, like "I am"—even if the verb "am" is merely implied and not actually present.

The only problem here is that great writers have been using "than" as a preposition as well as a conjunction since the sixteenth century. And as a preposition, "than" should be followed by "me"—or a similar personal pronoun, like "him," "her," "them," or "us." Who says? Well, Shakespeare, for one, used "than" as a preposition. So did Milton, Goldsmith, Johnson, Lamb, Scott, Thackeray, Kipling, and many others. Here's an example from a 1720 poem by Swift: "She suffers hourly more than me."

Until the mid-eighteenth century, writers routinely used "than" with whatever personal pronoun sounded best to them—"I" or "me," "she" or "her," "he" or "him," and so on. Common sense reigned, and everything was fine and dandy. In other words, it was a situation too good to last. Some Latinist was bound to take notice, and some Latinist did. Enter Robert Lowth, the fellow who helped popularize the myth that it's wrong to end a sentence with a preposition. In his *Short Introduction to English Grammar* (1762), Lowth decreed that "than" should be treated as a conjunction, not a preposition, when followed by a personal pronoun. Never mind Shakespeare, Milton, and all the rest.

Lowth must have had a hang-up about prepositions. At any rate, his pronouncement, like so many others dreamed up by Latinists, caught on. To this day, the more pedantic usage guides take the view that "than" is only a conjunction. Nevertheless, millions of educated people use "than" as a preposition too. And the more sensible authorities are on their side. "*Than* is both a preposition and a conjunction," says *Merriam-Webster's Dictionary of English Usage.* "In spite of much opinion to the contrary, the preposition has never been wrong." I'm one of the millions who see nothing wrong with using a sentence like "She's hotter than me" in speech or casual writing. In the unlikely event the subject came up in formal writing, I'd recommend "She's hotter than I am." But that's just what my ear tells me. Let your ear be your guide. Or, as Madonna says, "Express yourself."

Wake My Day

I got a letter (yes, people still write letters) from an old-media type who complained that English was changing so fast he couldn't keep up. "Am I living in a previous century?" he wrote. "Should I buy a lorgnette?" The last straw was hearing a young TV newscaster say "has woken" instead of "has waked," as in "A trapeze artist has woken after twelve years in a coma." I sympathized with my correspondent (though I like the idea of the lorgnette). English can seem bewildering as it adapts to the world of Facebook, iPods, texting, and Wikipedia. But "woken" isn't a creation of the YouTube generation. Anyone who thinks so is off by a few hundred years.

The AARP generation does tend to say "have waked," while its children and grandchildren prefer "have woken." But let's close the generation gap. Both are correct. Since the early 1600s, "woken" has been a bona-fide past participle (a verb form that among other things is used with the verb "have" to make compound tenses).

We've always had lots of ways to talk about getting up in the morning, perhaps too many. "Wake," "waken," "awake," and "awaken" are an intimidating bunch. The problem is an embarrassment of riches: There are so many correct ways to use them. Here are the acceptable present, past, and present perfect tenses, according to modern dictionaries.

- I wake / I woke or I waked / I have woken, I have waked, or I have woke.
- I waken / I wakened / I have wakened.
- I awake / I awoke or I awaked / I have awoken, I have awaked, or I have awoke.
- I awaken / I awakened / I have awakened.

How did we get all these verbs? It all began with two Old English words, *wacan* (to become awake) and *wacian* (to be or remain awake). Over the years, their descendants mixed and matched, giving us the words we have today. For the most part, the simple present and past tenses of these eye-opening verbs are a snap. It's the past participles that keep us awake nights. But rest easy. No matter which one you choose, you'll probably be right.

Before we call it a day, though, here's a thought. What, if anything, does all this have to do with the wake we hold for the dead? It seems that one old meaning of "wake" was to be awake or remain awake. This sense of "wake" also gave rise to related words having to do with guarding ("watch," "vigil"). And a "wake" for the dead is a vigil or watch kept over a body. By extension, the dead person is said to be "waked."

Interestingly, the phrase "to wake the dead" now has two distinct meanings in English—to be so noisy as to wake up the dead (a modern interpretation), and to hold a wake over the deceased (the traditional sense).

Is this a wonderful language, or what? Although the underpinnings of grammar—old faithfuls like subject-verb agreement—rarely change, English gives us wiggle room to reinvent words and phrases in creative ways. We have to use a singular verb with a singular subject, for instance, and a plural with a plural. But that doesn't mean we can't change our minds about what's singular, what's plural, and what's none of the above. Take the now-notorious use of "they" as an all-purpose pronoun, a practice that makes usage experts' hair stand on end. This was acceptable for many hundreds of years, and wasn't condemned by grammarians until the late eighteenth century. (See pages 141–42.) But after two hundred years of nagging, people by the millions still use "they," "them," "their," and such as singular pronouns ("Every teenager thinks they know it all").

In the end, it's not the grammarians and usage experts who decide what's right. It's you—the people who actually use the language day in and day out. In the eighteenth century, for example, grammarians tried to stamp out the use of "wrote" as the past tense of "write." They considered "writ" or "writt" the only correct forms. At least fifty-nine grammar books of the period pounced on "wrote," calling the usage "absurd," "bad," a "barbarism," "colloquial," "corrupt," "improper," "inelegant," "ungrammatical," a "solecism," or "vulgar." No matter. Once again, the people wrote the rules.

Chapter 3

Bad Boys of English
And Why We Still Love 'Em

Back in the early 1980s, soon after I joined *The New York Times,* I was grumbling to a colleague about a particularly woolly-minded writer I'd been editing. "What a putz!" I said. My friend smiled, then remarked, "You do know that 'putz' is a dirty word in Yiddish, don't you?" No, as it happened, I didn't. I thought it simply meant an idiot or a jerk.

I went to the newspaper's house dictionary, *Webster's New World.* No "putz" in sight. Uh-oh, this was ominous—in those days the *New World* didn't include "bad" words. Next I went to the *Times's* library and looked up "putz" in Leo Rosten's *The Joys of Yiddish.* Yes, it did mean an idiot or a jerk, Rosten said, but it was also "vulgar slang for 'penis.'" There was even a warning. "CAUTION: *Putz* is not to be used lightly, or when women or children are around." Rosten compared it with another Yiddish word for penis: "schmuck." Oh, no! Not "schmuck" too!

By the time I left the paper in the late 1990s, "putz" had made it into the house dictionary as a slang word meaning either a penis or a simpleton. It wasn't quite kosher yet, but it was on the way. As I got more involved in the language racket, I learned that we have two versions of "putz" in English. The older one, which showed up in the nineteenth century, comes from an archaic German word meaning ornament or decoration. That accounts for some rather startling citations in the *Oxford English Dictionary,* including this one from a 1902 article in *The New York Times Magazine:* "Only the chosen few can afford to have a really impressive 'putz' which fills half a room. . . . This more elaborate 'putz' requires not only money for its erection, but artistic handiwork." In Pennsylvania Dutch homes, a decorative Nativity scene was (and still is) called a "putz."

The unrelated Yiddish "putz," which refers to an entirely different kind of ornament, is of unknown origin. It entered English in its vulgar sense in 1934, the *OED* tells us, not via a Yiddish writer like Sholem Aleichem or Isaac Bashevis Singer but thanks to Henry Miller. His novel *Tropic of Cancer* refers to a woman who "ought to have better sense than be tripped up by every guy with a big putz who happens to come along." Since the late 1920s, "putz" has also been a slang term in English for fool or simpleton. Today that's the principal definition in *The American Heritage Dictionary of the English Language* (4th ed.). But the word is still considered vulgar by many, especially those familiar with Yiddish.

As for "schmuck," it lost much of its vulgarity when it entered English in the 1890s. English dictionaries define a "schmuck" as merely an oaf or a jerk, though the body part is noted in the word's etymology. I don't know how the FCC feels about "schmuck," but I'm not ready to use it on the air. Dictionary or no dictionary, it still raises too many eyebrows.

You've probably guessed where all this is heading. Like it or not, language changes—sometimes for the better, sometimes for the worse. Or rather, what I consider better or worse. Like you, I have only one vote, and no amount of finger wagging can change that.

Now let's look at some of the bad boys of English and why they've managed to survive despite all efforts to stamp them out. Perhaps they're not quite as naughty as we've been led to believe. But before we call the culprits into the principal's office, here's a letter I came across while researching "schmuck." In 1945, Groucho Marx wrote to his son, Arthur, in the voice of the family dog, Duke: "By the way, when you write to your father again, remember, not a word about this letter—he doesn't know I can write, in fact, he thinks I'm a complete schmuck. Well, take care of yourself. That's the leash you can do."

It Ain't Necessarily So

In 1941, the year Dizzy Dean left the pitcher's mound to become a radio announcer, he told his fans, "This job ain't gonna change me none." Sure enough, it didn't.

The four-time All-Star and future Hall of Famer began his new career at a local radio station in St. Louis, the scene of his glory days with the Cardinals. At the station, he did the play-by-play for home games of the Cardinals and their local rivals, the Browns. And he called the games like nobody else.

Players "swang" at pitches, "throwed" the ball, stood "confidentially" at bat, "slud" into home plate, and, when the "sityashun" called for it, they returned to their "respectable" bases. Dean would often sign off by saying, "Don't fail to miss tomorrow's game." Naturally he didn't fail to use the notorious "ain't" at every opportunity.

The St. Louis fans, who were used to urbane announcers with polished diction and perfect grammar, were wild about Ol' Diz and his mangled, Ozark-accented English. So was his sponsor, the Falstaff Brewing Corporation, whose beer sales soared after Dean was hired. Educators, however, were not amused. Dean's backwoods grammar—particularly his use of "ain't" and "them Cardinals"—was a bad influence on schoolchildren, claimed the St. Louis Board of Education. In 1942, the school board circulated a petition urging Falstaff to pull the plug. The company ignored the complaints, and Dean's response was typical: "You learn 'em English, and I'll learn 'em baseball." Two years later, when the baseball commissioner called Dean a national embarrassment for using "ain't" on the air, Dizzy shot back: "I ain't never met anybody that didn't know what 'ain't' means."

Then in July 1946, the syndicated columnist Leonard Lyons reported that the English Teachers Association of Missouri had filed a formal complaint against Dean with the Federal Communications Commission. Suddenly Dean was a nationwide cause célèbre (a phrase he wouldn't have used even if he'd known it). Loyal fans flooded newspaper offices and the radio station with impassioned letters and telegrams. In headlines across the country, delighted newspaper editors milked the controversy, dubbed the "School Marms' Uprising," for all it was worth. Even Norman Cousins, editor of the *Saturday Review of Literature,* came to Dean's defense.

Almost unnoticed in all the fuss was the teachers association itself, which was saying (more or less), "Uprising? What uprising?" In 2002 a pair of researchers, Patrick Huber and David Anderson, searched the FCC's files and found that no such complaint had ever been filed. But in postwar America, the fictional controversy was too delicious for a baseball-loving public to resist.

Huber and Anderson conclude that the whole thing was apparently a publicity stunt, cooked up by parties unknown. Whoever they were, the perpetrators of the hoax were wildly success-ful. In 1953, Dean became television's first national baseball broadcaster, calling the *Game of the Week* for ABC and later CBS (he left the show in 1966, after it was taken over by NBC). Dean stuck to his hokey, down-home delivery throughout his broad-cast career, but some colleagues thought that much of it was an act. "Once he said 'slid' correctly, by mistake, and he corrected himself," said fellow broadcaster Mel Allen.

Dean may have gotten away with using "ain't" over the air-waves, but even he couldn't make it respectable. The much-maligned contraction is the poster child for poor English and has been for generations, never mind that millions use it and every-one else knows what it means. But does "ain't" deserve a dunce cap? Well, it does and it doesn't. In other words, it ain't necessar-ily so.

Although "ain't" is now a symbol of the illiterati, it was rou-tinely used by the upper classes as well as the lower, by the edu-cated and otherwise, in the seventeenth, eighteenth, and nineteenth centuries. The word, or variations of it, can be found in the letters or diaries of Swift, Lamb, Byron, Tennyson, and Henry Adams, for example, as well as characters of all classes in the novels of Fielding, Austen, Dickens, Thackeray, George Eliot, and Trollope. Here's Arabella Trefoil, the daughter of Lady Augustus, in Trollope's *The American Senator:* "Two or three weeks ago I almost thought I loved Lord Rufford, and now I am quite sure that I hate him. But if I heard to-morrow that he had broken his neck out hunting, I ain't sure but what I should feel something."

Love it or hate it, everybody seems to feel something about "ain't." It was probably first used around 1600, just when most of our modern English contractions were being formed: "don't," "can't," "isn't," and so on. For centuries, "ain't" was just one of the crowd. It was first seen in print in the late 1600s, spelled "an't," "a'n't," and eventually "ain't." Some scholars believe the new spelling may have reflected the way the word was pronounced by certain speakers. Be that as it may, the "an't" and "a'n't" spellings had virtually disappeared by the late 1800s.

When the early versions of "ain't" arrived on the scene, the word was a contraction of "am not" and "are not." By the early 1700s, it was also being used as a contraction for "is not." And by the 1800s it was used for "have not" and "has not," too, replacing an earlier contraction, "ha'n't." As "ain't" took on more meanings, it drifted farther and farther from its roots. Contractions like "can't" and "don't" had clearly traceable parentage, but "ain't" claimed to have so many parents that it seemed illegitimate. No wonder language authorities turned up their noses. Since the late nineteenth century, they've considered "ain't" a crime against good English. In 1942, the slang lexicographer Eric Partridge said the use of "ain't" for "isn't" was "an error so illiterate that I blush to record it." Modern dictionaries still describe "ain't" as nonstandard, though acceptable when used informally in a folksy or humorous way ("You ain't heard nothin' yet").

It's a pity that "ain't" got too big for its britches. If it hadn't outgrown its old meanings of "am not" or "are not," it might be acceptable today. And we'd have a word to fill one of the most annoying gaps in English: the lack of a sensible contraction for "am I not." The clunky "amn't I" survives only in Scots and Irish English. The familiar alternative, "aren't I," clearly makes no sense—how can we justify it if we don't say "I aren't"? As it happens, "aren't I" didn't even exist until the early twentieth century, when British writers started using it to reproduce the way upper-class speakers pronounced "ain't I." (In the mouth of an old Etonian, "ain't" rhymed with "taunt" rather than "taint.")

Illogical it may be, but "aren't I" caught on in both Britain and the United States. It may have come out of left field, but today it's standard English while "ain't I" definitely isn't and probably never will be. Sorry about that, Diz.

The "Nucular" Family

Nobody ever said the W. in George W. Bush stood for Wordsmith. But our former president doesn't deserve the knuckle rapping that many wordies have given him for his famous pronunciation of "nuclear."

The word has been mispronounced so often and so publicly that NOO-kyuh-lur is gaining a foothold in dictionaries. *Merriam-Webster's Collegiate* (11th ed.), for example, lists the pronunciation as a variant "disapproved of by many," but "in widespread use among educated speakers including scientists, lawyers, professors, congressmen, US cabinet members, and at least two US presidents and one vice president." Actually, at least five presidents have had trouble pronouncing "nuclear." Bush's partners in crime include Dwight D. Eisenhower, Gerald Ford, Jimmy Carter, and Bill Clinton.

What is it about this three-syllable word that twists the tongues of so many people? Well, "nuclear" is a strange bird. No other English word is quite like it. The closest relatives are "likelier" and "cochlear" (ask your otolaryngologist what that one means). The problem, as linguists are always explaining, is that rare combination of an accented syllable followed by the sounds "klee-ur." Much more familiar, and easier to pronounce, is an accented syllable followed by the sounds "kyuh-lur," as in "circular," "muscular," "spectacular," "particular," "molecular," and others. "Nuclear" just wants to join the crowd.

Sure as shootin', this much-maligned usage will one day be considered just another standard pronunciation. Who knows—it may even become the most common. For now, though, NOO-kyuh-lur isn't ready for prime time. If you want to sound your best, stick with the usual pronunciation. But if your tongue simply isn't muscular enough to be particular, you're in distinguished company.

We can thank US presidents, by the way, for coining or popularizing many of our most common words and phrases. George Washington was particularly inventive, contributing such goodies as "indoors," "non-discrimination," "off-duty," "paroled," "reconnoiter," "bakery," "average" (the verb), "ravine," "rehire," and "hatchet-man" (a pioneer, not a thug, and certainly not someone who'd whack a cherry tree).

"I am a friend to neology," Thomas Jefferson wrote in a letter to John Adams in 1820. "It is the only way to give to a language copiousness and euphony." Jefferson introduced "lengthily," "belittle," "public relations," "electioneering," "indecipherable," "monotonously," "ottoman" (the furniture, not the empire), "pedicure," and the noun "bid." He liked inventing words so much that he even coined a verb for it: "neologize."

Jefferson's friend Adams popularized "caucus" and is responsible for "lengthy," "bobolink," "quixotic," "spec" (short for "speculation"), and the verb "net" in the financial sense. James Madison was the first to use "squatter." Abraham Lincoln came up with "relocate," "relocation," and "point well taken." Theodore Roosevelt popularized "muckraker" and invented "lunatic fringe" and "bully pulpit." Warren G. Harding revived two older words, "bloviation" and "normalcy." Franklin D. Roosevelt invented "cheerleader." Dwight D. Eisenhower gave us "military-industrial complex."

George W. Bush gave us many inventive wordings, too—

"malfeance," "uninalienable," "resignate," "subliminal," and "hispanically," among others. I don't think they're likely to stay the course. Then again, I may have misunderestimated them.

Axe, and It Shall Be Given

Everybody has a pet peeve, even the little man who lives inside my email software. He's always whining about the old mail clogging his arteries and slowing him down, especially the peeves I get from peevish language snobs. I could make his day by getting rid of all the messages about one item in particular: the pronunciation of "ask" as AX. Most people who vent about it blame African Americans for mangling poor old "ask."

Hold on a minute. The AX pronunciation isn't limited to African Americans. I heard it when I was growing up in Iowa, from whites as well as blacks. In fact, it's heard across the country, across racial lines, and even across the Atlantic. What's more, the word was spelled—and pronounced—"axe" in the fourteenth century, when it first appeared in writing.

Today this pronunciation is considered "nonstandard"— a term linguists now prefer for what used to be called "illiterate"—but it wasn't always so. The verb entered Old English in the eighth century and had two basic forms, *ascian* and *acsian.* During the Middle English period (1100–1500), the latter form (*acsian*) became *axsian* and finally "axe" (or "ax"), which was the accepted written form until about 1600. Chaucer, in *The Parson's Tale* (1386), writes of "a man that . . . cometh for to axe him of mercy." And in Miles Coverdale's 1535 translation of the Bible, there are lines like "Axe and it shal be giuen you" and "he axed for wrytinge tables."

In the early seventeenth century, "ask" (which had been lurking in the background) replaced "axe." Though the spelling changed and the consonant sounds were switched in standard English, the old pronunciation is still heard in the Midland and Southern dialects of England, according to the *Oxford English Dictionary*. And it's also heard in the United States, as we know. Is this bad boy ever going to make it back into our good graces? Not in my lifetime.

Disinterested Parties

You may not know much about the nineteenth-century French journalist Jean-Baptiste Alphonse Karr, but you're undoubtedly familiar with one of his epigrams: "The more things change, the more they stay the same." That pretty much sums up the story of the word "disinterested."

When it first showed up in print around 1612, "disinterested" meant not interested, according to the *Oxford English Dictionary*. In 1659, however, another meaning surfaced: impartial. Over the next couple of hundred years, respected writers including Samuel Johnson and Noah Webster merrily used both meanings and nobody seemed to mind.

It wasn't till the late nineteenth century that American usage writers decided "disinterested" should mean only one thing: impartial. Why? Because we already had a perfectly good word, "uninterested," that meant not interested. Our messy language, they figured, would be tidier if the two words had two different meanings. Never mind that "uninterested" had a messy upbringing too. It started out in the seventeenth century meaning impartial, but ended up meaning not interested a century later.

Forget the inconvenient history. To this day, most usage manuals and style guides will tell you that a juror who falls asleep is "uninterested," while an impartial judge is "disinterested." Of course, most of the people who actually speak and write English use "disinterested" both ways. And dictionaries include both meanings, while noting that usage authorities disagree. But, as we all know, in English the majority rules. All those usage experts will eventually come around. In the meantime, what is the conscientious writer to do? You can take a stand, use "disinterested" to mean not interested, and risk being thought an illiterate nincompoop by those who don't know any better. Or you can take the cowardly way out and use "disinterested" only to mean impartial.

My own feeling is that it's better to be understood than to be correct, especially when intelligent people can't agree on what is correct. If you mean not interested, say "not interested." If you mean impartial, say "impartial" (or "objective," "unbiased," "unprejudiced," "fair," "nonpartisan," "judicious," "incorruptible," and so on). That's my unbiased opinion.

Literal Minded

Early in my newspaper career, I was editing a story at the *Waterloo Courier* about a Pioneer Days celebration in rural Iowa. The event had all the trimmings—carnival rides, corn dogs and funnel cakes, live music, and a parade with covered wagons and costumed "settlers." There must have been a beer tent, too, or so I assumed from the copy handed in by the reporter. The spectators, he wrote, "were literally turned inside out and shot backwards in time." *Literally?* Gee, we should have sent a photographer along.

If I'd left the story the way it was, most readers wouldn't have batted an eyelash. But for the record, "literally" means "to the letter" or "word for word." Anyone who uses it in a less-than-literal way is literally wrong. Unfortunately, a lot of people do use it loosely in place of its opposite, "figuratively," which means metaphorically or imaginatively. (No one says "figuratively," of course, because it doesn't have enough oomph.) In fact, so many people have abused "literally" that this meaning is beginning to show up in dictionaries. *Merriam-Webster's Collegiate,* for instance, says "literally" can legitimately be used as "pure hyperbole intended to gain emphasis." I beg to disagree. I'm not willing to give up on the literal meaning of "literally."

To be honest, however, there is a case to be made for the looser meaning of the word. In the interest of fairness, here's the opposing point of view, brought to you by the lexicographer Jesse Sheidlower, the *OED*'s editor-at-large. Although "literally" meant "word for word" when it first showed up in English in 1533, it was being used more freely within a century and a half. Dryden, for instance, used it in the late 1600s merely to emphasize a point. By the late 1700s, it was being used to underscore figurative or metaphorical expressions, and well-known writers have been doing that ever since. Sheidlower cites Thoreau, Dickens, Twain, Thackeray, and others. In a bucolic picnic scene from *Little Women* (1868), for example, Louisa May Alcott writes: "The land literally flowed with milk and honey on such occasions."

All right, all right—the usage has a history. I admit that. But you won't find me using "literally" that way, at least not while editors blue-pencil it and educated speakers still cringe. You shouldn't either, especially if you hang around people who are "literal" minded.

Trying Times

I have nothing against grammarians as a class. After all, I'm one myself. But sometimes we get carried away. A case in point is the expression "try and," as in "try and make me," which language writers generally condemn as a trying usage that ought to be replaced by "try to." I'd like to try and change their minds. And yours too, if you're with them on this.

The expression "try and," which first showed up in the early 1600s, was considered perfectly good English until the late 1800s. Here it is in an 1813 letter from Jane Austen: "Now I will try and write of something else." In fact, etymologists say "try and" may be older than "try to." Similar expressions, like "come and" (as in "come and visit me") and "go and" (as in "go and see if it's there") have been around even longer, going back to the 1200s. As far as we know, not a word was said against any of them until 1864, when a book reviewer criticized a writer for hoping readers would "try and" not think him dull: "Try *and* think, indeed! Try *to,* we can understand." A popular language writer of the day, George Washington Moon, then included the criticism in an 1865 collection of essays on English.

The rest is history. Grammarians and usage experts have been piling on ever since, calling "try and" a "colloquialism," a "vulgarism," and more. Henry Fowler, the language mavens' language maven, defended the "literary dignity" of the usage in the 1920s, but he was the exception rather than the rule. I'm with Fowler on this. We often find "and" between two related verbs. It makes absolutely no sense to criticize a remark like "try and see him" when it's acceptable to say "come and see him" or "go and see him" or "stop and see him." Not convinced? Well, E. B. White, who knew a little something about the elements of style, wrote in a letter in 1936: "I'm going to try and see him today." And the usage didn't seem to bother Thackeray, Dickens, Melville, Twain, George Eliot, and many others.

No matter. Sticklers still condemn "try and," especially for formal occasions. And nearly two thirds of the usage panel for *The American Heritage Dictionary of the English Language* (4th ed.) reject it in writing.

Do I use "try and"? Sure I do. I may not use it in formal writing, but I don't hesitate to use it in casual writing and in conversation. Perhaps any sticklers who think otherwise should try and lighten up.

A Likely Story

When I was growing up, long before I became a logophile or even knew that a logophile was a word lover, my mom used to grumble about the misuse of the word "like" on TV. If it wasn't the Winston commercial, it was the teenage beatnik Maynard G. Krebs. She'd have plenty to say if she could hear how people use "like" today, and she'd have plenty of company.

The latest incarnation of "like" is a gossipy usage that has grammar purists—and many parents of teenagers—climbing the walls. This upstart "like" is the new "say," and users (or abusers, depending on which side you take) find it a handy tool for quoting or paraphrasing the speech of others, often with sarcasm or irony. Linguists call it the "quotative like," but any thirteen-year-old can show you how it works.

For example, it can introduce an actual quotation ("She's *like,* 'What unusual shoes you're wearing!' ") or a riff on one ("She's *like,* my shoes are weird!").

Or it can summarize the inner thoughts of either the quoter or the quotee ("She's *like,* yeah, as if I'd be caught dead in them! And I'm *like,* I care what you think?").

"Like" even lets a speaker imitate the behavior of the person being quoted ("She's *like . . .* " and the speaker smirks and rolls her eyes).

This "like" is not to be confused with Maynard G.'s favorite word, which most of us see as a meaningless verbal tic ("You mean, *like,* work?"). Even that one has its uses—to emphasize something ("I was, *like,* exhausted!") or to hedge a statement ("We had, *like,* six hours of homework!"). The new "like" is also not to be confused with the one that sticklers say should be "as" ("Winston tastes good *like* a cigarette should"), which I talked about on pages 35–37.

But back to the "like" that's used to introduce quotes (real or approximate) as well as thoughts, attitudes, and even gestures. It has a lot in common with the other quoting words commonly used in speech: the old standby "say," along with newcomers "go" ("He *goes,* 'Give me your wallet,' ") and "all" ("I'm *all,* 'Sure, dude, it's yours' "). But "like" does even more than these, and in just a generation or so it has spread throughout much of the English-speaking world.

OK, the new "like" is hot and it's useful, but is it legit? Aren't some rules of grammar or usage being broken here? Parents of teenagers may gnash their teeth (one dad, Calvin Trillin, writes, "Some of them can make do for days on end with hardly any words at all beyond the word 'like' "), but lexicographers are more relaxed about "like." The latest editions of *The American Heritage Dictionary of the English Language* and *Merriam-Webster's Collegiate Dictionary* now include it as a usage heard in informal speech. That's not a ringing endorsement, but it's not a condemnation either.

Linguists, meanwhile, argue that "like" is not exclusively a kid thing. Grown-ups use it too, men and women about equally. Another unfounded assumption, they say, is that "like" is used by the less educated among us—there's no evidence for that, either.

As for me, I'm convinced that this is a useful, even ingenious, addition to informal spoken English. And I believe that kids are capable of knowing the difference between formal and informal, written and spoken English. But let's be honest. For now, at least, the usage smacks of incorrectness to a great many people. My feeling is that it's OK in casual conversation with like-minded people, but not in writing, even on a BlackBerry.

Disrespectfully Yours

Perhaps you dis the verb "disrespect," snubbing it as a gangsta interloper from the world of hip-hop. Well, chill. This so-called bad boy is getting a bum rap. "Disrespect" is a perfectly respectable verb that's been around since the 1600s.

Nobody argues against using "disrespect" as a noun ("Beaver, don't show disrespect for your father"). But a lot of language lovers can't get their minds around using "disrespect" as a verb ("Beaver, don't disrespect your father"). Not only is the verb respectable, but it's been respectable even longer than the noun. The verb made its first known appearance in print in 1614, and the noun in 1631. In fact, the verb may actually be father to the noun, according to the *Oxford English Dictionary.*

It's also father to the verb "dis," as in "Don't dis me," which dictionaries promoted from "slang" to "informal" in a mere twenty years. The first citation in the *OED* is from a 1980 song by the rapper Spoonie Gee: "Ya wanna be dissed and then ya wanna be a crook. Ya find a old lady, take her pocketbook." But by 2000, "dis" had gone mainstream, as in this quote from the British newspaper *The Independent:* "Seething at seeing his life's work in pesticide research being dissed by the organic lobby, he called in the Advertising Standards Authority." Perhaps that watchdog group advised the seething scientist to chill.

As we all know, the verb "chill" means to grow cold—it's meant that for seven hundred years—but "chill" also has a long and sometimes contrary history as slang. At one time, it meant to warm something, or take the chill off. Dickens, in *Sketches by Boz* (1836), writes of a pint of beer "chilling" by the fire. In America's inner cities of the 1970s, "chill" meant to calm down or cool it or relax. Since the '80s, it has also meant to hang out or socialize with friends. Lately it's taken on another role, as an adjective meaning "cool." When street terms are useful, they gain cred and eventually make it into dictionaries—sometimes as slang (like "chill" and "phat"), sometimes as informal ("dis"), and sometimes as standard English ("cred," "gangsta," "bling").

"Cred" was once a slang word for (no surprise) "credibility." It first showed up in the early 1980s in the expression "street cred." Before long, everybody owned it, and by 1988 the *New Scientist* was referring to "lab cred," according to the *OED.* Today *Merriam-Webster's Collegiate Dictionary* (11th ed.) considers it standard English.

"Dis," "chill," and "cred," along with "phat" (first-rate), "bling" (flashy jewelry), and "gangsta" (you guessed it), are among the many African-American slang words that have come in off the streets and enriched the language. They don't deserve to be dissed.

Chapter 4

Once Upon a Time

The Whole Nine Yards of Etymology

Everyone knows what "the whole nine yards" means: the works, everything, the whole enchilada. And almost everyone has an opinion about where the expression comes from. At least that's what one would conclude from the response I get every time the subject is raised when I'm on the radio.

"It comes from World War II," a listener once wrote. "A ribbon of bullets on a warplane was twenty-seven feet long, and when they wanted to be sure to shoot down an enemy plane they would exhaust an entire ribbon." Many others agreed. "Machine gun ammunition clips had exactly nine yards of ammunition," one emailer explained. "The soldiers would say 'Give 'em the whole nine yards!' That is the origin."

But other listeners were equally sure that "the whole nine yards" was a seafaring phrase. "The people at the South Street Seaport had this one right," one said. "In sailing days, when they wanted to push their clippers to the limit, they put on the 'whole nine yards,' meaning the three yards, or long spars, on each of their three masts."

A husband and wife even sent dueling opinions. Hers: In olden times, nine yards of fabric were used to make a shroud. His: A ready-mix concrete truck, when fully loaded, carries nine cubic yards of concrete.

Unfortunately, many linguists and writers (including me) have spent way too much time trying to track down the phrase's origin. All those theories I mentioned, from ammo belts to loads of cement, have been debunked. The British language sleuth Michael Quinion has also ruled out suggestions that the phrase comes from the fabric needed for a nun's habit, a three-piece suit, or a Scottish kilt; the capacity of a coal-ore wagon or a garbage truck; the length of a maharaja's sash or a hangman's noose; the distance between the cellblock and the outer wall of a prison, and any number of measurements having to do with sports.

But the word detecting goes on. As of this writing, the first published references we have for the expression in its usual sense are from the early 1960s. Here's the one I find most promising. In an April 18, 1964, article about lingo in the space program, the *San Antonio Express and News* said, " 'Give 'em the whole nine yards' means an item-by-item report on any project." Of course, questions remain. Why "nine yards" instead of, say, "three pints" or "seven miles" or "ten pounds" or whatever? All we know as of now is that the expression may be an Americanism from the 1960s and a product of the space program.

That may not be the whole enchilada, but it's more than we know about a lot of other words and expressions. In many cases, we simply don't know—and may never know—where these things come from. But language lovers hate to take no for an answer. If a definitive origin is lacking, they'll be happy to supply one. Herewith, a few of the more inventive genealogies.

Jeepers Creepers!

Live radio can be hair-raising. You never know when someone will throw you a curve. This one seemed easy. A listener called to ask about the origin of the word "jeep." I explained that the word comes from GP, the Army's abbreviation for "general purpose" vehicle. I had *Merriam-Webster's Collegiate Dictionary* (10th ed.) at my elbow to back me up.

When I got home, I found an email from Florenz Eisman, whose husband, Hy, drew the *Popeye, Little Iodine,* and *Katzenjammer Kids* cartoons for many years. "The word 'jeep' originated in the Popeye strip many moons ago," she said, "before the Army vehicle was named." The true source, she said, was a cartoon character, Eugene the Jeep.

She was right, as I learned after some unusually entertaining research. The real story was a lot more fun than the one widely believed by Americans and found in many of their dictionaries, especially older ones.

I shared my news with listeners the next month and was delighted to get a call on the air from a Merriam-Webster's lexicographer. She said the company had made the same discovery and was planning to change its "jeep" entry. Sure enough, Eugene appeared in the dictionary's eleventh edition. Here's the whole nine yards about "jeep":

In 1936, a new cartoon character joined Popeye, Olive Oyl, Bluto, Wimpy, and Swee'pea in Elzie Segar's popular *Thimble Theater* comic strips. The newcomer was a cute little guy, a fuzzy fellow the size of a small dog with the ability to foresee the future and to disappear into the fourth dimension in an emergency. He ate a diet of orchids, and the only sound he could make was "jeep, jeep." Segar named him Eugene the Jeep.

An immediate hit, Eugene became the Snoopy of his day. In

the late 1930s he was adopted as a mascot by several government contractors and other corporations, which named planes, boats, trucks, and other vehicles after him. These were whimsically referred to as "jeeps," and some even had Eugene's picture painted on the side.

Meanwhile, in 1941 the Army introduced a small all-terrain reconnaissance vehicle manufactured mainly by two big companies, Willys-Overland and Ford. It just so happened that Ford used the factory designation GP on its models—G for "government contract" and P as a code for an 80-inch wheelbase.

So GP was not an Army designation, it did not stand for "general purpose," and it was not the origin of the name "Jeep."

When Willys-Overland unveiled a prototype, reporters wanted to know its name. "You can call it a jeep," said a company publicist. Later Willys began using the name officially, setting off furious legal battles over the commercial rights to the name. Willys changed hands over the years, and as of this writing the trademark "Jeep" is owned by Chrysler.

In case you're wondering, the British-based Wimpy fast-food chain is named after Popeye's freeloading pal J. Wellington Wimpy, who was always promising that he'd "gladly pay you Tuesday for a hamburger today." But the Popeyes fried-chicken restaurants have no connection to the comic strip. Their inspiration was Popeye Doyle, the hotheaded undercover cop played by Gene Hackman in the movie *The French Connection.* He wouldn't have been caught dead eating spinach.

The Cat's Meow

You're not going to like this one. The only time I get hissed or booed in public is when I talk about the origin of the expression "no room to swing a cat." So if you're squeamish, feel free to skip this section.

The usual explanation is that the "cat" in the saying refers to the infamous cat-o'-nine-tails once used to keep wayward sailors in line on British warships. This nasty piece of business consisted of a handle with nine branches, or tails, made of knotted rope. Supposedly there was such a crowd looking on and so little elbow room on deck that the flogger often had "no room to swing a cat."

That story sounds legit, except for one small detail. Expressions about not having enough room to swing a cat are older than the term "cat-o'-nine-tails"—and much older than the use of "cat" as a nickname for the dreaded lash. How do we know this? Let's go to the *OED*. The earliest published reference to this claustrophobic cat-swinging is from 1665: "They had not space enough (according to the vulgar saying) to swing a Cat in." That was thirty years before the first citation for "cat-o'-nine-tails" and 123 years before the short form "cat." All this suggests the cat-swinging business was in use well before a "cat" meant a whip.

The true story, which takes a bit of detective work, is just as gruesome in its own way. There's a clue in Shakespeare. In *Much Ado About Nothing,* written in 1599, the character Benedick jokingly insists he'll never marry. He goes on to say, "If I do, hang me in a bottle like a Cat, and shoot at me." In Elizabethan times, it turns out, archers stuffed cats into leather sacks (or "bottles") and swung them from trees for target practice. Well, I said you wouldn't like it.

By Mark Twain's time, the old Elizabethan reference to target practice had long been forgotten. But when Twain used the phrase "swing a cat" in the nineteenth century in *The Innocents Abroad,* he was obviously not referring to a cat-o'-nine-tails:

"Notwithstanding all this furniture, there was still room to turn around in, but not to swing a cat in, at least with entire security to the cat."

One final note. You may be wondering how the cat got into "cat-o'-nine-tails." The expression probably originated as "one of grim humour," a reference to a cat's "scratching" a miscreant's back, according to the *Oxford English Dictionary*. Ouch.

Red in the Face

Language lovers are a bloodthirsty lot. Some of their ideas about word and phrase origins make my hair stand on end.

It's widely believed, for example, that the expression "paint the town red" refers to the supposed savagery of the Roman legions. In ancient times, we're informed, soldiers drunk with victory (and who knows what else?) washed the walls of conquered towns with the blood of the defeated. Caligula meets Freddy Krueger.

Reality check: There's no evidence that the Romans had anything to do with this expression. Roman society depended heavily on slavery, and the Romans tended to enslave rather than massacre conquered people. If you don't believe me, check out accounts by Livy, Josephus, and the modern historian K. R. Bradley of the conquests of Carthage, Jerusalem, Epirus, and so on.

Another popular theory is that the expression originated in 1837, when the marquis of Waterford and a bunch of rowdy friends painted some public spots red in the English town of Melton Mowbray. Eric Partridge's *A Dictionary of Slang and Unconventional English* appears to accept the Melton Mowbray angle.

And the town's tourism industry trades heavily on it. But I have my doubts.

It's hardly likely that either Roman atrocities or aristocratic misbehavior would be the source of "paint the town red." That's because the expression is relatively recent. According to the *Oxford English Dictionary* it first appeared in American newspapers in the 1880s—half a century after the Melton Mowbray shenanigans and an ocean away, never mind the Roman Empire.

Then where did "paint the town red" come from? In the nineteenth century, according to *OED* citations, the verb "paint" was a slang term that meant to drink and alluded to a drunk's red nose. As for the original town, the language researcher Barry Popik suggests it may have been Chicago. Popik cites an article in a Lima, Ohio, newspaper saying the expression was coined to describe the exuberance of former President Ulysses S. Grant's supporters during the 1880 Republican National Convention in Chicago. Grant's delegates, the *Daily Democratic Times* said, "had not only drank all the whiskey but had painted the town red." The celebrating, though, was premature. When the convention ended after thirty-six ballots, the nomination went to James A. Garfield.

Blowin' in the Wind

I haven't done any sociolinguistic research on this issue, but I'm willing to bet that we have more popular expressions for bad behavior than for good. I can't think of very many colorful phrases for going to church, but look at all the ones we have for getting drunk. We can go on a bender, tie one on, pub-crawl, get a buzz on, go on a tear, wet our whistles, or get sloshed (or plastered or pickled or soused or tight or smashed or pie-eyed). And that's just the tip of the ice cube. If there's a lesson here, it's that popular expressions don't always show us at our best.

Take "three sheets to the wind." Everybody knows what it means, of course—inebriated. And almost everybody is sure where the expression comes from: the age of sailing ships. The three sheets supposedly are loose sails, flapping in the wind and out of control. The old schooner, meanwhile, lists—drunkenly—in the waves.

It's a good image, but it doesn't quite hold water. To a sailor, sheets are lines (ropes, to a landlubber), and not sails, as many people think. The sheets are used to trim, or adjust, the sails, making the most efficient use of the available wind. If the sheets are loose, the sails can't do their job, leaving the ship out of control, not unlike a drunken sailor stumbling back to port after a night on the town.

But why three sheets, instead of two, or four? One explanation may be that a sloop, the most common sailing boat, has one mast, two sails, and three sheets.

The expression was originally "three sheets *in* the wind." The earliest reference in the *Oxford English Dictionary* is from 1821, but I prefer a scene in the Dickens novel *Dombey and Son* (1848), where Captain Cuttle believes Bunsby is "three sheets in the wind, or, in plain words, drunk."

Before we go ashore, let's toss a couple of seafaring myths overboard.

"SOS," the international distress signal, doesn't stand for "Save Our Ship" or "Save Our Souls" or anything else. Wireless radio operators adopted it in the early twentieth century because the letters in Morse code (three dots, three dashes, three dots) were easy to send and unlikely to be misunderstood.

And the word "posh" isn't an acronym for "port out, starboard home," which supposedly designated the best (that is, the coolest) accommodations on a steamship voyage from England to India and back in the days before air-conditioning. The tickets of well-heeled passengers were supposedly stamped "P.O.S.H.," but no such ticket has ever been found.

In fact, the origin of the adjective "posh," meaning smart or fashionable, has never been pinned down. It first showed up during World War I, but it wasn't until decades later that anyone suggested "posh" was an acronym. Indeed, acronyms were rare before the 1930s, according to the lexicographer Jesse Sheidlower, and "etymologies of this sort—especially for older words—are almost always false."

Arrested Development

Like many writers of his day, Mark Twain was often paid by the word. At seven cents a pop, he'd get forty-nine cents for this sentence: "I met a policeman in the metropolis." Except that he wouldn't have written it like that, or so he once joked.

"I never write 'metropolis' for seven cents, because I can get the same money for 'city.' I never write 'policeman,' because I can get the same price for 'cop.'"

I like short words too. They're punchy, direct, and down-to-earth. But many people feel the need to dress up simple words by giving them colorful origins.

"Cop" is a good example, as it happens. The most popular myth about the word is that it comes from the copper buttons on police uniforms. Another is that it comes from the copper badges worn by New York City police in the nineteenth century. Yet another suggests that "cop" is an acronym for "constable on patrol" or "chief of police" or "custodian of the peace" or some such phrase.

In fact, cops were walking beats long before any of those phony acronyms arrived on the scene. And "cop" has nothing to do with any metals, copper or otherwise, whether in buttons or badges. Metal buttons on police uniforms have tended to be brass, and relatively few badges have been copper.

The best evidence, according to word detectives who have worked the case, is that the noun "cop" comes from the verb "cop," which has meant to seize or nab since at least 1704. The verb in turn may be a variation of an even earlier one, "cap," which meant to arrest as far back as 1589 (think of the word "capture").

Etymologists say the noun "cop" is short for "copper" (one who cops criminals), which first appeared in an 1846 British court document. The clipped version, "cop," appeared thirteen years later in an American book about underworld slang.

Speaking of gangster talk, I'm reminded of Raymond Chandler's complaint about scholars who study the subject: "The so-called experts in this line have their ear to the library, very seldom to the ground." If I'm guilty, I'll cop a plea.

Bird Brains

I've been a perfunctory birdwatcher for years, a slacker who often can't get her binoculars focused in time. But I don't need them to see the merlin that hunts field mice from our deck, or the goldfinches, grosbeaks, towhees, woodpeckers, turkeys, and pheasants at the feeders. Not to mention the bluebirds and swallows that negotiate with one another for nest boxes in the meadow. And I certainly didn't need binocs the evening a great horned owl dive-bombed my husband and me in the driveway.

There's not much chance, however, that I'll ever spot a rail—the skinny, secretive bird that many ornithologists, naturalists, and authors of birding guides insist is the source of the expression "thin as a rail." But here's where I'm one up on those bird eminences. While it's true that many of the feathered rails are skinny (or, as ornithologists are wont to say, "laterally compressed"), the evidence for an avian connection is thin. The rail in the expression, it just so happens, is the kind you find in a fence or a train track, not in *Birds of America.* The fence "rail" and the avian "rail" are two different species.

The man-made "rail" came into English in the fourteenth century from the Old French word *reille* ("iron bar"), which came from the Latin *regula,* meaning a straight stick—that is, a ruler. The ancient Indo-European root *reg,* meaning to move in a straight line, gave us a whole family of words including "right," "regular," "rule," "rigid," "straight," "reign," "rectify," "erect," "correct," and others. The feathered "rail," on the other hand, comes from a different Old French word, *raale,* and first appeared in English in two fifteenth-century cookbooks. Where the French got the word nobody seems to know, but it's probably related to the verb *raler,* or "rattle," which may describe the sound the bird makes.

As for "thin as a rail," the first writer known to have used the phrase was Mark Twain in *Roughing It* (1872): "You'll marry a combination of calico and consumption that's as thin as a rail." We can't tell from that whether he's referring to a bird or a fence. But a later quotation in the *Oxford English Dictionary,* "as thin as a lath or rake or rail" (1927), supports the idea that the rail involved was something man-made. All of the *OED*'s citations for "thin as a rail" or "lean as a rail" are listed under the noun meaning a rod, stick, bar, and so on.

If any birders out there still have doubts, I can cite a source that's up on both ornithology and etymology. Here's a quotation from the Audubon webpage for the Virginia rail (*Rallus limicola*): "Although 'thin as a rail' refers to the rail of a fence, it aptly describes the Virginia Rail, whose narrow body allows passage through the thick vegetation found in fresh and salt water wetlands."

Is Government the Issue?

The term "GI" shows up in many expressions: "GI Joe" and "GI Jane," "GI gin" and "GI party," "GI bath" and "GI shower." But what exactly does "GI" stand for? Most people seem to think "GI," which refers to an American soldier or things military, began life as an abbreviation for "government issue" or "general issue." And most people are wrong. Here's how the term got its marching orders.

In the early twentieth century, "GI" was a semiofficial US Army abbreviation for "galvanized iron." The term, dating back to 1907, was used in military inventories to describe iron cans, buckets, and so on, according to the *Random House Historical Dictionary of American Slang*.

By 1917, however, "GI" began to take on a wider meaning. In World War I, it was used to refer to all things Army, so military bricks became GI bricks and military Christmases became GI Christmases. Before long, we had GI soap and GI shoes and, eventually, plain old GIs. This new and improved term needed a new family tree, of course. In the minds of many, "galvanized iron" obligingly became "government issue" or "general issue."

During "the war to end all wars," the expression "GI cans" (remember those galvanized-iron buckets?) came to mean heavy artillery shells, especially ones that the Germans were firing at the Allies. As for other "GI" terms, here's a brief lexicon:

GI banjo: An army shovel.
GI bath: The forced scrubbing of a grungy trainee.
GI bride: A soldier's foreign wife.
GI gin: Military cough syrup.
GI Jane: A female soldier.
GI Jesus: A military chaplain.
GI Joe: A male soldier.
GI party: A barracks scrubbing.
GI runs: Diarrhea.
GI shower: See "GI bath."
GI trots: See "GI runs."

A Bun in the Oven

A few years ago, a radio host interviewed me about my latest book, then asked whether I had anything new in the works. "I have a bun in the oven," I replied. When I got home, I found a congratulatory email from a listener: "Good luck with your pregnancy."

Whoops! The "bun" in question meant one thing to me (a new book) but something quite different to the emailer. I shouldn't have been surprised. We've had metaphors and other kinds of figurative language as long as we've had writing, and probably longer. But confusion is the price we sometimes pay for using figurative speech, especially when we use it (as I did) in an unexpected way.

The expression "a bun in the oven," a euphemism for pregnancy, is relatively new. It first appeared in print, according to the *Oxford English Dictionary,* in *The Cruel Sea,* a 1951 novel by Nicholas Monsarrat. But the word "oven" has been used figuratively in English for the vagina or womb since the end of the seventeenth century. And the idea of baking as a metaphor for gestation goes back to classical times.

New metaphors are being created all the time—think of the "spam" in your in-box—but others have been around for so long that we've forgotten their literal meanings. How many people know what a "loophole" once was? Or a "dashboard"? Or a "deadline"? These words, and many others, are living ghosts. The original meanings all but died when history passed them by, but they've survived as metaphors. Linguists would argue that they're not true metaphors, since we're unaware of their original meanings when we use them. In fact, language experts often call them "dead metaphors." What do you say we resurrect a few of their late, unlamented histories from the metaphorical graveyard?

Loophole. In the 1300s a "loupe," later a "loop hole," was a small vertical slit in a castle wall for spotting enemies and shooting arrows at them. It probably came from a Middle Dutch word, *lupen,* meaning to lie in wait, watch, or peer. So an archer trapped in a besieged tower would shoot through a loophole at the surrounding forces. Today a loophole is usually an omission or ambiguity that gives you an opening to evade a legal provision.

Earmark. For centuries, farmers notched the ears of livestock as a means of identifying them, and many ranchers still do. The resulting noun, originally spelled "eare-marke," dates from 1523 and the verb from 1591, according to the *OED.* These days to "earmark" usually means to set aside funds for a specific purpose, a metaphorical usage dear to the hearts of politicians since the mid-nineteenth century.

Transfixed. It once meant pierced or stuck through with an arrow or a spear. The verb "transfix," according to the *OED,* first appeared in print in Edmund Spenser's epic poem *The Faerie Queene* (1590), where Semiramis, the queen of Assyria, is "transfixt" by her son's own sword. Nowadays someone who's "transfixed" is fascinated or mesmerized, as if stuck to the spot.

Tenterhooks. In the 1400s, tenterhooks were nails or pointed, L-shaped hooks set along the edges of a wooden frame (called a "tenter") for stretching and drying newly woven woolen cloth. In the eighteenth century, people began using the word figuratively, and "to be on tenterhooks" (no, not "tenderhooks"!) was to be tense or held in suspense. In today's far from relaxing times, that's the principal meaning.

Bellwether. Once upon a time, everybody knew that a wether was a castrated ram, and a bellwether the sheep that wore a bell to lead the flock. The word today has a literal meaning only in sheep-raising circles. Most of us now regard a bellwether as something that signals future trends.

Distaff. In the eleventh century a distaff (then spelled "distaef") was a staff wound with unspun flax or wool. The "dis" in "distaff" was probably from a Low German word *diesse,* meaning a bunch of unspun flax. The staff, about a yard long, was held under the left arm, and wisps of material were pulled through the fingers of the left hand, then twisted with the fingers of the right and wound onto a spindle. The word "distaff" came to be associated with women's work, and it's now a noun or adjective referring to the feminine side of things.

Dashboard. Believe it or not, we had dashboards before we had cars. In the early nineteenth century, a dashboard was a barrier of wood or leather used as a mud guard at the front, and sometimes the sides, of a horse-drawn carriage. The dashboard kept mud from being "dashed" into the interior by the horses' hooves. When you go for a spin today, the horses under your hood don't splatter mud on the passengers, but a dashboard is standard equipment.

Deadline. The original deadline was a four-foot-high fence that defined the no-man's-land inside the walls around the Confederate prisoner-of-war camp at Andersonville, Georgia, during the Civil War. Any captive Union soldiers who crossed the deadline were shot. The word first appeared in an inspection report written in August 1864 by a Confederate officer, Lieut. Col. D. T. Chandler: "A railing around the inside of the stockade and about 20 feet from it constitutes the 'dead-line,' beyond which the prisoners are not allowed to pass." After the war ended in 1865, Capt. Henry Wirtz, the commandant of the infamous camp, was tried and hanged for war crimes. Not until the early twentieth century did "deadline" come to mean a time limit. The *OED*'s first mention is in the title of a play about the newspaper business, *Deadline at Eleven* (1920). This usage may have been influenced by a somewhat earlier sense of the word: a guideline marked on the bed of a printing press. These days, as we all know, journalists aren't the only ones with deadlines to meet.

Linchpin. This word was born in the 1300s, when it meant a pin inserted into an axle or a shaft to keep a wheel from falling off. It was used exclusively in that way from the days of horse-drawn carriages to the T-Birds and Coupe de Villes of the 1950s. The metaphorical use of "linchpin" (as a vital person or thing) is relatively new—the *OED*'s first citation is a 1954 diary entry by the author Malcolm Muggeridge, though Winston Churchill used it in the 1930s and '40s. Today only mechanics and hobbyists still use the word in its original sense.

I'll Be Home for Xmas

The language lady's Christmas: A hangover after too much eggnog. Carpal tunnel syndrome from writing all those cards. A reminder to call Weight Watchers. Chapter 7 bankruptcy. And, of course, an in-box stuffed with indignant mail about Xmas (not the holiday—the spelling).

"Who took Christ out of Christmas?" somebody always asks. The usual suggestion is that "Xmas" is a secular plot, an attempt by the ungodly to x-out Jesus and banish religion from the holiday. In other words, we're told, it's all part of the War on Christmas.

I won't get into any of the other battles on the Christmas front. But I'd like to throw a very heavy book (maybe even all twenty volumes of the *Oxford English Dictionary*) at the grinches who dis "Xmas." A little research would show them that "Xmas" isn't part of a modern plot against Christmas. In fact, the usage has been around for nearly a thousand years. Here's the real "Xmas" story.

The first recorded use of the letter X for "Christ" was back in 1021, according to the *OED*. But don't blame secularists. If you want, blame the monks in Great Britain who used the X while transcribing classical manuscripts into Old English.

Christos, the Greek word for Christ, begins with the letter *chi,* or X. It's spelled in Greek letters this way: ΧΡΙΣΤΟΣ. In early times the Greek letters *chi* and *rho* together (XP) and in more recent centuries just *chi* (X) were used in writing as an abbreviation for "Christ." Sometimes a cross was placed before the X and sometimes not.

Thus for nearly ten centuries, books and diaries and manuscripts and letters routinely used X or XP for "Christ" in words like "christen," "christened," "Christian," "Christianity," and of course "Christmas." The *OED*'s first recorded use of "Xmas" for "Christmas" dates back to 1551.

There was certainly no disrespect intended. And one other point. Although St. Andrew's Cross is shaped like an X, there's no basis for the belief that the X used in place of "Christ" is supposed to represent the Cross on Calvary.

And a Happy New Year.

Chapter 5

Lex Education

Cleaning Up Dirty Words

I love this story. It's surely a myth, but this is a book about myths, right?

When the late Queen Mother visited Newcastle, so it goes, the Lord Mayor escorted her to the River Tyne to see the picturesque punts and canoes. In all the excitement, his tongue got tangled and he called her attention to "the colorful cunts and panoes." After a short silence, the Queen Mum replied: "What exactly is a panoe?"

We have many ways of dealing with raunchy words. We concoct funny stories about them, like the one you just read. We camouflage them in puns ("cunning linguist"), double entendres ("Did you get scrod?"), and euphemisms ("the family jewels"). We compose raunchy limericks about them ("Prince Hamlet thought uncle a traitor / For having it off with his Mater"). We bleep them, we delete them, we ban them, and we "!#@%&" them.

If all else fails, we try to rehabilitate these sexual or scatological rascals. We turn etymology on its head to prove that they aren't so bad after all. We convince ourselves that a shocking word may once have been innocent. Or maybe it has noble roots, now long forgotten. Or perhaps it's only an acronym, made from harmless words.

George Carlin, who knew a thing or two about dirty words, wrote a comic monologue back in the 1970s called "Seven Words You Can Never Say on Television." Of course that was before cable TV, shock radio, and the Internet. Today the Big Seven are heard almost routinely. Here they are, in the original order of presentation: "shit," "piss," "fuck," "cunt," "cocksucker," "motherfucker," and "tits." Carlin later expanded the list to include "fart," "turd," and "twat." That pretty much covers all the bases, wouldn't you say?

Now let's look at the etymological gymnastics we've gone through to clean up four of those naughty words, plus one that Carlin skipped. (Maybe it wasn't bad enough.)

Ship High in Transport

I'm a great believer in the beauty of short, simple words, and I never miss an opportunity to plug them on the air. I once quoted from my favorite poem, composed mostly of one-syllable words: "When you are old and grey and full of sleep, / And nodding by the fire, take down this book, / And slowly read, and dream of the soft look / Your eyes had once, and of their shadows deep."

Boy, was I eloquent (thanks to Yeats)! In passing, I happened to mention that dirty words are short and simple, too. Most of them sprang from short and simple Anglo-Saxon terms. You can guess which part of the discussion was memorable to the audience.

When I got home, my in-box was bulging with email from

listeners offering to enlighten me on the subject of four-letter words. One of those forbidden words, they said, did not have Anglo-Saxon roots. Here's their explanation for the origin of "shit."

Back when manure was shipped from the New World to the Old as fertilizer, it had to be kept dry. If the manure got wet in the hold, it would produce dangerous methane gas. A sailor who was careless with a candle or lantern could blow ship and crew to smithereens. So the label SHIP HIGH IN TRANSPORT was stenciled on the crates, and the acronym "S.H.I.T." became a new word for manure. End of story.

Numerous webpages say it's so (though many say the "T" is for "Transit").

Well, it didn't happen that way. "Shit" (the word) has been around a long time, probably longer than transatlantic shipping. It entered the language more than a thousand years ago as the Old English verb *scitan,* meaning—what else?—"defecate" (the *sc* was pronounced "sh"). The word's roots in old Germanic languages go back even further.

Linguistics aside, the "Ship High" story is wildly improbable. Farm manure is always plentiful—to say the least—wherever animals are domesticated, so why import it from another continent?

Now, bat or seabird excrement, high in nitrogen and phosphorus, is another story. Droppings collected from remote islands were fiercely fought over in the nineteenth century, until the development of synthetic fertilizers ended the so-called guano wars. But cow manure? Didn't happen.

"Shit" is a source of many other made-up acronyms. Army officers who didn't go to West Point, as well as disgruntled cadets, have referred to it as the South Hudson Institute of Technology. And Quang Phuc Dong of the South Hanoi Institute of Technology (aka James D. McCawley, a University of Chicago linguist) created the field of "scatolinguistics." Of course not all S.H.I.T. acronyms are made up. Dan Rather's alma mater changed its name from the Sam Houston Institute of Teaching to Sam Houston State Teachers College to avoid the unfortunate acronym.

Well, shit happens. But what about "shat"? In Anglo-Saxon times, a word that sounded like "shat" was indeed the past tense of "shit." But that usage fell by the wayside (so to speak), leaving "shit" to serve for both present and past until modern times. The word "shat" was revived as a humorous past tense in the early twentieth century, according to the slang lexicographer Eric Partridge. Dictionaries now list both "shit" and "shat" as accepted past tenses of "shit"—that is, if either version can be described as acceptable.

You C_nt Say That

Some time ago, three high school girls in Cross River, New York, created an uproar by using the v-word in a reading from *The Vagina Monologues*. Imagine what would have happened if they'd used the c-word, perhaps the most forbidden term in the English language! Or is it? Maybe I missed something and "cunt" isn't so naughty after all.

Just type "cunt" and "goddess" into your search engine and stand back. Tens of thousands of websites claim that "cunt," a four-letter word with a long English pedigree, is actually a sacred word derived from the title of a Hindu goddess. It stands for all that's warm, loving, sensitive, sensual, life-affirming, and empowering about womanhood.

Is this the outline for a seminar on the semantic bleaching

(i.e., rehabilitation) of naughty words? Or the plotline for a steamy Bollywood movie?

Perhaps more nonsense has been written about "cunt" in recent years than about any other word in English. The usual story, which is quoted from one end of the blogosphere to the other, goes something like this: "cunt" is a sacred ancient word derived from the terms *cunti* or *kunda,* titles of the Hindu goddess Kali.

The truth is more down-to-earth. There's no evidence that "cunt" comes from the title of a goddess, Hindu or otherwise. It's a very old English word going back to the Middle Ages, when it meant, as it does today, "the female external genital organs," according to the *OED.* The earliest surviving reference (spelled "cunte") appeared around 1325 in the *Proverbs of Hendyng,* a collection of religious and moral advice from the 1200s and perhaps earlier. In one of the precepts (I'm roughly translating the Middle English), women are advised to "Give thy cunte wisely and ask for marriage."

Language researchers have discovered even older references within English surnames and street names. The last name Sitbithecunte (sounds like a spoof, doesn't it?) appeared in 1156 in the Norfolk public records. And Gropecuntelane was a red-light district in London around 1230. It was later called Grub Street (Samuel Johnson lived there), then Milton Street, near what is now the Barbican Centre for performing arts.

The *Oxford English Dictionary,* the mother of all language authorities, says "cunt" is related to similar words in many medieval Germanic languages (*kunta* in Old Norse, *kunte* in Old Frisian, etc.). The source of all these words, according to the *OED,* is believed to be a prehistoric Germanic root that linguists have reconstructed as *kunton.*

That's about all we can say for sure about the origin of "cunt."

Everything else is speculation, some of it more plausible than the rest. The most unlikely theory is that "cunt" comes from a similar-sounding word like *cunti* or *kunda* in Sanskrit, the language of the Hindu holy books.

English has borrowed lots of words from the languages of India: "candy," "guru," "mantra," "nirvana," "yoga," "bandanna," "cot," "dungaree," "juggernaut," "jungle," "loot," "pundit," "thug," and many others. But I haven't found a single reputable linguist or etymologist who believes "cunt" is one of them. Most of the words that we've adopted from India entered the language during the English colonization of the subcontinent, from the early 1600s until the mid-1900s, well after "cunt" was established in England. And the majority of the Indian words either didn't have English equivalents or were trendy alternatives. It's unlikely that we would have adopted an Indian word for such a basic body part.

Granted, *cunti* and *kunda* sound like "cunt." But could a sound-alike in Sanskrit have given birth to that ancient Germanic root *kunton,* which presumably gave us the c-word? No way, according to linguists who have studied the ancient languages of Europe and Asia.

It gets a bit complicated now, so you can skip this paragraph if you're already convinced. Way back when, both Sanskrit and ancient Germanic evolved from Indo-European, a prehistoric language that developed in different ways in different parts of the world. An Indo-European word something like *peter,* for instance, evolved into *pitar* in Sanskrit and *fadar* in ancient Germanic, giving us the modern words *vater* in German and "father" in English. In ancient times, a "k" sound in a Sanskrit word (like *kunda*) would have been an "h" sound in Germanic. And a "k" sound in an ancient Germanic root (like *kunton*) would have been a "g" sound in Sanskrit. Linguists call this sound shift Grimm's

Law. In plain English, we couldn't have gotten "cunt" from *cunti* or *kunda* or any Hindu holy word starting with a "k" sound.

So where does the goddess stuff come from? The source most often quoted is *The Woman's Encyclopedia of Myths and Secrets,* by Barbara G. Walker, a former journalist who has also written books about crystals, tarot, divination, and goddess worship.

Though the root of "cunt" isn't divine, it's not smutty, either. The "cu" sound in Old English (spelled *cwe*), like the "gu" sound in ancient Sanskrit, stood for the essence of femininity. The Old English *cwithe* ("womb") was certainly nothing to be ashamed of, and neither was *cwene* ("queen"). Sharing this ancestry is our "cow" and the sacred *go* (pronounced "gow") in Sanskrit. Good words all, but they hardly justify redefining "cunt" itself as a word for everything that's positive about womanhood.

Nevertheless, a "Cunt Power" movement, complete with buttons and T-shirts and campus festivals, has sprung up among some feminists who want to rehabilitate the c-word. I can sympathize with efforts to take back "cunt," but I think this is a losing battle. Despite its innocent prehistoric roots, "cunt" has been considered taboo or bawdy for nearly all of its existence. Buttons and T-shirts aren't likely to change that.

The word is still so shocking that the *Chicago Tribune* pulled an article on this very subject a few years ago although the c-word wasn't even in it. The headline? "You C_nt Say That."

As for the three high-school girls who dared to say "vagina" at a school program, the principal suspended them but quickly backed down under pressure from parents, teachers, and the public. One of the people who came to their support was Eve Ensler, author of *The Vagina Monologues.* Her play has done much to make girls and women comfortable about using a perfectly acceptable word.

But in a foreword to the book version of the *Monologues,* Gloria Steinem perpetuates the myth that we have a goddess to thank for the c-word: "By the time feminists were putting CUNT POWER! on buttons and T-shirts as a way of reclaiming that devalued word, I could recognize the restoration of an ancient power. After all, the Indo-European word *cunt* was derived from the goddess Kali's title of Kunda or Cunti."

Let's Do It

Birds do it, bees do it, even educated fleas do it. We do it too, but we go through more contortions in talking about it than in doing it. One of the more entertaining ways we deal with the word "fuck" is to invent fanciful acronyms for it.

Contrary to what some people believe, it did not come from a World War II handbook warning US Army recruits of penalties "For Unlawful Carnal Knowledge." Nor did it come from a royal seal of approval ("Fornication Under Consent of the King") posted on bawdy houses in Merrie Olde England—or, for that matter, from a royal seal of disapproval ("Forbidden Under Charter of the King").

Other fictitious origins include "Forced Unlawful Carnal Knowledge," a reference to the crime of rape, and "File Under Carnal Knowledge," a Scotland Yard designation for rape cases. And the aforementioned "For Unlawful Carnal Knowledge" supposedly appeared on placards shaming adulterers from medieval England to colonial New England.

It doesn't take Scotland Yard to get to the bottom of all this. The word "fuck" was offending sensibilities for centuries before anybody suggested that it might be an acronym. In fact, none of the apocryphal acronyms seem to have existed before the 1960s, according to the lexicographer Jesse Sheidlower, who edited a book called *The F-Word,* a fount of wisdom on the subject. (And you thought lexicographers led dull lives!)

The real roots of "fuck" aren't quite so colorful. As far as we know, it first appeared in print (spelled "fukkit") in a poem around 1503, though it was hinted at in another poem (coyly disguised in code) published sometime in the 1400s. In speech it's no doubt much, much older. Linguists believe it has Germanic origins. There are similar words in archaic Dutch (*fokken*) and old Scandinavian dialects (*fukka* in Norwegian and *focka* in Swedish).

For obvious reasons, "fuck" has been used more often in speech than in print over the centuries, which explains why the early paper trail is meager. No wonder it's been an irresistible subject for pseudohistory.

Until recent times, publishers have cringed at putting "fuck" in print. The word was bowdlerized as "fug," for example, in Norman Mailer's 1948 novel *The Naked and the Dead* (a euphemism later adopted by the underground rock group the Fugs).

And herein lies another myth. When Mailer was introduced to Tallulah Bankhead, according to popular legend, she remarked, "You're the man who doesn't know how to spell 'fuck.' " (Some accounts credit the quip to Dorothy Parker.) But Mailer insisted years later that nobody said any such thing. Bankhead's enterprising publicity agent, he said, made the story up.

Bitch Craft

I love dogs. I'm a dog person. Naturally, I watch the Westminster Kennel Club dog show on TV every February. But I have to admit that my ears twitch when a commentator admires "a promising young bitch" or "the top-winning bitch in her group." You know what I mean.

Granted, "bitch" is a perfectly good word meaning female dog. It's meant that for a thousand years, probably longer. But it also means a lewd, malicious, treacherous, difficult, unpleasant, or otherwise bitchy woman, and it's had that other meaning for six hundred years.

Dog breeders are about the only ones who feel comfortable using "bitch" in ordinary conversation. Or are they? A lot of women are trying to redefine "bitch" as a positive term for an assertive, powerful, smart, sensual woman. I agree that language has been used to demean women. But I wish these well-meaning folks would get their facts straight. Not to mention their myths!

The revisionists say "bitch" is at heart not only a good word but also a sacred one, with roots going back to the "bitch goddesses" of antiquity. Christian Europe, so the story goes, turned "bitch" into a bad word because of its association with paganism. In making their case, those who want to redefine "bitch" say the goddess of the hunt (Artemis to the Greeks, Diana to the Romans) was referred to as a "bitch goddess" because she led a pack of dogs. Another "bitch goddess," we're told, was herself a dog (Sarama, in Hindu mythology), and still another was a she-wolf (Lupa, who suckled Romulus and Remus).

I won't go into the religious mythology here, though I find some of the latter-day interpretations questionable. The language mythology is what concerns me. It's beside the point whether any deities were referred to as "bitch goddesses" in ancient Greek, Latin, or Sanskrit. In English, "bitch" is a very old word, going back to Anglo-Saxon days, and it had nothing to do with goddesses until the twentieth century. It first appeared in writing as "bicce" about the year 1000, when it meant a female dog in Old English. The word's ancestry is unclear, but it may come from *bikkja,* an ancient Norse word, or *pittja,* a word in an ancient language spoken by herdsmen in Lapland.

For several hundred years, a "bitch" was just a female dog and nobody's ears twitched at the word. It was treated much the same as "dog," the word for a male canine or a generic member of the species. In fact, the word "dog" became a slur before "bitch" did. In the Middle Ages, to call a man a "dog" was the worst kind of insult. It meant he was despicable, cowardly, ill tempered, and worthless. The first published reference to "dog" used this way dates from about 1325, according to the *Oxford English Dictionary.*

Interestingly, "bitch" was first used in a negative way to put down men, not women. The phrase "son of a bitch," meaning a despicable or hateful man, dates from around 1330, some seventy years before the word was turned against women. That's right. It wasn't until about 1400 that people began using "bitch" as an insult for a woman. If Christian Europe wanted to demonize "bitch," it certainly took its time. The truth is that women were by no means singled out in the canine-insults department. The word "bitch" itself was used as a masculine insult around 1500, when the *OED* has a man referred to as "a schrewed byche."

Which brings us to "bitch goddess," an English expression that originated in the early twentieth century, not in pagan times, and has nothing to do with mythology. In 1906 the American philosopher William James (brother to the novelist Henry) coined the expression when he wrote that people who valued money over accomplishment were worshiping "the bitch-goddess SUCCESS." Since then, we've used "bitch goddess" so often as a metaphor for worldly success that it's almost a cliché.

Speaking of success, will the revisionists succeed in rehabilitating the word "bitch"? I doubt it. I don't like being called a bitch, and I don't know anyone who does.

Twat Not

English can be a risqué business. Here's a myth with a very limited circulation—only one person, the poet Robert Browning, believed it. But I like this one so much that I'm including it anyway.

You're probably familiar with these lines from *Pippa Passes*, Browning's famous poem about a little Italian girl named Pippa who briefly passes through the lives of several characters, changing their destinies:

> *The year's at the spring*
> *And day's at the morn;*
> *Morning's at seven;*
> *The hill-side's dew-pearled;*
> *The lark's on the wing;*
> *The snail's on the thorn:*
> *God's in his heaven—*
> *All's right with the world!*

You'll find that inspiring excerpt from Browning's long dramatic poem in any anthology of nineteenth-century English poetry. But you may not find these seldom-quoted lines, from later in the poem, comparing the owls and bats of evening to monks and nuns:

> *Then, owls and bats,*
> *Cowls and twats,*
> *Monks and nuns, in a cloister's moods,*
> *Adjourn to the oak-stump pantry!*

Twats? Whatever was he thinking?

The editors of the *Oxford English Dictionary* apparently wondered the same thing as they were gathering quotations four decades after the poem's 1841 publication. So they asked Browning—at least that's what one supposes from a rather cryptic note in the *OED*'s entry on "twat": "Erroneously used (after quot. 1660) by Browning *Pippa Passes* IV. ii. 96 under the impression that it denoted some part of a nun's attire."

It doesn't take much imagination to fill out the story between the lines. Browning apparently told the *OED* that a "twat" was a nun's headdress, comparable to a monk's cowl. When the curious editors asked him why he thought so, he told them he'd learned the word from an anonymous seventeenth-century poem, "Vanity of Vanities," about an ambitious clergyman. Here are the key lines, quoted in the *OED* entry:

> *They talk't of his having a Cardinall's Hat,*
> *They'd send him as soon an Old Nun's Twat.*

Browning had lived a sheltered life, so it's not surprising that he thought the "twat" in the naughty satirical poem was a nun's hat, not (God forbid) a nun's vulva. One wonders how he got hold of the poem in the first place. One also wonders how he and his equally sheltered wife, Elizabeth Barrett Browning, managed to produce a son.

"Twat" wasn't the only word that Browning tripped over. Sir James A. H. Murray, the original lexicographer of the *OED*, complained to his son Oswyn that "Browning constantly used words without regard to their proper meaning. He has added greatly to the difficulties of the Dictionary."

If any of Browning's readers were startled to find the word "twats" in *Pippa Passes* before the *OED* did, they were too tactful to tell him. Though he was ignorant of its true meaning, "twat" wasn't unknown in Victorian England. It was a slang expression, first recorded in the mid-1600s, meaning just what you'd think—the female pudendum.

The word's origins are obscure, but Eric Partridge, in *A Dictionary of Slang and Unconventional English,* suggests that "twat" may be related to "twachylle," a word from the 1400s meaning a passage or lane. ("Twachylle," according to the *OED,* comes from an even older word for a fork in a road.) Other sources suggest a link to the Old Norse word *thveit,* a forest clearing.

Partridge calls Browning's blunder "a hairraising misapprehension—the literary world's worst 'brick.'" More hairraising to me is the thought that for years Browning might have dropped "twat" into casual conversation over the teacups.

What makes a word dirty? The short answer is that we do. We decide that "shit" is forbidden, "crap" is not quite so bad, and "defecate" is OK. A lot of this goes back a thousand years to the Norman Conquest. England's new ruling classes spoke Norman French, so that became the language of the elite. Saxon speech, meanwhile, was considered crude. So formerly neutral Saxon terms for bodily functions were branded as low-class and eventually obscene, while their French and Latin counterparts were above reproach.

Many of today's four-letter unmentionables ("shit," "fuck," "cunt," "twat," and probably "cock") come from Anglo-Saxon or other old Germanic languages. But their cousins derived from Romance languages ("defecate," "fornicate," "pudendum," "penis," and so on) are acceptable in polite society. In other words, it's all in our minds.

Chapter 6

Identity Theft

The Great Impostors

Next to food and sex, the urge to talk about other people may be the single most compelling force driving human civilization. I don't know if anthropologists will back me up on this, but gossip columnists certainly will. If we aren't eating or having sex, we're probably talking about one another.

We're social animals, after all. We like talking about people so much that we sometimes make words out of their names. This propensity is behind words like "sandwich" (named for John Montagu, the fourth earl of Sandwich), "masochism" (the novelist Leopold von Sacher-Masoch), "leotard" (the aerialist Jules Léotard, who inspired the song "The Daring Young Man on the Flying Trapeze"), and "Kafkaesque" (you know who).

Predictably, we even have a word for a word named after a person: "eponym," from a Greek word that means "named after." The practice was already booming in classical times, when legend has it that Athens was named for the goddess Athena and Rome for the mythological Romulus. We've been doing as the Romans ever since.

Real as well as mythical figures have lent their names to many words over the centuries. But sometimes the relationship is mythical: A word that we think comes from a name actually doesn't. For every "sandwich" or "leotard," it seems, there's a "crapper"—a wannabe-eponym with a fake ID. Let's unmask a few of the more notorious impostors.

Toilet Training

You run across all kinds of people when you're an author, but one woman in particular sticks in my mind. We met in the greenroom before appearing on *Oprah* to talk about our new books, mine on grammar and hers on the history of the toilet.

Yes, I know. She was a hard act to follow. But back to the greenroom. While we were having our hair and makeup done, we chatted nervously and exchanged books.

It wasn't until the flight home that I had a chance to look through hers. Amid illustrations of Louis XIV on his commode and English aristocrats pooping in the bushes, a familiar name caught my eye—Thomas Crapper. The book claimed that the Victorian plumbing magnate was the source of the word "crap," thus abetting one of the most notorious myths of English etymology.

Lowly "crap" has been used to mean debris or discarded by-products since the 1400s. And "crapping" meant defecating at least as far back as 1846, when Crapper was barely out of diapers, not yet privy to the inner workings of the water closet. In fact, there's some evidence, though not conclusive, that "crapping" might have meant the same thing as far back as the 1600s.

Another widespread legend about Crapper is that he invented the flush toilet. This myth was helped along by a comic biography, *Flushed with Pride: The Story of Thomas Crapper* (1969), by the British humorist Wallace Reyburn. In fact, the flush toilet was around well before Crapper was born. He did, however, help popularize it, and he patented some toilet-related inventions, not all of them improvements. One in particular, a spring-loaded toilet seat, was nicknamed the "bottom-slapper" for its inclination to paddle Victorian users as they rose.

Crapper's business prospered nevertheless. He introduced the first bathroom showrooms and startled Victorians by putting the goods in display windows. Despite his success, he was never knighted (another myth), although Thomas Crapper & Company did supply toilets to the royal family.

One final claim is that his name is the source of "crapper," slang for the device itself. American doughboys in England during World War I, so the story goes, saw the name "Crapper" on British toilets and brought the word home as a noun meaning toilet. But in fact the word was already in use in 1911, when it meant a lavatory or bathroom and not the fixture itself. The apparatus wasn't referred to as a "crapper" until 1932, long after the war. It's likely that any connection with Mr. Crapper himself is coincidental. Linguistically speaking, he's an innocent bystander.

Another innocent bystander, at least etymologically, is the brutal Roman emperor Commodus. Despite rumors to the contrary, he did not design the first commode. (I'm as disappointed as you are.) The word "commode" comes from the Latin *commodus,* which means convenient (think "convenience," a handy Victorian euphemism for "toilet").

One more dubious etymology down the drain.

Great Caesar's Ghost

Not many people can tell you when Julius Caesar was born, but a lot will tell you how: by caesarean section. Isn't that why the operation was named after him? Hold your chariots. Let's not render unto Caesar more than he deserves. Fortunately for the Roman ruler (not to mention his mother), this story is one of the oldest and most durable urban legends of them all.

It can be traced back to one sentence in Pliny the Elder's *Historia Naturalis,* a thirty-seven-volume exploration of such wide-ranging subjects as astronomy, botany, architecture, animal husbandry, and human physiology. In discussing the human birth process, the Roman naturalist coldly argues that children positioned feetfirst in the womb should be delivered surgically, even though such an operation would cost the mother's life. To make his case he cites the emperor Nero, born feetfirst and widely regarded as a plague on humanity. Even surgery, Pliny says, would have been better than that.

In passing, Pliny notes that the first person to be called Caesar got the name because he was cut from his mother's womb (*a caeso matris utero*). He was plainly referring to the first of the many Caesars who preceded the great ruler. But over the centuries a lot of readers thought the first Caesar was a reference to the leader himself. Ergo, a myth was born!

As for the man himself, Gaius Julius Caesar was born on July 12 or 13 in the year 100 or possibly 102 BC. The exact date is uncertain. (Perhaps, like many celebrities, Caesar liked to shave a year or two off his age.) What is certain is that his mother, Aurelia, the daughter of Lucius Aurelius Cotta, lived long into her son's adulthood, which would have been impossible if she'd delivered him by caesarean.

In ancient times, surgical deliveries were performed only on women who were dead or dying. Back then, the child's survival was barely possible after such an operation, but not the unfortunate mother's. The first documented caesarean survived by the mother was supposedly performed in 1500, by the patient's swineherd husband. But even that case is doubtful, since it wasn't reported until eighty-two years later.

As for the cognomen "Caesar" (a cognomen is the last of a Roman citizen's three names), its origin is still in dispute. Did it have anything to do with surgery? It could be that the original Caesar was born surgically, as Pliny suggested, but several other theories have been proposed. One of the more interesting comes from a Roman grammarian, Sextus Pompeius Festus, who believed the name came from the Latin word *caesaries,* or "hair," and suggested the first Caesar was born with a full head of hair.

If the surgical procedure had nothing to do with Julius Caesar, how did it come to be called a "caesarean"? The Latin word *caeso* (from the verb *caedere,* meaning to cut) does appear to be the likely source. But Caesar will probably always be associated with surgical birth. Even the venerable *Oxford English Dictionary* has repeated the myth.

By the way, Julius bears no responsibility for Caesar salad, either. The king of salads was invented in 1924 by Caesar Cardini, a chef and restaurateur in Tijuana, Mexico.

Whose Name Is Mud?

On June 29, 1865, Dr. Samuel Mudd was found guilty of taking part in the conspiracy to murder Abraham Lincoln. Since then, historians have debated the extent of his involvement.

Word lovers have put Dr. Mudd at the center of another controversy—whether he's the source of the expression "his name is mud." The circumstantial evidence is strong. By the time Dr. Mudd was led to prison in irons, his name was a detested symbol of villainy. It was perhaps inevitable that people would come to associate him with the expression. But some stories are just too good to be true.

First, a little history. John Wilkes Booth, an actor and a Confederate sympathizer, shot Lincoln in the president's box at Ford's Theatre in Washington during a performance of the play *Our American Cousin.* After firing the fatal shot, Booth leaped to the stage, breaking a leg. (No, this did not inspire the theatrical expression "break a leg.")

Despite his injury, Booth managed to escape and made his way to Dr. Mudd's house in Maryland, where the doctor set the fugitive's broken leg. Booth was later killed by Union soldiers and Dr. Mudd was tried as a conspirator. He escaped the death penalty by one vote and was eventually pardoned by President Andrew Johnson.

Mudd's descendants are still trying to clear his name, but etymologists have already cleared him of any association with "his name is mud." The noun "mud," meaning a stupid (or thick) person, dates back to 1708, according to the *Oxford English Dictionary.* And the expression "his name is mud" dates from 1823, more than forty years before Lincoln was assassinated. Incidentally, the television journalist Roger Mudd is a distant relative of Dr. Mudd, not a direct descendant as some people have claimed.

The word "mud," it turns out, makes appearances in quite a few other expressions, including "here's mud in your eye," "muddy the waters," "clear as mud," and "drag through the mud." Dr. Mudd is innocent on all counts.

His Wicked, Wicked Ways

The swashbuckling actor Errol Flynn was notorious for his womanizing, his drunken brawls, and his run-ins with the police. He had a lot to answer for, but probably not the expression "in like Flynn."

Popular opinion traces the expression to Flynn's most notorious off-the-set scandal. In late 1942, two underage girls accused him of statutory rape. He was cleared in 1943 after a sensational trial, but his reputation as the archetypal Hollywood bad boy was sealed forever.

Flynn himself bragged in his autobiography, *My Wicked, Wicked Ways,* that "in like Flynn" was inspired by the verdict and was an allusion to his legendary success with women. In the public's mind as well as his own, Flynn was now firmly identified with the expression, and generations of reference books cited him as its source. But there's a hitch: the phrase predated his rape trial.

During the 1939–40 New York World's Fair, which ended a couple of years before Flynn's trial, an official at the fair was quoted as telling a party of people who were to receive passes for a show, "Your name is Flynn . . . you're in." And in early 1942, before the scandal broke, a columnist wrote in *The San Francisco Examiner:* "Answer these questions correctly and your name is Flynn, meaning you're in."

Those earlier references allude to success in general rather than to sexual prowess. (The actor had been a household name since *Captain Blood* in 1935, so these could have been roundabout references to his pretrial cinematic feats.) But the expression took on sexual overtones after Flynn's highly publicized trial. A more salacious interpretation, that the reference was to the sex act itself, is hardly credible, since the phrase was so widely and unblushingly used in the news media.

A competing theory links the expression to Edward J. "Boss" Flynn, the Bronx Democratic machine politician whose candidates were considered shoo-ins. Although there's no evidence that he's the source, Boss Flynn's heyday was the 1920s, '30s, and early '40s. As chairman of the Democratic National Committee in 1940, he helped elect FDR to a third term.

But the word sleuth Barry Popik is dubious about both the Boss Flynn and Errol Flynn theories. He suggests instead that there could be a connection with *Flynn's Detective Weekly,* a popular magazine in the twenties and thirties. But until there's better evidence, we can't say for sure where the expression comes from.

I think another explanation may be closer to the truth. "In like Flynn" may be an example of serendipitous rhyming slang ("Joe Blow," "even Steven," "jeepers creepers," "loose as a goose," "drunk as a skunk," and so on). The expression may have already existed and just happened to attach itself to a popular figure of the day, whether Boss Flynn or Errol Flynn or both.

The phrase's history took an odd turn in the 1960s with the release of the James Coburn movie *In Like Flint.* The title was intended as a takeoff on "in like Flynn." But the popularity of the film, a sequel to *Our Man Flint,* led many to believe that the movie version of the phrase was in fact the original.

Without Foundation

One of the most titillating but, alas, insupportable word origins connects a Frenchman named Philippe de Brassière with the undergarment of the same name. Sadly, there was no corsetiere named Brassière. The French don't even call a brassiere a *brassière,* for that matter. They call it a *soutien-gorge*. A *brassière* is a baby's undershirt.

Although the story of M. de Brassière is celebrated on and off the Internet, the man himself is a hoax, the invention of our old friend Wallace Reyburn, the same guy who gave us the phony biography of Thomas Crapper. In a spoof history of the bra published in 1971, Reyburn claimed that in the 1930s Brassière made a mint selling supportive undergarments based on designs stolen from the supposed inventor of the bra, German-born Otto Titzling.

The two ersatz entrepreneurs, Brassière and Titzling, fought a long and vicious court battle, the story goes. Brassière emerged largely unscathed and Titzling never recovered from the blow, according to Reyburn's book, *Bust-Up: The Uplifting Tale of Otto Titzling and the Development of the Bra.*

Clearly meant as a send-up, the "uplifting tale" was apparently swallowed whole by some gullible readers. It was kept alive by the Bette Midler song "Otto Titsling," by a Trivial Pursuit game card ("What did Otto Titzling invent?"), and later of course by the Internet, that fount of language legend, lore, and lies.

The biggest problem with the Brassière-Titzling myth, apart from the far-fetched surnames, is that women have been using breast supports of one kind or another since ancient times. In Greece, for example, a fitness buff would wear a band of cloth known as an *apodesmos* or *mastodeton* to support her breasts during exercise. The Roman version, which was sometimes made of leather, looked a lot like a modern sports bra. And in China's Han Dynasty (206 BC to AD 220), ladies wore strappy underthings resembling camisoles. They'd be a hit at Neiman Marcus.

In more recent times, a variety of bra-like devices were patented in the 1860s, '70s, and '80s. These designs were refined in the late nineteenth and early twentieth centuries by Herminie Cadolle in Paris and Mary Phelps Jacob in New York, but clothing historians say no single person can be credited with inventing the brassiere. As for the word, it's almost as hard to pin down as the garment itself.

Over the years, we've had many English words for the garments that shape a woman's upper body. In fact, a "body" in Elizabethan times was, among other things, a contraption much like a corset. This feat of engineering, made of two parts laced together, was also referred to as "bodies," "pair of bodies," and eventually "bodice." In the late nineteenth century, bra-like devices were called "bust supporters," "breast supporters," or "bust corsets."

The word "brassiere" (no accent, please) apparently showed up in English for the first time in 1893. The wordsmith Michael Quinion has traced it to a Syracuse, New York, newspaper article singing the praises of "the six inch straight boned band or brassiere which Sarah Bernhardt made a necessity with her directoire gowns." But why "brassiere"? What does a breast supporter have to do with the French word for a baby's undershirt? It seems that in the 1890s, when we borrowed the word, the French did indeed call a brassiere a *brassière.* But by 1904 French dictionaries were calling it a *soutien-gorge,* and *brassière* was relegated to the nursery.

This wasn't the first time the French had changed their minds about the word *brassière.* It got its start on the battlefield in the Middle Ages as an arm guard (arm is *bras* in French). Over the centuries, the word in different spellings has referred to a military breastplate, a shield, a bodice, a blouse, a camisole, a corset, a strap, a restraint, a life preserver, a baby's undershirt, and more.

In English, though, a brassiere is a brassiere is a brassiere—unless, of course, it's a "bra." The short form has been around since the mid-1930s, and it has my full support.

Horseplay

Since the fifteenth century, we've had a perfectly good word, "cramp," to describe the gripping muscle pain we get while playing touch football or moving cartons of old LPs in the attic or lying in bed doing nothing at all. But somehow mere "cramp" doesn't do justice to such torment, so we've been calling it a "charley horse" since the 1880s. Why "charley horse"? That question has given word sleuths a pain for over a hundred years.

Etymologists may be puzzled, but lots of other people can tell you exactly how the phrase came about. Here's the story that's been making the rounds for generations. Back in the 1890s, a white horse named Charley had the unenviable job of pulling a roller across the infield at the White Sox ballpark in Chicago. He was old and stiff, and limped as he dragged the roller back and forth. Baseball players, whose language was picturesque even then, thought of the horse whenever they had a muscle cramp. Before you could say "neigh," the term "charley horse" was born.

As it turns out, that story puts the cart before the horse. Charley may have toiled in the 1890s for the Chicago White Stockings (the Sox didn't exist yet), but the expression was around before then. So what's the real source? Etymologists and baseball historians have turned up a half dozen or so theories, none of them home runs, but the most likely is a "hoss" of a different color.

The Charley in this version is the Hall of Fame pitcher Charles Gardner Radbourn, who played in the major leagues from 1880 to 1891. Known affectionately as "Old Hoss," he got a killer cramp after hitting a homer for Boston in a game against Providence in the 1880s. As Radbourn limped to home plate, according to a 1907 *Washington Post* article dug up by Barry Popik, a teammate shouted, "What's a mattah wit you, Charley Hoss?" Radbourn replied, "My leg is tied up in knots."

Baseball reporters started using the phrase "charley horse" in 1886. And by the 1920s the rest of us were using it too. Even doctors began skipping the medical jargon when it came to injuries of the quadriceps femoris. In November 1946 the *Journal of the American Medical Association* published an item entitled "Treatment of *Charley Horse*."

Flack Attack

We live in an age of self-promotion. People are brand names, and even celebrity chefs hire publicists, otherwise known as flacks, to manipulate their images. So it's ironic that the press agent behind the word "flack" should be all but forgotten today.

Ask almost anyone and you'll hear that "flack" is a misspelling of "flak," a term coined during World War II to describe enemy antiaircraft fire. ("Flak" was an acronym for *fliegerabwehrkanone*, a German antiaircraft gun.) After the war, "flak" also came to mean a barrage of criticism or disapproval. It's understandable, then, that the flacks who bombarded newshounds relentlessly with press releases got confused with flak. Even slang lexicographers have described "flack" as a misspelling of "flak."

In the interest of giving credit where credit is due, let's do some public relations on behalf of the now-obscure PR man who gave us "flack." His name was Gene Flack (yes, that was his real name), and in the 1920s and '30s he was a movie publicist without peer. He was so good at his job that *Variety*, the showbiz weekly, starting calling all publicists "flacks."

When your name becomes a lowercase noun—think "bloomers" (Amelia Bloomer), "boycott" (Charles Boycott), "chauvinism" (Nicolas Chauvin), "diesel" (Rudolf Diesel), "saxophone" (Adolphe Sax), "silhouette" (Étienne de Silhouette)—

then you know you've arrived. In other words, you've got legs, to use another *Variety* coinage.

The scribblers at *Variety,* as we all know, have made profound contributions to the vocabulary of stage and screen. Besides the venerable "showbiz" itself, they've given us such beauts as "socko" (very good), "boffo" (even better), "whammo" (better yet), and "flopperoo" (forget about it).

Hat Tricks

Charlie Chaplin wore one. Laurel and Hardy, too. So did Henry Ford, Sir Winston, and Toulouse-Lautrec. We can't imagine them without their bowler hats. But we can easily imagine how the bowler got its name.

It looks for all the world like a bowl worn upside down. A child of six could figure this one out. Well, don't toss your hat in the air just yet. It may seem logical that "bowler" comes from "bowl," and many people have made that assumption, but (with apologies to Oliver Hardy) this is another fine mess such logic has gotten us into. Herewith, a lesson in sartorial history.

The bowler was created in 1850 for William Coke II, later the earl of Leicester, who wanted a snug hat with a hard, rounded crown to protect his gamekeepers from branches as they rode on horseback. His purveyors of headgear, James and George Lock of No. 6 St. James's Street, London, designed the hat and had it produced by their chief suppliers, Thomas and William Bowler of Southwark.

The hat, which took its name from the Bowler label inside and not from its bowl-like shape, was tremendously popular in Britain in the late nineteenth and early twentieth centuries. It was a democratic piece of headgear, worn by businessmen and laborers as well as toffs. A compromise between the rigid top hat and the softer felt hat or cloth cap, the bowler could be donned with equal dignity by Bertie Wooster or his man Jeeves or Lady Chatterley's gamekeeper.

The bowler has also been called a "derby," especially in the United States, apparently because of its association with horseback riding and races, or "derbies." (We say DUR-bee, by the way, and the Brits say DAR-bee.) The original Derby, run in 1780 at Epsom Downs in Surrey, was named after Edward Stanley, twelfth earl of Derby. He had earned the right to name the race by winning a coin toss with Sir Charles Bunbury, but Sir Charles got the last laugh when his horse Diomed won.

Meanwhile, back at the ranch, we find another popular myth—that the ten-gallon hat got its name because it could hold ten gallons of water. No, the cowboy hat doesn't hold ten gallons. It doesn't even hold one. No one knows for sure how the ten-gallon hat got its name, but there are several theories. One explanation is that it comes from *sombrero galoneado,* Spanish for a hat decorated with a *galón,* or braid, worn by Mexican *vaqueros,* or cowboys. Another possibility is that it comes from the phrase *tan galán,* Spanish for "such a gallant" (in other words, "what a dude"). A third theory is that it's a jokingly hyperbolic reference to the hat's size.

Spanish, by the way, has given us lots of cowboy lingo, words like "buckaroo" (from *vaquero*), "lariat" (*la reata*), "stampede" (*estampida*), "pinto" (*pinta,* or "spot"), "bronco" (Spanish for "wild"), and "rodeo" (Spanish for "roundup"). And, of course, "sombrero," which brings us back to our bowl-shaped friend.

In some other languages, the bowler hat is indeed named for its round shape. In Spanish, it's a *hongo* ("mushroom"); in French, a *melon* (yes, "melon"); in German, a *melone* (ditto); in Dutch, a *bolhoed* ("globe hat"); and in Italian—here's my favorite—a *bombetta* ("little bomb"). Hats off to the Italians!

Nasty Business

In 1871, *Harper's Weekly* published an editorial cartoon by Thomas Nast showing William M. Tweed, the corrupt political boss, as a potbellied vulture feeding on the carcass of New York City. The caption read: "Let Us Prey." It was typical Nast—sarcastic, merciless, and nasty. No wonder Boss Tweed offered him a half-million dollars to skip town. And no wonder people came to believe that we got the word "nasty" from the granddaddy of political cartoonists. Here's a typical comment, from an art gallery in the Berkshires that deals in Nast's scathing caricatures: "His cutting political wit gave us the name based expression 'Nasty.' "

Not even close. It's an interesting theory, but about five hundred years off.

The word "nasty" first showed up in English in a book of religious lyrics from the late 1300s. At first, it meant "filthy" or "dirty" (as it still does), but in the late 1400s it also came to mean "annoying" or "contemptible." By the early 1800s, years before Nast was born, the meaning had widened to include "bad tempered," "spiteful," and "unkind." So Nast is in the clear, as far as the derivation of "nasty" is concerned. He's also in the clear on that hush money he was offered. The cartoonist turned down the bribe, then turned up the heat in the pages of *Harper's*. As for Boss Tweed, he died in 1878 in New York's Ludlow Street Jail.

Camp Followers

We can't talk about words and the people behind them without stumbling across Maj. Gen. Joseph Hooker, the hard-drinking, skirt-chasing Union commander who briefly led the Army of the Potomac during the Civil War. The goings-on at Hooker's headquarters so shocked a young cavalry officer that he described it as "a combination of barroom and brothel." Hooker's affinity for working girls was so well known, in fact, that he's credited with inspiring the name of a red-light district in Washington, "Hooker's Division."

It's only natural that Civil War buffs would put this all together and conclude that Fighting Joe Hooker was the source of the word "hooker." Even the historian Shelby Foote has written that "from this time on, the general's surname entered the language as one of the many lowercase slang words for prostitute." It's a great story, but once again there's a historical catch. Streetwalkers were called "hookers" back in the 1830s, when the young general-to-be was still at West Point. In 1835, the *New York Transcript* reported a courtroom exchange in which a female defendant complained that a witness had "called me a hooker."

The word may ultimately come from the sixteenth century, when to "hook in" customers meant to draw them in, as with a hook. In those days, a "hook" or "hooker" meant a thief or a pickpocket. Over the centuries, "hook" has appeared in many other figures of speech, including "hook, line, and sinker" (what a gullible sucker is likely to swallow) and "by hook or by crook" (a medieval expression for "by means fair or foul").

It strikes me that there's something off-putting about many "hook" expressions. Thieves, pickpockets, prostitutes, con men, carnies, hucksters—what a world! In recent years, even the innocent "hook up" has taken on a salacious meaning—to have casual sex. Words make strange bedfellows, don't they?

Chapter 7

An Oeuf Is an Oeuf

Fractured French

S ometimes a *cigare* is just a cigar. But our love/hate relationship with the French is never that simple. Not even Woody Allen's psychoanalyst would take the case.

The arbiters of French culture look down their noses at Hollywood, then award the Légion d'Honneur to Jerry Lewis, Clint Eastwood, and Sylvester Stallone (not to mention making M. Allen a Commandeur des Arts et des Lettres). Is it any surprise that we got the word "condescension" from the French? As for world affairs, the best you can say is that we agree to disagree. When Americans have had it up to here with Gallic critiques, we rename our foods "freedom fries" and "freedom toast," and politicians suspected of being too Frenchified take to wearing cowboy hats.

Let's admit it, though. We love the Louvre, Châteauneuf du Pape, haute couture, and haute cuisine (but forget the frogs' legs and the escargots). Yes, French women dress divinely and they really *are* thinner, even if it's because they smoke too much. And the language is beautiful—which is fortunate for us, since we've gotten more than a quarter of our English words from French (of course, the Norman Conquest had a little something to do with that). But instead of being flattered that we've adopted so many of their words, the French complain that we abuse their language. Many Americans think so too. Sometimes, though, abuse is in the eye (or the ear) of the beholder. Let's look at a few common misconceptions about the French—and not-so-French—words in our language.

Author! Author!

When people hear that I'm a writer, they unfailingly ask what I've written. "Oh, books about English," I usually reply, and their eyes glaze over. Well, I can't help it that I'm not a block-buster novelist. Once I jokingly said, "The Harry Potter books. I write under a pen name." (Insert shriek of delight, followed by author's sheepish denial.) No, J. K. Rowling is not my pen name. I have, however, done some research into the phrase "pen name." As we all know, it's English for an old French expression, *nom de plume.* Or is it?

Well, "pen name" is indeed the literal meaning of *nom de plume.* But *nom de plume* is not an old French expression—or a new one, either. The British made it up.

The real French expression for an assumed name is *nom de guerre,* which the British adopted in the late seventeenth century. But in the nineteenth century, British writers apparently thought the original French might be confusing. One can see why *nom de guerre,* literally "war name," could puzzle readers. The French initially used it for the fictitious name that a soldier often assumed on enlisting, but by the time the British started using the expression, it could mean any assumed name—in English as well as French.

The faux-French *nom de plume* was introduced in English in the nineteenth century. An obscure Victorian novelist, Emerson Bennett, is responsible for the first citation in the *Oxford English Dictionary* (perhaps the only feather in his cap). In his 1850 novel *Oliver Goldfinch,* the title character is said to be "better known to our readers as a gifted poet, under the *nom de plume* of 'Orion.' " Bennett could have used the word "pseudonym," which we had borrowed from the French around the same time *nom de plume* was invented. But perhaps he felt "pseudonym" lacked a certain *je ne sais quoi.* Whatever his reasons, *nom de plume* was a hit with the literary crowd—such a hit that it inspired an English translation, "pen name," which made its debut in 1864 in *Webster's American Dictionary of the English Language.*

The old French expression *nom de guerre* is still with us, though. It's defined in English dictionaries as "pseudonym" or "fictional name," but these days it seems to be used most often for the sobriquets of terrorists (or freedom fighters, depending on your point of view). I'm reminded of a story about the poet Coleridge, who not only used *noms de plume* ("Cuddy" and "Gnome," among others) but once had a *nom de guerre* as well. When a young lady refused his hand, the rejected suitor dropped out of Cambridge and enlisted in the Fifteenth Light Dragoons under the assumed name "Silas Tomkyn Comberbache." (He'd seen the name Comberbache over a door in Lincoln's Inn Fields in London.) All's fair in love and war.

A Niche in Time

Paula Abdul has been a lot of things—a cheerleader for the LA Lakers, a Grammy-winning pop singer, an Emmy-winning choreographer, a judge on *American Idol*—but as far as I know she hasn't won any awards for her oratorical skills. So it wasn't big news when fans of the popular TV show jumped all over her for saying to a contestant, "This is your niche." Or, rather, for how she said it. The gripe was her pronunciation: NITCH instead of NEESH. The critics showed no mercy. "FOR THE LOVE OF GOD!!!" went a typical comment in the blogosphere. "Would someone please tell Paula Abdul that there is no such word as NITCH?!"

The only problem here is that the ex-cheerleader got it right and the wired Miss Grundys who criticized her got it wrong. Traditionally the word "niche" has been pronounced NITCH, though the pseudo-Gallic NEESH has been gaining in popularity in recent decades. American dictionaries now accept both versions, but NITCH is more widely used here. In Britain, however, the affected NEESH is now the usual pronunciation.

We borrowed "niche" from the French in the seventeenth century, but the French had borrowed it in turn from the Romans (it ultimately comes from the Latin *nidus,* meaning nest). The word, which was first spelled "neece" or "niece" or "nice" in English, originally referred to a recess set into a wall, usually for a statue or other decorative object. But the first citation in the *Oxford English Dictionary,* from a 1610 play by the poet Samuel Daniel, speaks of the "Neeces wherein the Ladies sate," an apparent reference to seating alcoves.

How was the word pronounced way back then? It seems that nobody knows for sure. The earliest pronouncing guide for "niche," from a 1907 entry in what would become the first edition of the *OED,* lists only NITCH. The NEESH pronunciation "is apparently not recorded before this date," according to lexicographers at the *OED.* NEESH didn't show up until ten years later, and it was described then as an alternative to the usual pronunciation. All fourteen editions of Daniel Jones's influential

English Pronouncing Dictionary from 1917 to 1977 give NITCH as the typical pronunciation and NEESH as a variant, according to the *OED*.

So there, all you *American Idol* fans! But, as I've said before, English is a living language. And if enough of us decide to pronounce "niche" as if we were on the rue de la Paix in Paris instead of State Street in Chicago, NEESH may become the usual pronunciation on both sides of the Atlantic. More's the pity.

It's a Frog's Life

I have a thing for amphibians of the order Anura (from the Greek for "without a tail"). But I usually refer to them by their common names: "frogs" and "toads" (*frogga* and *tadige* in Old English). I'm very fond of the wood frog (*Rana sylvatica*) and the spring peeper (*Pseudacris crucifer*), but my heart belongs to the eastern spadefoot toad (*Scaphiopus holbrookii*), which is an endangered species in my neck of the woods. As you can imagine, I'm not especially fond of *cuisses de grenouille,* a French culinary favorite better known to Americans as frogs' legs. If you ask me, amphibians belong in the wild, not in the sauté pan.

But enough sermonizing. Why do English speakers refer contemptuously to their Gallic brethren as "frogs"? Ninety-nine out of a hundred people will tell you it's because the French eat frogs' legs. But the answer isn't quite so simple. The word "frog" has been a term of abuse in English since the fourteenth century, well before anyone ever used it to abuse the French. For hundreds of years, in fact, the typical object of scorn was another Englishman, though the epithet was sometimes used for a Dutchman (aka Froglander).

Not until the late eighteenth century did "frog" begin showing up in English as a derogatory term for the French. The usage is thought to have made its first appearance in 1772, in a satirical poem in *Westminster Magazine* about the British routing the French: "They will fly at the French with the stomach of hogs, / And, like storks, in a trice clear the sea of the frogs." Etymologists generally attribute this usage to the French custom of eating frogs' legs, which the English frequently poked fun at, as in this example of froggerel from an anti-French song that made the rounds in 1803: "Brave Nelson's sea thunder / Shall strike them with wonder, / And make the frogs leap in their bellies."

Some slang dictionaries, though, offer another source for the epithet, the fleur-de-lis, noting that the French coat of arms has been described as three frogs or toads saluting. But the late language sleuth James N. Tidwell, in "Frogs and Frog-Eaters," perhaps the most definitive study of the subject, comes down squarely on the side of frog eating as the source of the slur.

I'm with Tidwell on the etymology, but I'm with Kermit the Frog on amphibian cuisine. It's not easy being green. If the French aren't sautéing you, the English are using you to roast the French.

Jam Session

I like marmalade with my toast in the morning, so my ears perked up when I heard that the English actor Michael Caine had an interesting idea about the origin of the word. In an interview on British TV, he traced "marmalade" to Mary Queen of Scots. When she was ill, her French-speaking attendants would supposedly bring her citrus preserves and say, "*Ma'am est malade.*" I'd heard the story before. In some versions, the attendants said, "*Marie est malade.*" And sometimes the sufferer was Marie Antoinette.

The truth is that the word "marmalade" was around long before either Mary or Marie. The first appearance of the word is believed to be in a 1480 letter about a gift of oranges and marmalade, apparently sent to a student at Exeter. It's derived from *marmelo,* the Portuguese word for "quince," which is what marmalade was originally made of.

The only thing to be said for the phony French etymology is that *malade* can help you remember how to spell the last two syllables of "marmalade."

Franglais Speaking

If you're a fan of *The Simpsons,* you'll remember the episode from 1995 when Willie, the grumpy Scottish groundskeeper at Springfield Elementary School, calls the French "cheese-eating surrender monkeys." The expression went mainstream when France opposed the American invasion of Iraq in 2003. But it was just the latest addition to our anti-French lexicon. As far back as the sixteenth century, English speakers called venereal disease the "Frenche pox," the "French marbles," or the "French disease" (in France, of course, it was the "English disease").

You'd think we didn't like these guys. Never mind. We may not be the best of friends, but we've always had a love affair with their language. We've borrowed umpteen thousand Gallic words, but some of them no longer mean what they once did in France. What's more, we've dressed up many of our own words to make them look French. Nowadays, most Americans think these fossilized or fake expressions are the real thing. Let's separate the faux from the French.

Double entendre. Although the expression, adopted into English in the seventeenth century, was once French for double meaning, there's no exact equivalent in modern French. Two near misses, *double entente* and *double sens,* don't have the suggestiveness of the English version. How should one pronounce our illegitimate offspring? Illegitimately, of course. Dictionaries are all over the place on this, but I treat "double" as an English word (DUB-ul) and "entendre" as if it's French (ahn-TAN-dr).

Négligee. No, the French don't call that frilly, come-hither nightie a *négligée,* though in the eighteenth century a *négligé* was indeed a simple, loose gown worn by a Frenchwoman at home. In France, the nightie is a *peignoir* or a *chemise de nuit.* The French verb *négliger* means to neglect, and a person who's *négligé* is careless or sloppy or poorly dressed.

Encore. The word we shout when we want Sam to play it again isn't used that way in France, except by tourists. Although "again" is one meaning of *encore* in French, a Parisian usually shouts *"Bis!"* to call for a repeat performance. English speakers have been shouting *"Encore!"* since at least the early 1700s, but nobody seems to know why. Perhaps we can blame the eighteenth-century vogue for all things French.

Pièce de résistance. The French don't use this for the main dish or the main part of something. In fact, they don't use it at all. The closest thing to it in France is *plat de résistance,* meaning the main dish. But in the eighteenth century, when so many French expressions crossed the Channel, a *pièce de résistance* was a main dish or a dishy woman.

Idiot savant. This invention would sound idiotic to a Frenchman, though the inventor may have been a French-born physician living in the United States, according to the *OED.* In "New Facts and Remarks Concerning Idiocy," an 1869 lecture to a New York medical association, Dr. Edouard Séguin used the term "idiot savant" to describe someone with a "useless protrusion of a single faculty, accompanied by a woful general impotence." The actual French phrase for the condition is *savant autiste,* similar to the current medical term for the condition in English, "autistic savant."

Résumé. A job hunter in France doesn't polish up her *résumé.* She updates her *curriculum vitae,* or *CV.* In French, a *résumé* is a summing up, as in a plot summary. And that's what it meant when the word entered English in the early nineteenth century. The term wasn't used for a career summary until the mid-twentieth century, when this sense began appearing in the United States and Canada. Maybe it was easier to pronounce than "curriculum vitae."

Affaire d'amour. This would be meaningless in France, where an *affaire* is a business deal, not a romance. The French for "love affair" is *histoire d'amour.* Where did our faux French come from? It's a froufrou version of an old English expression, "love affair," which dates from Elizabethan times, when Shakespeare used the original in *The Two Gentlemen of Verona.* (And by the way, it's a myth that the term "love" in tennis comes from *l'oeuf,* though an egg is more or less round like a zero. Mere folklore.)

Toupee. This word is unknown to the French, who call a hairpiece a *moumoute* or *postiche.* The English probably adapted it from the French word *toupet,* a tuft of hair (real hair) over the forehead, like a person's bangs or a horse's forelock.

Risqué. Nope, *risqué* isn't titillating or sexy in French. It's merely "risky" or "dangerous," which aptly describes the dubious practice of using these faux French expressions when you're in France.

As I said up above, we've "borrowed" beaucoup from the French. But a correspondent in Paris once wrote me about a word we borrowed and then returned with interest: "budget." We got it (originally spelled "bowgette") in the 1400s from the French *bougette,* a diminutive of *bouge* (a leather bag). The English word initially referred to a leather pouch or wallet, but a century later it meant the contents of the pouch or wallet.

By the early eighteenth century (after an etymological hop, skip, and jump), a "budget" had become a statement of projected revenues and expenses. The earliest *OED* citation for the new financial usage, dating from 1733, refers to a budget of "publick Revenues" as "this Art of political legerdemain." (Sound familiar?) So handy was this new usage that the French borrowed it back in the early nineteenth century, spelled the English way: *budget.* For this word, at least, the budget is balanced.

French Provincial

I love that bit in Mark Twain's *The Innocents Abroad* where a young American named Blucher writes a note to a Paris hotel-keeper, demanding a bar of soap for his room and complaining that he's been overcharged for candles:

> "*Pourquois* don't you *mettez* some *savon* in your bed-chambers? *Est-ce que vous pensez* I will steal it? *La nuit passée* you charged me *pour deux chandelles* when I only had one; *hier vous avez* charged me *avec glace* when I had none at all; *tout les jours* you are coming some fresh game or other on me, *mais vous ne pouvez pas* play this *savon* dodge on me twice. *Savon* is a necessary *de la vie* to any body but a Frenchman, *et je l'aurai hors de cet hôtel* or make trouble. You hear me. *Allons.*"

Well, *plus ça change.* If Americans aren't sprinkling their English with real or imagined French, they're mixing both languages in a stew of Franglais. And if a word looks the slightest bit French, we'll pronounce it like French, even a word that's been ye olde Englische since Chaucer's day. I'm thinking of "homage," which has been part of the English language since 1290. It should be pronounced HOM-idge or OM-idge. Whether or not the *h* is pronounced, the accent is on the first syllable. The French pronunciation oh-MAHJ is incorrect—and affected to boot—unless you're in Marseilles (where it's spelled *hommage*). Yes, we did get "homage" from the French way back when, but we also got "adroit" and "toilet" and "voyage" from them, but we don't say ah-DWAH, twa-LAY, and vwah-YAZH.

On the other hand, many of the words and expressions we've borrowed from French are still pronounced pretty much the way the French do: "à la carte," "au naturel," "café," "cliché," "connoisseur," "derrière," "éclair," "gauche," "gourmet," "grotesque," "quiche," "rendezvous," "séance," and lots more. Then there are those that we try to pronounce like the originals and turn into grotesqueries. The most common pronunciation of "lingerie," for example, is a Frenchified lawn-zhuh-RAY that's nowhere near the real French LANZH-ree, though English dictionaries now find the faux French acceptable. And many Americans, including a fair number of talking heads, pronounce "cache" and "cachet" the same way. Not acceptable, say dictionaries. The first is CASH, the second ca-SHAY.

I can't retire to my Adirondack chair without mentioning an expression that sounds wrong no matter how you say it. We got the phrase "chaise longue" from the French, and dictionaries say we should pronounce it in the French way: shays-LONG. But countless Americans ignore the dictionaries and say chase-LOUNGE. I usually take the coward's way out and say "lounge chair." But this is another example of English changing under our very noses. If I had to bet on how "chaise longue" will be pronounced in the longue run, I'd put my money on chase-LOUNGE. And I wouldn't bet against "chaise lounge" as the accepted spelling someday. It's already the dominant one on Google.

Chapter 8

Sense and Sensitivity

PC Fact and Fiction

"The auctioneer's block in Maryland," said the abolitionist Frederick Douglass, "is the place to witness the heartrending cruelties of slavery." In a speech to an English audience in 1846, Douglass described a slave woman "at an auction block," her limbs "brutally exposed" for the inspection of bidders with money in their pockets. "Give us a bid, gentlemen," he quoted the auctioneer as saying, "here is a fine, able-bodied woman, capable of undertaking field or house-work, sound in wind and limb, look for yourselves." Pretty horrifying stuff. And, yes, the expressions "auction block" and "auctioneer's block" were indeed products of the slave trade.

A generation or so after slavery ended, segregationists enacted Jim Crow laws that made it impossible for most blacks to vote in the South. The laws, adopted in the late nineteenth and early twentieth centuries, established poll taxes and literacy requirements but provided escape clauses that effectively exempted whites. Anyone who could vote before freed slaves were enfranchised was exempt from the anti-black requirements, and so were his descendants: sons, grandsons, and so on. That's why the exemptions were called "grandfather clauses"—another product of our country's racist history.

Although the origins of these expressions reflect America at its worst, no one seems to find them offensive today. The term "auction block" is routinely used in news articles about the latest sales at Sotheby's or Christie's. And lawmakers just as routinely use "grandfather clause" to mean a provision that exempts an existing activity from a new regulation. Most people, of course, have no idea how we got the two expressions, and even the people who do know aren't bothered by them. Yet many words or phrases without any skeletons in their closets are unfairly accused of being racist or sexist or otherwise bigoted—that is, politically incorrect.

The whole business of political correctness, which got out of hand in the twentieth century, has given rise to many myths about English. Before we get to them, however, consider the expression "politically correct" itself. When it was first used, back in the early days of the Republic, the phrase merely meant politically accurate. In 1793, Justice James Wilson used it in a US Supreme Court opinion to protest slipshod political language. "Sentiments and expressions of this inaccurate kind prevail in our common, even in our convivial, language," he wrote. Someone proposing a toast to the country will say, "The United States," not "the People of the United States," Wilson complained. "This is not politically correct."

It wasn't until the twentieth century that the phrase was used to describe people with the "right" (in this case, left) beliefs. In 1934 the British author John Strachey, a Communist firebrand who would later become a Labor MP, said Marxist writers were "more politically correct" than other leftists. In the 1970s the expression took on new life in the United States, where it meant considerate of racial, sexual, class, and other sensitivities. "A man cannot be politically correct and a chauvinist too," the feminist Toni Cade Bambara wrote in 1970. The phrase also became a mantra of liberal conformity, which may have contributed to the PC backlash that followed in the more conservative '80s and '90s. An article in *The Nation* in 1987, for instance, referred to an author's "insistent effort to keep literature from becoming a weapon—he would say casualty—of the politically correct or incorrect."

I have nothing against political correctness. Why trample on someone's feelings unnecessarily? But too often what passes for political correctness is more political than correct. So let's call a spade a spade (see below), examine the herstory (ditto), and set the record straight.

Thumbs Down

When I was an editor at *The New York Times Book Review*, we published a glowing review of a new book on domestic violence. The distinguished reviewer called it "feminist scholarship at its best" and an important work that put the raw facts in their historical, social, and legal contexts. The fact of wife beating, the reviewer said, "was once acceptable if it conformed to the 'rule of thumb' (no rod thicker than the husband's thumb could be used)." The headline on the review was a natural: "Wife Beating and the Rule of Thumb." I didn't raise an eyebrow at the time. In fact, a few years later I tweaked a radio caller for using the sexist expression "rule of thumb" on the air. Wow, did I get an earful from another listener! And no, he didn't spare the rod.

I admit it. I helped perpetuate one of the most persistent myths of political correctness. For the record, the phrase "rule of thumb" does not come from an old English law allowing a husband to beat his wife with a rod or stick no thicker than his thumb. No one has ever found such a law on the books—not in England, not in the United States, not anywhere else. William L. Prosser, author of perhaps the leading American textbook on civil law, put his mind to this question of husband, wife, and thumb. His conclusion: "There is probably no truth whatever in the legend that he was permitted to beat her with a stick no thicker than his thumb."

The expression "rule of thumb," meaning a method based on experience or approximation, first appeared in writing, as far as we know, in a sermon preached in the mid-1600s by James Durham, a Presbyterian minister in Glasgow. In *Heaven Upon Earth* (1685), a collection of Durham's sermons published twenty-seven years after his death, he said that "many profest Christians are like to foolish builders, who build by guess, and by rule of thumb, (as we use to speak) and not by Square and Rule." No wife beating here, nor in a 1785 dictionary that defined "by rule of thumb" as "to do a thing by dint of practice."

The phrase is believed to come from the old custom of using parts of one's body as rough units of measure. A man's foot is a foot long or thereabouts, and it's still used in a pinch to pace off the size of a room. The palm of the hand is about four inches wide, a unit once called a "hand's breadth"—even now, horses are measured in hands (a mare standing fifteen hands would be sixty inches tall at the withers). And the thumb is about an inch wide, a unit once called a "thumb's breadth" and common in the textile trades. As for the "rule" in "rule of thumb," think of a ruler or measuring stick.

So how did wife beating enter the picture? Well, a husband once did have the right under English common law to "give his wife moderate correction," according to Sir William Blackstone's

Commentaries on the Laws of England (1765). But the old right, Blackstone said, began to wane in the 1600s. He offered this rationale for the old practice: Since a husband had to answer for his wife's misbehavior, "the law thought it reasonable to intrust him with this power of restraining her, by domestic chastisement, in the same moderation that a man is allowed to correct his apprentices or children."

Thumbs didn't come up, so to speak, until 1782, when an English judge, Francis Buller, supposedly ruled that a husband could beat his wife if the rod or stick were no thicker than his thumb. There's no published record of his comments, but the judge was ridiculed in the press and viciously caricatured in cartoons that labeled him "Judge Thumb" and "Mr. Justice Thumb." In the following century, judges in three American court cases—two in North Carolina and one in Mississippi—also referred to such a doctrine. But none of the judges, on either side of the Atlantic, offered a shred of verifiable evidence that the doctrine had ever existed. (As we know, it never did.) And none of the judges actually used the expression "rule of thumb."

The real mystery here is how "rule of thumb," a seventeenth-century term for a rough measurement, got linked with a mythological legal doctrine. As far as we know, the expression wasn't mentioned in relation to wife beating until 1976, when the feminist Del Martin used it, apparently as a pun, in a report on domestic violence. She presented the debunked legal doctrine as if it were fact, then followed it with her unfortunate play on words. "For instance," she wrote, "the common-law doctrine had been modified to allow the husband 'the right to whip his wife, provided that he used a switch no bigger than his thumb'— a rule of thumb, so to speak."

Not long after her report was made public, other writers took Martin's wordplay seriously. They began referring to this ficti-

tious legal doctrine as the "rule of thumb" and spreading a fictitious etymology in the process. Within a few years this myth was
so entrenched that the US Commission on Civil Rights entitled
its 1982 report on battered women "Under the Rule of Thumb."

Classical Spadework

I'm often asked to suggest a kinder, gentler way of saying "call a
spade a spade." I routinely oblige by offering things like "call
them as you see them," "don't beat around the bush," "tell it as
it is," "don't mince words," or just "speak plainly." Then I
kindly, gently inform whoever's asking that there's actually
nothing bigoted about calling a spade a spade. Avoid the expression if you think your audience will take offense. But be aware
that it isn't racist, it never was, and it never will be—unless
enough well-meaning though misinformed people keep on saying that it is. In its earliest incarnations, we find, the saying was
about figs and troughs, not spades. The real story is a mystery
worthy of Hercule Poirot.

To begin at the beginning, the ancient Greeks described a
plainspoken person as someone who'd call a fig a fig, a trough a
trough. They used the expression, sometimes mockingly and
sometimes not, for someone who preferred plain words. But why
"figs" and "troughs"? Well, for one thing both words were as
common to the ancient Greeks as, say, "balls" and "jugs" are to
us. And like those words, "figs" and "troughs" had double meanings (think "double entendres") in classical times. So the choice
of words was no doubt an ancient joke.

The Greek word for "fig," *sukon,* had them laughing in the
aisles in antiquity, when it had sexual and scatological overtones.
"The bridegroom's fig is great and thick; the bride's very soft and

tender," sings the leader of the chorus in Aristophanes' *Peace,* a bawdy fifth-century BC comedy. And *skaphe,* which has been translated as "trough" or "basin" or "bowl" (it literally means something hollowed out), got its share of catcalls too. In *The Clouds,* Aristophanes uses the image of a kneading trough (a bowl for making bread) in some suggestive wordplay about kneading—i.e., masturbation.

Thus, someone who called a fig a fig and a trough a trough was either a straight talker or a rube unaware of the finer (or cruder) shades of meaning. The expression evidently first appears, minus the figs, in the writings of the first-century Greek historian Plutarch, who attributes it to Philip of Macedon. In Plutarch's *Moralia,* Philip says it's in the nature of the plainspoken Macedonians "to call a trough a trough." Variations on the theme—this time with figs—appear twice in the works of the second-century satirist Lucian. In *De Conscribenda Historia,* for example, he says a historian has to be "fearless, impartial, frank, a friend of free speech and the truth, one who, as the comic poet says, names the figs figs and the trough a trough." Some word detectives have speculated that the "comic poet" was Menander or Aristophanes, but classical scholars haven't found the expression in the writings of either of them. (A tantalizing fragment about figs and troughs is often attributed to Menander, but most authorities are skeptical.)

During the Renaissance, the Dutch scholar Erasmus translated the works of Plutarch, Lucian, and many other Greek writers into Latin, which was then the common language of learned Europeans. Unfortunately, his scholarship had a hole in it. In his translations of Plutarch and Lucian, he mistook the Greek word *skaphe* ("trough") for the similar *skapheion* (a digging tool), and translated it into Latin as *ligo* ("spade").

The translators who then turned Erasmus's Latin into English immortalized his mistake. In 1542, Nicolas Udall rendered the Plutarch version of the expression (the remark about the blunt Macedonians) as "to calle a spade by any other name then a spade." Three decades later, the Protestant reformer John Knox, apparently influenced by an Erasmus translation of Lucian, wrote, "I have learned, plainly and boldly, to call wickedness by its own terms—a fig, a fig, and a spade, a spade."

Pretty soon, English speakers dispensed with the figs, as in these lines from a 1580 poem by Humfrey Gifford: "I cannot say the crow is white, / But needes must call a spade a spade." And in these words from a Puritan pamphlet attacking the Church of England in 1589: "I am plaine, I must needs call a Spade a Spade."

Before we dispense with figs ourselves, a figurative digression. Physicians in ancient Greece used the word for "fig," *sukon,* as a euphemism for hemorrhoid, an inventive usage that survived in Latin (where *ficus* can mean both fig and hemorrhoid) and even, for a time, in English. Until well into the sixteenth century, someone suffering from piles was said to have "ye Figes," "the fyge," or "the fygge." In ancient times, the "sign of the fig," a gesture made by putting the thumb through the fingers of the clenched fist, was a symbol of fertility or good luck. Today "the fig" is used in Italy, Greece, and other Mediterranean countries much the way a rude American might give someone "the finger." Just another kind of digital communication, I guess.

But where were we? Oh yes, spades. So how did an innocuous expression like "call a spade a spade" get mixed up in racial politics? Well, we find that "spade" in the sense of "Negro" emerged as black slang during the flowering of African-American art and literature known as the Harlem Renaissance. It first appeared in print, according to the *Oxford English Dictionary,* in the 1928 novel *Home to Harlem,* by Claude McKay: "Jake is such a fool spade. Don't know how to handle the womens." A year later, the novelist Wallace Thurman used it in *The Blacker the Berry:* "Wonder where all the spades keep themselves?" The word in this sense is thought to come from the color of the spades suit in a deck of cards. Though it wasn't meant to be hateful in the early examples, dictionaries now label the term offensive, especially when used by whites.

It's no surprise that some people take offense, and others wonder if they're giving offense, when "call a spade a spade" is in the air—even people who are aware of the expression's harmless origins. But I think it's a handy figure of speech (though a bit of a cliché), and Lord knows it's stood the test of time. So go ahead and use it if the occasion calls for it, but be mindful of your audience. If a little warning bell goes off in your brain, choose another expression. The same holds true for the expressions "in spades" and "coming up spades," which also have innocent origins. Spades is the highest-ranked suit in cards (the values of the suits, in ascending order, are clubs, diamonds, hearts, spades). So to have something "in spades" is to have a great deal of it, and to "come up spades" is to be in luck.

A final note. The ancient Greek saying "call a fig a fig and a trough a trough" has lost its figs and troughs in English, but the original expression is alive and well in modern Greece. Those naughty double meanings, though, are gone. When a Greek says "call a fig a fig, a trough a trough" today, what he means is speak plainly—in other words, call a spade a spade.

Don't Know Much About Herstory

If you've seen the musical *South Pacific,* you'll remember the on-again, off-again romance between Nellie, the Navy nurse, and

Émile, the rich planter. During an off moment, Nellie vows to "wash that man right outa my hair." Nellie eventually gets her man, but offstage some women have been trying to wash "man" right out of the feminist lexicon. So we find a student house at Beloit College called the Womyn's Center; an FM station in California with a *Wimmin's Music Program;* a Canadian musical group named the Dorchester Wymyn Drummers, and an Iowa social-service group, the Rainbow wÝmYn's Circle.

We can trace this lexical inventiveness back to the late 1960s and early '70s, when some feminists began playfully altering the spellings of a few common words to remove real or fanciful traces of maleness. They gleefully took etymological liberties to lay siege to—and poke fun at—the boys' club orientation of history and language. So "history," retold from a woman's point of view, became "herstory." The word "women" became "womyn" and "wimmin." Before long we had "wymyn," "womben," "womon," "womin," and other whimsies. Meanwhile, some females gave up "female" in favor of "femina" or "femelle." And cheeky girls turned "girls" inside out, calling themselves "grrrls," "gurls," "grrlz," and so on.

To be fair, the feminist writers who started all this were making a political, not an etymological, statement. But politics, as we know, has a way of twisting etymology to its own ends. A lot of younger womyn who use these creative spellings today mistakenly believe that the "his" in "history" really has something to do with maleness, that "female" is derived from "male," and that "woman" is sexist because it includes the word "man."

First a little herstory. I'm not a big fan of this word, but I'd better get used to it. You should too, since "herstory" has earned a place in dictionaries and is now standard English. Lexicographers describe it as a blend of "her" and "history," circa 1970. It's usually defined as history told from a feminist viewpoint or emphasizing the contributions of women. Instead of making up a new word, though, I'd rather see history do the job it's supposed to do—tell women's stories as well as men's. Besides, there's nothing masculine about the word "history," no matter how many websites make claims to the contrary. The "his" in "history" is not the masculine pronoun that's the opposite of "her." We got the word from the Latin *historia,* which means an "account" or "narrative," and the Romans got it from a similar word in Greek. No pronouns here, male or otherwise.

Which brings us to "female." We can thank the Romans for this one too. We got it from the Latin *femella,* a diminutive form of *femina,* or "woman." Here again, no maleness intended. *Femella* was strictly a female female. When the word entered English in the early 1300s it was spelled "femelle," similar to a word in Old French. This spelling was short-lived, however. By the end of the century it had become "female" because of confusion with "male," which comes from an entirely different Latin root, *masculus.* Did sexism rear its medieval head? Perhaps. And since "female" isn't related etymologically to "male," I guess one could make a case for using "femina" or "femelle" instead. But why bother? I'm not changing my vocabulary to fix a slip of the quill by an obscure scrivener (male, no doubt!) in the Middle Ages.

You won't catch me adding "womyn," "wimmin," and the rest to my spell-checker's dictionary either. There's nothing sexist about the word "woman." Here's the history—or, if you prefer, the herstory. In Anglo-Saxon times, when words were bubbling away in the stewpot of Old English, there were several ways to refer to men and women. For a few hundred years, *manna* and other early versions of our modern word "man" referred merely to a person regardless of sex—that is, a human being. So how did the Anglo-Saxons tell one sex from the other? A single or married man was a *wer* or a *waepman* (literally a "weapon-person"). A single or married woman was a *wif* or a *wifman.*

By the year 900 or so, *wifman* began to lose its *f.* Over the next five hundred years, it went through many spellings until it settled down as our modern word "woman." Meanwhile, *wif,* which had its own share of spellings before becoming "wife" in the 1400s, led a double life. It could mean a married woman, as it does today, but also a woman, married or single, in a humble trade—an archaic usage that survives in the quaint terms "fishwife" and "alewife."

Speaking of quaint terms, whatever happened to the weapon-people? Around the year 1000, the various versions of *manna* began to mean an adult male as well as a human being. By the 1400s, *manna* had become our modern word "man," while the old macho terms *wer* and *waepman* had fallen out of use. (Too bad. I rather like them.) That left the guys without a unique word for an adult male. They had to share "man" with humanity in general. If you ask me, it was the men who got screwed, etymologically speaking. We women ended up with a word all our own. And that, boys and girls, is the real herstory.

As for "girls," remember the "Hans and Franz" sketches on *Saturday Night Live* in the late 1980s and early '90s? When the two bodybuilders weren't pumping up or boasting about their famous cousin Arnold, they were sneering at "girlie men." Cousin Arnold himself, as we know, later ridiculed his political opponents as "girlie men." Hey, guys, forget the abs and pecs for a minute. Here's a news flash: "girl" wasn't always a girlie word.

In about 1300, when the word made its first known appearance in print, a "girl" was a child of either sex, and "girls" meant children, period. In the fourteenth-century poem *Piers Plowman,* for example, a children's Latin grammar book is called a "gramer for girles." And in the *Canterbury Tales,* Chaucer refers to small children as "yonge gerles." But in the late fourteenth and early fifteenth centuries, the word began to mean female children, and by the end of the fifteenth century the androgynous meaning of "girls" was lost.

The word "girls" has come a long way since the Middle Ages. When I was in college and the women's liberation movement was in its heyday, I took offense at the use of "girl" to mean "woman," especially if the offender was a man. To some extent, I still feel that way, but I may be behind the times. The term "girl" has taken on a sassy, in-your-face pride that it didn't have in my college days. Young women (and women not so young) routinely call themselves "girls" now. It's not uncommon for these girls (or "grrrls" or "gurls" or "grrlz") to spend a "girlie" afternoon together, doing "girl" things and talking "girl talk."

Those grrrowly spellings arrived on the scene in the early nineties, as young women were redefining feminism. The terms "grrrl" and "grrl," according to the *OED*, appeared in print for the first time in 1992, when *Billboard* referred to the "riot grrls" punk-music movement. Within a couple of years, young women with an edgy, playful attitude were borrowing "grrrls" for themselves and improvising fanciful new spellings. I may be inconsistent, but I'm not particularly bothered by all the inventive spellings of "girl." The big difference here is that the "gurls" using all these "grrrly" words are merely having fun with language, not misunderstanding it. And girls just want to have fun.

The Other N-Word

In early 1999, as the world braced itself for a computer meltdown come the millennium, word lovers were having a nervous breakdown over an etymological squabble in our nation's capital.

A white city official got himself into deep doo-doo when he told two aides that money was tight and he'd have to be "niggardly" with expenses. One of the aides mistook the remark for a racial slur, the Washington rumor mill went to work, and all hell broke loose. Ten days later, the official quit under fire and the city's black mayor accepted his resignation.

Wordies, both black and white, had conniptions, and no wonder. "Niggardly" means tightfisted, as lexicographers and newspaper editorials pointed out, and has no connection at all with the despised word "nigger." The whole ugly mess, in short, was just an etymological misunderstanding. In the end, the storm blew over and the official was rehired. But more than a decade later, "niggardly" remains a tainted word. I hate to see an innocent word wrongly convicted. But perhaps this one, no matter how innocent, is just too close for comfort, never mind its etymology.

"Niggardly" has roots going back to around 1300, when "nig" or "nygge," probably borrowed from old Scandinavian languages, meant a miser. In the later 1300s, "niggard" was used as both a noun and an adjective to refer to a stingy person. It appeared in the Wycliffe Bible in the 1380s and in the *Canterbury Tales* a decade later. "Niggardly" came along in the sixteenth century, with the same parsimonious meaning.

The word "nigger" is no relation. It's derived from the Latin *niger* (black), which is also the source of *negro,* the Spanish and Portuguese word that gave us "Negro." The n-word that's such a notorious and hated slur today wasn't always a term of contempt. When it first showed up, in the sixteenth century, spelled "niger," it was a neutral, sometimes positive, term for a dark-skinned person. The earliest known published use of the word, from 1574, refers to "the Nigers of Aethiop, bearing witnes." But by the late 1700s it was a hostile word, used by whites to refer to blacks in a demeaning way. It has become more highly charged over the centuries, and is now the most bitterly resented racial slur a white person can utter. When it's used by black people to refer to other blacks, however, the story is different. Since as far back as the early 1800s, "nigger" has had three personalities among African Americans: sometimes derogatory, sometimes neutral, sometimes even affectionate. In fact, young rappers now treat it as an honorific of the 'hood—repackaged as "nigga," "niggahz," etc.—to the dismay of some of their elders who have painful associations with the original.

It was probably inevitable in our race-conscious times that "niggardly" would get rounded up with the usual suspects. I don't like losing a word, but if ever a word could go missing without being missed, this is the one. To begin with, it hasn't been a household word in modern times. It reminds me of snuffboxes and whalebone stays. I'll bet many people never heard of it before all the fuss in Washington, and its obscurity is well deserved: There are so many better words. "Stingy" is pretty good, and so are "grudging," "parsimonious," "grasping," "greedy," "cheap," "miserly," "money-grubbing," "tight-fisted," and "penny-pinching." With such riches, why use "niggardly" at all? Somebody who uses it is in effect telling his audience: "I'm smarter than anyone who's dumb enough to get mad."

I'm not saying we should ban "niggardly" (or any other word, for that matter). Use it if you must, but use it with care. I suspect, though, that anyone who can't come up with a better word has a tin ear.

On the other hand, I'd hate to lose *bête noire*, an expression that some people (mainly oversensitive whites, in my experience) mistakenly think is racist. *Bête noire* literally means "black beast" in French, but its modern meaning is closer to "pet peeve." It's a figurative expression for something (or someone) that's particularly annoying, and it's been used in English since the mid-nineteenth century. The *OED*'s earliest published reference is in a Thackeray novel, *The Luck of Barry Lyndon* (1844): "Calling me her bête noire, her dark spirit, her murderous adorer, and a thousand other names indicative of her extreme disquietude and terror." Among those thousand other names, of course, are many common phrases in which "black" means dismal or bleak— "black mood," "black day," "black outlook," and so on. No one who uses them is thinking of race.

Almost any word or expression is capable of offending somebody if the circumstances are right. Words themselves (except for the notorious exceptions) aren't insensitive; people are insensitive. For instance, there's nothing wrong with "offhand remark," but you wouldn't want to use it to describe a comment by someone who'd had a hand amputated. Similarly, there's nothing wrong with *bête noire,* but it might be unwise to use it in reference to, say, an African-American councilman.

If we were to forbid every term that might offend someone, we'd have to go around with duct tape over our mouths. Bird lovers, for example, couldn't fill their feeders with "niger," a small black seed much relished by finches. Believe it or not, the Wild Bird Feeding Institute, a trade association, coined the name Nyjer in 1998 to avoid, among other things, the "offensive" mispronunciation of "niger." Another euphemism for "niger" is "thistle," though niger comes from an entirely different plant. Some sources trace the name "niger" to the River Niger in Africa, while others say it refers to the color of the seed. Whatever its source, "niger" is pronounced with a long *i,* as in "dine," which the goldfinches on my most popular feeder love to do.

To He or Not to He

Political junkies will remember this one. A retired lawyer in Reno asked a state court to keep Hillary Clinton off the ballot in Nevada if she won the Democratic nomination for president in 2008. His argument: The Constitution never intended a woman to be president. "The use of female gendered pronouns 'she' or 'her' are not present in the document," his suit argued, "making it conclusive that the framers never intended that a woman would be president of the United States."

The case didn't get anywhere (the legal thinking was as muddled as the grammar). But it raised an interesting question: Why do we use "he," "him," and "his" to refer to both men and women? Many people see the generic "he" as a good olde usage dating back to Anglo-Saxon days, like the generic "man." Others see it as one more ancient and outdated example of male chauvinism. Think again, people. The generic "he" isn't very old and it isn't the handiwork of the testosterone crowd.

If any single person is responsible for this clunky usage, it's Anne Fisher, an eighteenth-century schoolmistress in England and the first woman to write an English grammar book, according to the linguist Ingrid Tieken-Boon van Ostade. We don't have a surviving copy of the first edition of Fisher's popular guide, *A New Grammar with Exercises of Bad English,* but an advertisement for it appeared in 1745 in the *Newcastle Journal.* The second edition came out five years later, followed by thirty other editions, making the grammar guide one of the most successful of its time.

A New Grammar, according to Tieken-Boon van Ostade, was the first grammar book to say the pronoun "he" should apply to both sexes. "The *Masculine Person,*" Fisher wrote, "answers to the *general Name,* which comprehends both *Male* and *Female;* as, *any Person who knows what he says.*" (A male grammarian, John Kirkby, said the same thing soon after Fisher's first edition came out, but language scholars feel he plagiarized the idea from her.)

I like a lot of what Fisher had to say about English. She believed in making grammar easy to understand by using simple terms (she called an auxiliary a "helping verb," for example) and by eliminating some of the nonsense that Latinists had introduced. A woman after my own heart! I recognize a kindred spirit here: "Most of our *English* Grammars are so dependent on the *Latin,*" she wrote, "that they appear only translations of them, introducing many needless perplexities; as superfluous cases, genders, moods, tenses, &c. peculiarities which our language is exempt from." Amen. But I wish Fisher had left "he" alone. I'm a she who has never got used to being called a he. I'll have more to say about this he-ing and she-ing business later in the chapter.

Why a Duck?

I used to watch Groucho Marx's *You Bet Your Life* on television every Thursday night when I was a kid in the late 1950s. I was too young to get the jokes, but I loved seeing the stuffed duck fall from the ceiling with a hundred-dollar bill for the guest who happened to say the secret word. I wasn't around in the early thirties, when Groucho had a radio show named for a fly-by-night law firm, *Flywheel, Shyster and Flywheel.* He played Waldorf T. Flywheel and Chico played his assistant, Emmanuel Ravelli. Groucho was the only Flywheel in the firm, but he talked enough for two. As for Shyster, he was just a guy who ran off with Flywheel's wife and got his name put on the firm's door as a token of gratitude.

Here's a typical scene between Flywheel and his secretary:

> Flywheel: Miss Dimple, put down that telephone book. This office is no place for a bookworm.
>
> Miss Dimple: Yes, Mr. Flywheel.
>
> Flywheel: Any mail this morning?
>
> Miss Dimple: Yes, there's a letter from the typewriter company. They say you haven't paid for the typewriter yet.
>
> Flywheel: Why should *I* pay for the typewriter? You're the one who uses it.
>
> Miss Dimple: But Mr. Flywheel, I—
>
> Flywheel: Never mind. Take a letter to those cheap chiselers. Ah . . . Gentlemen . . . I never *ordered* that typewriter. *(Pause.)* If I did, you didn't send it. . . . If you sent it, I never got it. . . . If I got it, I paid for it. . . . And if I *didn't,* I won't. Best regards . . .

Now that's a shyster! Which brings me neatly to my point. Many people feel uncomfortable about "shyster," a word for an unethical or unscrupulous person, especially a lawyer. In their minds it's an anti-Semitic allusion to Shylock, the ruthless Jewish moneylender in *The Merchant of Venice,* whose name has come to mean a loan shark. Let's examine the evidence.

We can rule out Shylock as a suspect right away. There's no paper trail connecting Shakespeare's character with the word "shyster," which first showed up in the New York underworld in the 1840s, centuries after the original Shylock asked for his pound of flesh. Word detectives have also dismissed the notion that "shyster" refers to an unscrupulous New York lawyer named Schuester. No such person has been traced. The *Oxford English Dictionary* has suggested the word may be derived from "shy," which once had the slang meaning of shady or disreputable. But all of the *OED* citations for this usage of "shy" are from Britain, across the Atlantic from where "shyster" first appeared, and all of them showed up after "shyster" did. Another suspect cleared.

Just when the language world needed a Sherlock Holmes to solve this case, along came the slang etymologist Gerald L. Cohen. He traced "shyster" back to a defunct nineteenth-century newspaper, *The Subterranean,* which covered New York's courts and jails. In an 1843 article about legal corruption, the editor of the paper said he'd heard an attorney use "shiseter" for an unscrupulous lawyer. When the editor asked where the term came from, the attorney offered an explanation "which we would now give our readers, were it not that it would certainly subject us to a prosecution for libel and obscenity." Aha, the missing clue! It led Cohen to conclude that "shyster" (a spelling adopted soon afterward by *The Subterranean*) came from a vulgar German word for an incompetent or contemptible person, *scheisser,* literally "one who shits." Or, as an American might put it, an asshole. Cohen felt the term would have been familiar in New York because of the many German-speaking immigrants there at the time. Most lexicographers accept that explanation today.

OK, "shyster" isn't anti-Semitic, or at least it didn't begin life that way. But a few minutes of googling will turn up endless examples of the word used as a slur, as in this definition on Urban Dictionary, whose entries are written by users: "A Jewish professional who cons people. Taken from the Shakespearian character Shylock, in *The Merchant of Venice.*" And bigots aren't the only ones who think "shylock" when they hear "shyster." For many (if not most) of us, the word is guilty by association. That may be unfair, but I'd think twice before using it.

Gender Bending

We have countless words in English, literally countless, since nobody knows quite how to count them. Is "sleep" one word or two (a noun as well as a verb)? Is "sleeps" yet another one (or two)? Does "sleepy" count as a separate word? And should we count the gazillion (give or take) scientific and medical and technological terms ("2,4,5-Trimethylbenzaldehyde," for example) that only specialized dictionaries include, not to mention all the acronyms and abbreviations and texting wrds and so on? The lexicographers at Oxford University Press, publisher of the *OED*, think we probably have a quarter to three quarters of a million English words, minus all those 2,4,5-Trimethyl-whatevers— way more than French, German, Spanish, Italian, Swedish, Dutch, and so on. No matter how you count them, we have more words than anybody will ever use, even if he or she lives to be a hundred. But one word is missing, and it's left a great big hole in English—the word I would have used instead of "he or she" in that last sentence.

What we need is an all-purpose pronoun for people that can be masculine or feminine, singular or plural. As it turns out, we once did have such a word. For hundreds of years, people used "they," "them," or "their" to refer to people in general, whether one or more, male or female. Although "they" was originally plural when English borrowed it from Old Norse around 1200, people began using it as a singular in the 1300s to refer to a generic person, an everyman (or everywoman). Here's an example from Chaucer's *Canterbury Tales* (1395): "And whoso fyndeth hym out of swich blame, / They wol come up and offre on goddes name." (In case your Middle English is rusty: "And whoever finds himself without such blame, / They will come up and offer in God's name.") Great writers, including Shakespeare, Defoe, Swift, Fielding, Richardson, Goldsmith, and Johnson all made great use of the sexless, numberless "they/them/their" without raising eyebrows. It wasn't until the end of the eighteenth century, when all of them were late as well as great, that eyebrows were raised.

One of the most influential of those eyebrows belonged to the grammarian Lindley Murray, who was widely popular on both sides of the Atlantic. Perhaps influenced by Anne Fisher (see pages 137–38), he ruled in 1795 that it was a violation of good English to use the plural pronouns "they" and company to refer to technically singular words. In his bestselling *English Grammar,* he gave this as an example of a lousy sentence: "Can any one, on their entrance into the world, be fully secure that they shall not be deceived?" He insisted "their" should be "his" and "they" should be "he." The idea caught on with other, popular grammarians, who saw English in black and white, and were uncomfortable with the gray area occupied by "they." It didn't seem logical to them that a pronoun could be plural one moment and singular the next.

By the early nineteenth century, the prohibition against using "they" in a singular way was firmly entrenched in standard English. In 1828 Noah Webster defined "they," "them," and "their" as strictly plural, basically what grammar, usage, and style guides have been telling us since. For example, a century later Henry Fowler, the father of *Modern English Usage* as well as modern English usage, said treating "they/them/their" as singular "sets the literary man's teeth on edge." And more recently, an update of Wilson Follett's *Modern American Usage* insists that "*they* is unfit to represent a singular antecedent." Meanwhile, great writers—like Byron, Shelley, Austen, Scott, Thackeray, Eliot, Dickens, Trollope, Kipling, Wharton, Shaw, Auden, and more recently Doris Lessing—have continued to use "they" and its rel-atives in a singular sense, grammarians be damned.

Of course, great writers make their own rules, but the rest of us risk looking like fools if we call a "someone" a "they" in edu-cated company. That's the way things stand now, though we may be witnessing a seismic change. So many people are now using "they" in the old singular way, especially in Britain, that diction-aries and usage guides are taking a critical look at Lindley Mur-ray's prohibition. In fact, the newest edition of Fowler's manual, edited by R. W. Burchfield, suggests it's only a matter of time before this usage becomes standard English: "The process now seems irreversible." *Merriam-Webster's Collegiate Dictionary* (11th ed.) already includes the singular "they" as standard English, but the practice is still condemned by a majority of the usage panel for *The American Heritage Dictionary of the English Language* (4th ed.).

Eventually, the fate of "they" will be decided by the ladies and gentlemen of the jury—the people who actually speak the lan-guage. In the meantime, with experts at odds over the issue, the safest course is to avoid using "they" and its cousins in a singular sense, especially in writing. I'm not entirely satisfied with the al-ternatives available, but let me share some of the verbal contor-tions I go through to deal with the problem.

One solution is to refer to the generic person with "he" or "him" or "his" in some places, and with "she" or "her" or "hers" in others. Simply alternate masculine and feminine pronouns. (When I worked at the *Des Moines Register* in the mid-1970s, that was the thinking on the Op-Ed pages. The shifts back and forth didn't seem to bother anyone.) Another solution is to avoid the problem pronoun entirely. Instead of "Someone forgot to pay his or her bill," say "Someone forgot to pay the bill." If you must use "they," "them," or "their," then make the pronoun refer to something plural, not singular. Instead of "Every parent dotes on their child," make it "All parents dote on their children." There's always a way. No, it's not a perfect answer. But disregarding two centuries of opposition to the all-purpose "they" is no answer either—at least not until it's recognized by most educated speakers as legitimate.

No doubt many sticklers cringe at the idea of living in a world where a pronoun can be either singular or plural. But they don't seem to mind "you," which everybody knows can be both. What everybody doesn't know is that "you" started out as a plural. In Old English, there were four ways of expressing "you"-ness: the singulars "thou" and "thee," and the plurals "ye" and "you." The Anglo-Saxons used "thou" and "ye" as subjects, "thee" and "you" as objects. But by the end of the sixteenth century, the all-purpose "you" was firmly established as standard English, though some "thee"-ing and "thou"-ing survived, notably among the Quakers and in rural dialects.

OK, there's a good case to be made for using "they" to refer to a singular, indefinite person. To tell you the truth, though, I still can't get my mind around the idea. I wish there were another solution. Many other people have wished for one too, and some have gone further and dreamed up new pronouns. If only it were that easy! Made-up pronouns are almost impossible to introduce into a language.

In 1884, there was a serious attempt to introduce "thon," a sexless third-person pronoun, into English, and it actually made it into dictionaries. (The guy behind the idea was the American lawyer and composer Charles Crozat Converse, whose other claim to fame is that he wrote the tune to "What a Friend We Have in Jesus.") Though you can still find "thon" in fifty-year-old dictionaries, it eventually went the way of "ne" (1850s), "heer" (1913), "ha" (pre-1936), and several other attempts to in-

vent a genderless pronoun. They just didn't fly. "Among the
many reforms proposed for the English language," the linguist
Dennis E. Baron has written, "the creation of an epicene or bisexual
pronoun stands out as the one most often advocated and at-
tempted, and the one that has most often failed." Or, as Ogden
Nash said in another context, "No, thonx."

Italian Dressing

What does Fiat stand for? Frenzied Italian at traffic light. Pretty
lame, huh? That's what you get for checking out word origins on
the Web. Actually, the carmaker's name is an acronym for Fab-
brica Italiana Automobili Torino (Italian Automobile Factory of
Turin). You'll find more etymological bologna if you google the
word "wop," an ethnic slur for an Italian. Supposedly it's an
acronym for "without papers" or "without passport" or "works
on pavement." Nope, nope, and nope.

"Wop," which originated in the United States, has been a
derogatory term for an Italian since 1908. But it's not an
acronym and it has nothing to do with immigration documents,
which weren't even required of newcomers until 1918. The word
comes from *guappo,* a word in Sicilian and Neapolitan dialects
that means a swaggering thug. It's ultimately derived from the
Latin *vappa,* or "sour wine," a word the Romans used figuratively
for a worthless guy.

Many people mistakenly believe that "wop" originated at Ellis
Island, where inspectors supposedly used stamps or chalk or
placards to identify immigrants without proper papers. Although chalk markings were used to identify those with health
problems (G for goiter, H for heart, L for lameness, and so on),
the symbols didn't include WOP. Despite the absence of evi-

dence, this myth has persisted even among Italian-Americans, who should know better.

In his autobiography *The Good Life,* the singer Tony Bennett says many illiterate immigrants arrived without the right documents. "The derogatory term 'wop,' an acronym for 'With Out Papers,' would be stamped on the forms of these unfortunates, and officials would call out, 'We have another "wop." Send him home.' "

Well, he didn't get his Grammys for etymology.

Snow Job

It's almost impossible to kill a myth once it starts spreading, especially on the Internet. Psychologists have a field day with stuff like this. The more we see or hear something, even if it's being debunked, the more we believe it, studies show. So I'm probably wasting my time here, but IT'S A MYTH that Eskimos have dozens or even hundreds of words for snow. (Maybe capital letters will help.) It may be politically correct to believe that primitive cultures are every bit as complex as our own, but the number of Eskimo words for snow won't make the case. In fact, English probably has just as many, depending on how you count them.

Where did all this come from? Lucky for me, I don't have to do the research. Laura Martin, a linguistic anthropologist, traced the myth back to an innocent comment by the anthropologist Franz Boas in a 1911 book. He happened to say that the Eskimo languages had four words for snow: *aput* ("snow on the ground"), *qana* ("falling snow"), *piqsirpoq* ("drifting snow"), and *qimuqsuq* ("snowdrift"). In 1940 the linguist Benjamin Whorf expanded the list to seven, and gave the issue a cultural spin by saying

English had only one. In the decades since then, the number of words has snowballed with each retelling. As Martin wrote in a 1986 article, "Boas's small example—ironically, one intended as a caution against superficial linguistic comparisons—has transcended its source and become part of academic oral tradition." Some scholars used the Eskimo story to support the theory that language determines how we view the world, others to make the point that every language is sophisticated in its own way. The cultural relativists were as happy as clams. Martin's 1986 article in a scholarly journal had little or no impact on the avalanche of snow stories. Neither did the linguist Geoffrey Pullum's 1991 book *The Great Eskimo Vocabulary Hoax.* As I said, these things aren't easy to stop.

In truth, the Eskimos have about a dozen words for snow "counting generously," according to the Harvard psychologist Steven Pinker. But he points out that "by such standards" English has just about as many: "snow," "sleet," "slush," "blizzard," "avalanche," "hail," "hardpack," "powder," "flurry," "dusting," and even "snizzling" (a humorous coinage from a meteorologist at Boston's WBZ-TV). As someone who plows her own snow in rural Connecticut, I think that's quite enough.

How to Unmake an American Quilt

I love old African-American quilts, especially those made from scraps of material that happened to be at hand: a threadbare work shirt, worn-out jeans, a dress beyond repair, a flour sack, whatever. I was blown away when I saw the quilts made by the women of Gee's Bend, Alabama, on display at the Whitney Museum of American Art in Manhattan some years ago. They spoke to me about the hard lives the quilt makers had lived and the hard lives those old fabrics had seen. Out of such hardship came such beauty. The quilts, most from the 1930s to the 1970s, spoke a language beyond words.

We have only a few surviving examples of the quilts that slaves sewed for their own use a century or more earlier. I haven't seen any, but I imagine they would also tell a story of hard lives and making do. There's one thing they wouldn't tell, though. Those old quilts didn't use secret codes to tell slaves how to escape to safety along the Underground Railroad. Nevertheless, numerous schoolchildren have been taught that secret messages in the patterns of quilts hung out to air told slaves when to flee, what to take with them, the best routes to follow, and how to find a safe house. And this isn't just a kid thing. *The New York Times, USA Today, National Geographic, The Oprah Winfrey Show,* and even the secretive National Security Agency's museum of codes have at one time or another repeated the story, sometimes with a caution or two, sometimes not.

Yes, it's made of whole cloth, and the cloth isn't very old. The first suggestion that quilts were used to help slaves escape came in a 1990 book by Gladys-Marie Fry, *Stitched from the Soul.* In a single paragraph, Fry wrote that quilts "with the color black" in them were hung on clotheslines to indicate safe houses. She didn't offer any evidence, and the quilt historian Leigh Fellner says she has found nothing to support the claim.

Nine years later, Jacqueline Tobin, a writer, and Raymond Dobard, an art historian, published a book, *Hidden in Plain View,* with a new and expanded version of the quilt story. The book was featured on *Oprah* two months before it was published, and the show was rebroadcast on the eve of publication in January 1999. The authors, according to the book, relied on the recollections of Ozella McDaniel Williams, a Charleston, South Carolina, quilt maker who had died before *Hidden in Plain View* came out. Escaping slaves, the book says, were guided by ten quilt patterns: the Monkey Wrench told them "to gather all the tools they might need," the Shoofly advised them "to dress up in cotton," the Wagon Wheel signaled them "to pack all the things that would go in a wagon," the Tumbling Boxes meant "it was time to escape," the Bear's Paw told them a bear's footprints "would undoubtedly indicate the best path," the Flying Geese indicated "the best season for slaves to escape" and "pointed to the direction, north."

The holes in this story are so big that you could drive a buckboard wagon full of monkey wrenches through them. Apart from the obvious nonsense (why couldn't the slaves simply talk among themselves, maybe during all those quilting bees?), most of the ten quilt patterns weren't even around until the late nineteenth or early twentieth centuries. But that's only for starters. Giles R. Wright, director of the Afro-American History Program at the New Jersey Historical Commission, summed up the criticism this way: (1) No coded slave quilt has survived. (2) None of the former slaves interviewed by the Works Progress Administration in the 1930s ever mentioned such quilts. (3) Not one of the diaries or memoirs from the time mentions them. In other words, there's not a thread of evidence to support the myth. Yet it lives on, and it's been nurtured by a host of children's books with titles like *Sweet Clara and the Freedom Quilt, The Patchwork Path,* and *Under the Quilt of Night.*

But who needs evidence? Certainly not the designer who came up with the idea of incorporating a coded slave quilt in a memorial to Frederick Douglass in New York's Central Park. Scholars were not pleased to hear about the plans for an eight-foot-tall bronze statue of the former slave, standing on a granite quilt carved with the "secret" patterns. "Frederick Douglass never saw, nor did he even hear of, a quilt used to signal a runaway slave like himself, on his or her desperate journey to freedom," said David Blight, a Yale historian and an authority on Douglass. He called the whole quilt-code business "a myth, bordering on a hoax." In the words of Marsha MacDowell, an art professor at Michigan State University and an authority on quilting, "It's like Washington chopping down the cherry tree." As for the Douglass memorial, the granite quilt stayed, but some of the wording on the monument was changed to avoid perpetuating the myth. It seems like a patchwork solution to me.

He Said, She Said

Take Henny Youngman, please: "My wife is breathtaking; every few hours she stops to take a breath." Oh, yeah? I could say the same about my husband, who insists on discussing the newspaper at breakfast while my nose is buried in a book. But who really talks more—men or women? The accepted wisdom these days seems to be that women are the bigmouths. At least that's what one would believe after reading all the books and articles published on the subject over the last couple of decades, not to mention googles and googles of information on the Internet.

Let's talk numbers. Women use anywhere from twice to three times as many words a day as men, according to three bestselling authors. Dr. Scott Haltzman, a psychiatrist and marriage counselor, puts the figure at 7,000 words for her versus 2,000 for him. The evangelist and broadcaster James Dobson prefers 50,000 versus 25,000. And Dr. Louann Brizendine, a neuropsychiatrist, has given us 20,000 versus 7,000. But you'll find all kinds of numbers from all kinds of authors: 25,000 versus 12,000, 5,000 versus 2,500, and so on.

What you won't find, however, is a single scientific study showing that women talk much more than men. In fact, the best evidence suggests that men are at least as chatty as women, and perhaps a little chattier. Two social psychologists, Campbell Leaper and Melanie Ayres, examined the available scientific evidence—sixty-three studies of men, women, and talkativeness—in a paper published in 2007. Their conclusion: Men talk somewhat more than women, but the difference isn't much. In another study published the same year, a team of psychologists led by Matthias R. Mehl attached voice-activated digital recorders to 396 people and actually counted the words they spoke. The results: Both men and women used an average of about 16,000 words a day.

What I'd really like to see is a study of who listens more, men or women. The accepted wisdom here is that women listen better. But I suspect that's not true either. My husband may talk a lot, but he listens a lot too. So don't take my husband, please!

Disoriented

An acronym is a word made up of the initial letters or syllables of other words. "Radar," for instance, is an acronym for "radio detecting and ranging." The term "acronym" was coined in the twentieth century from the Greek words for limb, *akros,* and name, *onoma.* So you might say an acronym is a name made from the limbs of other words. One thing you develop pretty quickly in the language racket is radar to detect phony acronyms. The more interesting they are, the more likely they'll leave you out on a limb, waiting for the guy with a chainsaw.

Which brings us to "wog," an offensive term used mostly by the British for a dark-skinned foreigner, especially one from the Middle East or the Far East. But some of the sceptred isle's more inclusive-minded bigots may extend "wog" to encompass an

Italian or a Spaniard (though the last I heard a Frenchman was still a frog and a German a Hun).

If you've read much twentieth-century British literature, you've probably seen "wog" or variations of it. The first two citations in the *Oxford English Dictionary* come from James Joyce's *Ulysses* (1922): "She called him wogger. . . . She may have noticed that her wogger people were always going away." The *OED*'s first reference for "wog" itself comes from a 1929 book on sea slang: "*Wogs,* lower class Babu shipping clerks on the Indian coast."

And if you've spent much time in the mother country or around expatriate Brits, you've probably heard the story that "wog" is an acronym—for "wily oriental gentleman" or "worthy oriental gentleman" or "we oriental gentlemen." I see a blip on the radar screen! No, "wog" isn't an acronym, but it's sometimes called a backronym, a false acronym created after the fact from an existing word. (There's a word for almost everything!)

Where does "wog" really come from? We don't know for sure, but some lexicographers have traced it to the Golliwogg, a black rag-doll character in the children's stories of Florence Kate Upton. The American-born British author and artist, who wrote in the late nineteenth and early twentieth centuries, was widely successful but failed to protect her creation. The name soon became public property (spelled "golliwog") and inspired dolls, toys, books, and many other products. A golliwog named Golly was featured on the Robertson & Sons jam and marmalade jars from 1910 until 2001. And the popularity of golliwogs may also have inspired a mid-twentieth-century revival of blackface minstrel shows in Britain. *The Black and White Minstrel Show* ran on BBC television from 1958 until 1978. A stage version of the variety show ran in London from 1960 to 1972, and traveling troupes performed it for another fifteen years.

Good golly! Where are the PC police when you need them?

Chapter 9

In High Dungeon
And Other Moat Points

During one of my appearances on WNYC, a caller asked me to explain the difference between metonymy and synecdoche, two figures of speech. "Isn't the second one a town in upstate New York?" asked Leonard Lopate, the host of the show. (The pun later cropped up in a movie title.) Ever since, I've had to think twice to keep from blurting out "Schenectady" on the rare occasions when I have to use the term.

Leonard, a world-class punster, was joking, of course, but many of us unwittingly mangle the English language when our ears and tongues play tricks on us. Most of the time, we just embarrass ourselves and provide entertainment for those who are better informed. But as we mishear, misspeak, or mis-whatever, our bloopers can sometimes change the very language that they affront. The words "gantlet" and "gauntlet," for example, have become so mixed up in people's mouths—and minds—that dictionaries now say it's OK to use them interchangeably.

We're often more creative at abusing language than using it, and as you might expect we have names for the various species of abuse. Mixing up two similar-sounding words (like "synec-doche" and "Schenectady") is called a malapropism (from the French *mal à propos,* or inappropriate). The name was popularized by a character in *The Rivals,* an eighteenth-century play by Richard Brinsley Sheridan. Just about every time Mrs. Malaprop opens her mouth, she bobbles her words. She wants her niece, Lydia Languish, to marry for money instead of love, but Mrs. M complains that the reluctant young woman is "as headstrong as an allegory on the banks of the Nile." She regrets that "my afflu-ence over my niece is very small," but she praises the stubborn Lydia as "an object not altogether illegible." When her elo-quence is called into question, Mrs. Malaprop exclaims: "Sure, if I reprehend anything in this world, it is the use of my oracular tongue, and a nice derangement of epitaphs!"

If malapropisms tickle your fancy, then spoonerisms ought to tickle your funny bone. A spoonerism, a slip of the tongue in which parts of words are switched around, is a "different fettle of kitsch," as the essayist Roger Rosenblatt once put it. The term comes from William Archibald Spooner (1844–1930), a scholar, dean, and warden at New College, Oxford. He was known for his slips of the tongue, though most of those attributed to him (like "It is kisstomary to cuss the bride") are apocryphal. In fact, many of the spoonerisms I've come across weren't slips at all but the deliberate work of punsters. One of my favorites is the song-writer Tom Waits's quip, "I'd rather have a bottle in front of me than a frontal lobotomy." Of course, we don't have to search far to find legitimate slips of the tongue. Here's one from our forty-third president: "If the terriers and bariffs are torn down, the economy will grow."

If you like rock music, you've probably misheard a lyric or two. There's also a name for this one. A mondegreen is a misun-derstanding in which a familiar song lyric, bit of poetry, or popular expression is misinterpreted or misheard. Many schoolchildren, for example, have begun the Pledge of Allegiance with "I led the pigeons to the flag," and sung in church about "Round John Virgin" or "Gladly, the cross-eyed bear." The term "mondegreen" was coined by an American writer, Sylvia Wright, who'd misheard an old Scottish ballad when she was a child. What she heard was "They hae slain the Earl o' Moray, / And Lady Mondegreen." The real second line was "And laid him on the green." Rock songs are a rich source of mondegreens. Creedence Clearwater fans, perhaps under the influence of controlled substances, have heard "There's a bathroom on the right" instead of "There's a bad moon on the rise." And many a Jimi Hendrix audience used to join in and sing "'Scuse me while I kiss this guy" instead of "while I kiss the sky." After a while, it became a running joke and even Hendrix joined in. He'd sometimes point to a guy onstage—his bassist, Noel Redding, for instance—while singing the mondegreen version.

The linguists Geoffrey Pullum and Mark Liberman came up with the term "eggcorn" to describe another kind of blooper: mistaking a word or phrase for a similar-sounding one. The expression was inspired by a woman who used "egg corn" for "acorn." Think of "duck tape" (for "duct tape") or "tough road to hoe" (it's "row," not "road") or "tow the line" (nope, "toe"). Now let's resurrect a few blunders that aren't quite dead as a doorknob.

Tortured Chamber

I can't resist mentioning one more of Leonard Lopate's puns. This time it was when someone called WNYC to ask about the expression "in high dungeon." The puzzled listener was wondering how a dungeon could be upstairs, not down. Leonard quipped, "That's a moat point."

It's "dudgeon," not "dungeon," but the point wasn't all that "moat." In the Middle Ages, dungeons could indeed be upstairs. When the word "dungeon" entered English around 1300, it referred to the keep, or main tower, of a castle. The dungeon, the most secure part of the castle, was where the nobleman and his family could seek safety, where the armory was kept, and where defending forces retreated to make a last stand. But the keep was also used to hold prisoners, sometimes upstairs and sometimes down, and a "dungeon" came to mean a prison cell in the fourteenth century. By the way, we got the word "dungeon" from France, where *donjon* still means the keep of a castle, and what we think of as a dungeon is called a *cachot*.

I suspect that Thomas More, Anne Boleyn, and other famous prisoners were in high dudgeon no matter how high or low their quarters were—which brings us to an interesting question: What exactly is a dudgeon? When the word first showed up in English in the fourteenth century, it meant a kind of wood, perhaps boxwood, once used for the handles of knives and daggers. In the sixteenth century, it came to mean the wooden hilt of a dagger, as in Macbeth's famous "Is this a dagger which I see before me" soliloquy: "I see thee still, and on thy blade and dudgeon gouts of blood." About the same time, the word took on a new meaning: a feeling of anger or resentment. So people in a snit were "in dudgeon," and when they were really snitty, "in high (or great or deep) dudgeon."

But how did the handle of a dagger come to mean hard feelings? Nobody seems to know for sure, though that hasn't kept people from taking a stab at it. The most likely theory is that it had something to do with grabbing a dagger in anger. Some word detectives have tried to link "dudgeon" with *dygen,* a Welsh word that means malice or resentment, but the *Oxford English Dictionary* doesn't see a connection. Interestingly, two similar-sounding words, "bludgeon" and "curmudgeon," are also etymological mysteries. But "gudgeon," a small fish used for bait, as well as a gullible person who'll swallow anything, has a clear pedigree: It comes from *goujon,* the French word for the fish, which in turn is from *gobius,* the Latin for it.

Whatever "dudgeon" is, "dungeon" it isn't. So let's bury that tortured usage.

Hic Transit Gloria

A bunch of famous people come from my home state, Iowa: John Wayne, Herbert Hoover, Johnny Carson, Buffalo Bill, Ann Landers, and Abigail Van Buren. Then there's Charles Osborne, a pig farmer whose claim to fame was that he had the longest hiccup attack on record—from 1922 until 1990. Whoa, sixty-eight years! As my Gramps would have said, better him than me.

Note that I didn't spell the word "hiccough," though many dictionaries list that as an acceptable variant of the more common "hiccup." The *Oxford English Dictionary,* however, says the variant "ought to be abandoned as a mere error." I'm with the *OED* on this.

When the word first appeared in English in the sixteenth century, it was written every which way—"hicket," "hickot," "hickop," "hikup," and so on—all onomatopoeic spellings of the sound itself. "Hiccup" and "hiccough" showed up in the seventeenth century, but etymologists say the second spelling was apparently the result of a mistaken idea that hiccupping had something to do with coughing. You might call this a hiccup in the history of English.

The Horns of a "Dilemna"

Welcome to the Twilight Zone. The word "dilemma," which has been in English since the 1500s, has always been spelled with a double *m*. And yet legions of people around the English-speaking world not only spell it "dilemna," but also (and here's where Rod Serling steps out from behind a tree) insist that their teachers drummed this into them and ridiculed any "mistaken" efforts to spell it with two *m*'s.

No matter what you were taught, the correct spelling is "dilemma." The word is derived from the Greek *di* ("twice") and *lemma* ("assumption"). What it means, as you probably know, is a choice between two or more alternatives, all unfavorable. (Despite the *di-* prefix, the word is now widely accepted as applying to more than two choices.) The alternatives are sometimes called the "horns" of the dilemma.

The only published reference for "dilemna" in the *Oxford English Dictionary* comes from a book on logic written by Thomas Wilson in 1551, and that was probably a typo, since printing was rather primitive in those days and spellings were sometimes arbitrary. The phantom spelling isn't in any other reference book I know of, including obscure nineteenth-century dictionaries and spellers. No dice. Or, rather, no "dilemna."

But in googling "dilemna," I got hundreds of thousands of hits, including the CNN headline "Seoul's Missile Dilemna," and in searching the *New York Times* archive, I found fifty-eight appearances of "dilemna" since 1851. Mostly, though, I found cries in the wilderness from people whose teachers apparently insisted on the spelling "dilemna" so vigorously that it became engraved on their brains! Who were these teachers and where did they get this harebrained idea? Did they descend from a single Proto-Teacher born on another planet?

The odd "mn" spelling does have parallels in English: "condemn," "solemn," "limn," "autumn," and others. Curiously, the French word for "dilemma," *dilemme,* is widely misspelled in France as *dilemne.* As one French language website points out, "*En effet, la forme 'dilemne' n'existe pas.*" Another calls it "*un barbarisme.*" This gets curiouser and curiouser.

Some things, and this apparently is one of them, are beyond me. I can't account for the bizarre phenomenon of so very many people being taught—and taught insistently—that "dilemna" is correct. With apologies to Churchill, this is a dilemma wrapped in a mystery inside an enigma.

Hoedown

I don't know if hoeing a road is illegal, but one made of asphalt must be a mighty tough road to hoe. Still, numerous people, including politicians, journalists, academics, and corporate types, are hoeing tough roads from sea to shining sea. Senator Charles Schumer of New York, for example, has hoed roads on CBS, NBC, and CNN. The correct expression is, of course, "a tough row to hoe," and it refers to hoeing rows in a farm field. To have a tough or hard or long or difficult row to hoe means to have a daunting task to perform.

The *Oxford English Dictionary* says the expression is of American origin and dates back to 1835. The first known published reference is from *Tour Down East* by the frontiersman Davy Crockett: "I know it was a hard row to hoe." But within a few years, there was a fork in the row. An 1840 political cartoon about President Martin Van Buren's reelection campaign showed him laboring along a fanciful White House Turnpike. The caption: "A Hard Road to Hoe."

In the grand scheme of things, substituting "road" for "row" is only a misdemeanor, and doesn't deserve hard time. Definitely no more than an hour on a road crew.

Name Dropping

The last time I brought home a new puppy, I went to a baby-name discussion site on the Web for ideas about what to call her. I didn't find a name, but I did get a subject to discuss on the radio the next day: the baloney that people believe about names.

Some people awaiting their little bundles of joy thought that "Aaron" and "Erin" were simply male and female versions of the same name. Others believed that "Mary" and "Merry" were the identical name, just differently spelled. And still others thought "Carrie" and "Kerry" were merely variations on a theme—either male/female or unisex versions. No, no, and no. These are entirely different names with entirely different histories.

"Mary" is a name from the Bible, where it most often refers to the mother of Jesus. The *Oxford English Dictionary* says it can probably be traced to the Hebrew name "Miriam," which in turn may have its origin in an ancient Amorite word meaning "gift of God." But "Merry" is of Old English origin and comes from the adjective "merry," meaning festive or full of gaiety. The two ladies aren't even distantly related.

"Carrie" is commonly a pet name for "Caroline," while "Kerry" is a cross-gender name that was originally a place name. There were (and still are) Kerrys in both southwest Ireland and the Welsh border country.

As for "Erin," which has been used for both boys and girls, it's the Irish Gaelic word for "peace" and a poetic name for Ireland. But "Aaron" is another biblical name, from the Hebrew word for "enlightened." The most famous Aaron was a Jewish patriarch, the elder brother of Moses.

After that radio discussion about names, a college student wrote me to ask about some nicknames that he'd run across in an English literature course: "Ned" (for Edward), "Dick" (for Richard), "Hal" (for Harry), and an especially odd one, "Noll" (for Oliver).

It turns out that "Noll" was once a common nickname for "Oliver." (One of Oliver Cromwell's nicknames among the English people, when they weren't calling him something worse, was "Old Noll.") In a custom dating from medieval times, people added an affectionate "mine" before first names starting with a vowel, and they often dropped syllables as well. Thus "mine Oliver" led to "Noll"; "mine Edward" led to "Ned"; "mine Abel" became "Nab"; "mine Ann" gave us "Nan"; and "mine Ellen" ended up as "Nell." And sometimes an *r* in the middle of a name would somehow become an *l,* as in "Hal" (from Harry); "Mol" (Mary or Martha); "Dolly" (Dorothy); or "Sally" (Sarah). "Dick," I'm afraid, remains a mystery.

The word "nickname" itself has an interesting history. It's derived from an extremely old word, "ekename," which first appeared in print in 1303, according to the *OED.* (An "eke" in those days was an addition or a piece added on.) The pronunciation of the phrase "an ekename" was misunderstood as "a nekename," which in turn led to the modern word "nickname," first recorded in the seventeenth century.

As for the puppy (a yellow Lab), I decided to call her Gracie. I wanted to be able to end the day by saying, "Good night, Gracie."

Glove Affair

When I went to work for *The New York Times* in the early 1980s, the house stylebook insisted that one threw down a gauntlet and ran a gantlet. No ifs, ands, or buts. The latest *Times* stylebook still makes the distinction, though it acknowledges that some authorities ("but not this one") disagree. Never mind that dictionaries on both sides of the Atlantic now recommend "gauntlet" for all occasions and consider "gantlet" a mere variant. I fear that my old employer is fighting a losing battle here, one that's probably not worth winning. Mind you, this isn't another case of a wrongheaded usage worming its way into dictionaries by winning a popularity contest. People have been running gauntlets and throwing them down for hundreds of years. So how did this "gantlet"-vs.-"gauntlet" thing get started?

The word for what a knight throws down as a challenge (the glove worn with his medieval armor) comes from the French *gantelet,* which means little glove. It was spelled all sorts of ways—"gantelet," "gauntelote," "gauntelette," "gantlet," "gauntlet," and so on—after arriving in English in the early 1400s. By the mid-1500s, though, English writers had settled on the "gauntlet" spelling.

The thing that's run (or the ordeal one faces) refers to an old military punishment in which the miscreant had to strip to the waist and pass between two rows of men who struck him with sticks or knotted cords. Ow! We got the word during the Thirty Years' War (1618–48) from the Swedish term for the punishment, *gatlopp,* according to the *Oxford English Dictionary.* It was spelled "gantlop," "gantloop," "gauntlope," "gantelope," "gauntlet," "gantlet," and so on in English in the 1600s and 1700s. The *OED's* first published reference for running the "gantlet" is from 1661, and the first for running the "gauntlet" is from 1676. Both spellings have been used over the years, as well as the now-obscure "gantlope."

So what do we make of all this? In theory, I'm hand in glove with the lexicographers. But in practice I'm not so sure. English is often untidy, and we can find something in the disorder to support just about any position. No doubt the sticklers among us, including my old friends at the *Times*, will continue to uphold the "gantlet/gauntlet" distinction. For people who like things neat and tidy, it's an easy rule to follow. I'm a bit tidy myself, and I'm not quite ready to give up "gantlet" when I mean the thing one runs. But I won't throw down the gauntlet over this one.

Hold the Forte

When I think of fencing, I think of the fight scene with Ronald Colman and Douglas Fairbanks Jr. in *The Prisoner of Zenda*. Nice moves, guys! At least they looked good to me, but David O. Selznick, the producer, wasn't happy at first and had the scene reshot until he was satisfied. I can't vouch for the boys' technique. All I know about fencing is that you parry with the "forte" (the strong part of the blade near the hilt) against your opponent's "foible" (the weak part near the tip). We got both words from French fencing terms: *fort de la lame* (strong part of the blade) and *faible de la lame* (weak part of the blade). The words evidently first appeared in English in the autobiography of Edward Lord Herbert, baron of Cherbury, written in about 1648. A good fencing-master in France, Lord Herbert wrote, tells his students that "a Foyle . . . hath two Parts, one of which he calleth the Fort or strong, and the other the Foyble or weak."

I know this is a feeble segue, but we're not here to talk about swordplay. It enters the picture only because the French fencing term *fort* gave us "forte," our word for a strong point or specialty. And sticklers are ready to cross swords over how to pronounce it. Is it FORT, like Fort Knox, as traditionalists insist? Or is it, as most people think, FOR-tay, like the musical thunderclap that surprises us in Haydn's "Surprise" Symphony? The short answer to each question is yes, according to dictionaries. The longer answer: etymologists say that FORT and FOR-tay are equally legitimate and equally illegitimate. Historically, both pronunciations resulted from mistakes.

If you remember, we borrowed the word "forte" from the French *fort* in the seventeenth century and it was originally spelled "fort." To be true to its Gallic roots, it should be pronounced FOR, but never mind. The English added an *e* to the end in the eighteenth century, apparently in a misguided attempt to make the word look more French. As in many other adoptions of French words, the *OED* explains, a feminine form was "ignorantly substituted for the masculine." So both the spelling "forte" and the pronunciation FORT were etymological errors. What's more, the new spelling created confusion with the Italian word for "loud," *forte,* which is correctly pronounced FOR-tay.

Etymologists trace the FOR-tay pronunciation to a couple of misconceptions. First, that "forte" (meaning a strength) came from the Italian musical term. Second, that it came from an ersatz French word, *forté,* which would be pronounced for-TAY if it existed.

No matter what inspired FOR-tay, it's far and away the most popular pronunciation today and no longer condemned by usage experts, though many traditionalists haven't gotten the message. So pick the historical error you prefer. Both FORT and FOR-tay are good English. Besides, they're not worth fighting over. The

French and the Italian originals each came from the Latin *fortis* (strong).

I still say FORT out of habit when talking about someone's strong point and FOR-tay when I'm listening to music. But I admit that when I say FORT for anything that's not an army post, people give me odd looks. At least I hope that's why I'm getting the odd looks.

Wrong Division

An old radio hand once scolded me for pronouncing the *ch* in "schism" as if it were a *k*. "I was a radio announcer for many years and was raised by a very Victorian mother who insisted on proper speech," he wrote. "With that in mind, 'schism' is pronounced SIZ-em, not SKIZ-em, as I thought I heard you say on WNYC." I was sorry to disappoint him, but the word "schism" has evolved, and not for the first time.

When "schism" came into English in the fourteenth century, it was spelled "scisme" and was pronounced SIZ-em. The word apparently first showed up in print in the Wycliffe version of the Bible in 1382, and it originally referred to divisions in the church. We got the spelling "scisme" from Old French, but the ultimate source is *schisma,* Latin and Greek for "split" or "division." (The Latin *ch* and the Greek letter *chi* are pronounced like *k*).

Latin scholars got into the act in the sixteenth century, when they decided to stick an *h* in the middle of "scisme" to reflect its classical roots. Despite the new spelling, the pronunciation remained SIZ-em for another couple of hundred years—until it began to annoy an eighteenth-century lexicographer named John Walker. In his influential and widely popular *Critical Pronouncing*

Dictionary (1791), Walker wrote that in Greek-derived words, *ch* should be pronounced as *k,* so SKIZ-em "is the only true and analogical pronunciation." His opinion probably seemed reasonable to many people because *ch* was pronounced as *k* in two similarly spelled words of classical origin, "school" and "scheme."

For the next 150 years or so, Walker's new pronunciation was more popular with the people speaking the language than with those writing the dictionaries and usage guides. The experts insisted SKIZ-em was an error until the 1960s, when the pronunciation started gaining a foothold in American dictionaries. Today it's listed as the more popular choice in *The American Heritage Dictionary of the English Language* (4th ed.). The old SIZ-em is a distant second.

Ivory League

I was a guest speaker at a college fund-raiser when a benefactor in the audience proposed a novel origin for the expression "ivory tower." She'd read about the discovery in Ukraine of ancient huts made of mammoth tusks, and thought this could be a prehistoric clue. An interesting idea, and I can picture a tower of ivory tusks silhouetted against the tundra, but the real explanation is more interesting still.

The expression isn't quite as old as the woolly mammoth, though it does date back to the Old Testament. The ivory in the original, as it happens, referred not to construction material but to the beauty of a woman's neck. In the Song of Solomon, a lover sings to his beloved: "Thy neck is as a tower of ivory; thine eyes like the fishpools in Heshbon." Several English writers in the seventeenth century used the phrase in poems influenced by the Song of Solomon. In *A Paraphrase Upon the Canticles* (1679), for example, Samuel Woodford wrote: "Thy Neck is like a Tower of Ivory, / Hung with the Trophies of Love's Victory."

All the early references seem to refer to beauty or purity. But in 1837, the French literary critic Charles-Augustin Sainte-Beuve used the expression *tour d'ivoire* to describe what he considered the aloof, unworldly poetry of Alfred de Vigny. This usage of "ivory tower," which the *Oxford English Dictionary* defines as "a condition of seclusion or separation from the world" or "shelter from the harsh realities of life," made its way into English in the early twentieth century. The *OED*'s first English citation for this sense is from a 1911 translation of an essay in which the French philosopher Henri Bergson says each member of society "must avoid shutting himself up in his own peculiar character as a philosopher in his ivory tower."

For decades, the phrase was primarily used to describe writers, artists, and public officials isolated from the real world. In fact, none of the early citations refer to academia, perhaps the most common meaning of the phrase today. The first writer to put "ivory tower" on campus was Mary McCarthy in her novel *The Group* (1963): "We called you the Ivory Tower group. Aloof from the battle." An article in *The Economist* that same year referred to dons "attached to academic ivory-toweredness."

Which brings us to ivy, a common feature of leafy college campuses and the source of many ivied expressions about academic life. The earliest of these in the *OED* is from William Black's novel *Green Pastures and Piccadilly* (1877), which refers to "the ivied wall of the Bodleian," the library at Oxford. A half century later, a similar usage appeared on this side of the Atlantic.

In 1933, a sportswriter at *The New York Herald Tribune* referred to football at "our eastern ivy colleges." In 1935, other sportswriters started using the term "Ivy League" to refer to elite

Northeastern colleges, a usage dismissed by the *Princeton Alumni Weekly* in 1939: "The 'Ivy League' is something which does not exist and is simply a term which has been increasingly used in recent years by sports writers, applied rather loosely to a group of eastern colleges." The eight schools in the athletic conference now called the Ivy League signed an "Ivy Group" agreement for football in 1945, but the official founding of the Ivy League is considered to be 1954, when the agreement was extended to all sports.

With both "ivy" and "ivory" clinging to academia, it was inevitable that the two would become entwined and a malapropism would be born: "ivy tower." Let's hope this vine doesn't become invasive.

Palm Oil

Perhaps the biggest sin among traditionalists is not being backward-looking enough. A good example is their beef against people who say "pawn off" instead of "palm off." Or, as one of my correspondents wrote: "Don't they understand the deception involved? The underhandedness implied (pun intended)?" Well, some usage and writing guides agree, but "pawn off" is by far the more common of the two phrases today. And dictionaries now accept both as standard English for passing something off deceptively.

Dictionaries notwithstanding, traditionalists still cling to what they see as the oldie but goodie, blissfully unaware that the two expressions have been in English for hundreds of years. The "palm" version apparently showed up first, but both of them are long in the tooth. The earliest "palm" examples involved palming something "on" or "upon" somebody. The first citation in the

Oxford English Dictionary comes from John Crowne's *The Ambitious Statesman* (1679), a Restoration tragedy in which a character says, "Thinking you cou'd pawme such stuffe on me." Yes, that's how "palm" was spelled in those days.

The "pawn" version appeared a century later, thanks to the economist Adam Smith. In a 1763 lecture at the University of Glasgow, he said, "The teller of wonderful or lamentable stories is disagreeable because he endeavours to pawn them upon us for true ones." The *OED* suggests that this usage was the result of confusing "palm" and "pawn." If Smith did indeed mix them up, it's understandable. The spellings of the two words were all over the place in the 1600s and 1700s. "Palm" could be "paume," "pawme," "pawm," and so on, while "pawn" might be "paune," "pawne," "paun," etc.

Charles Lamb, in his 1822 essay "Distant Correspondents," was apparently the first writer to use the wording "palm off": "Have you not tried in some instances to palm off a yesterday's pun upon a gentleman, and has it answered?" The *OED*'s earliest citation for "pawn off" comes from *Newton Forster* (1832), a seafaring novel by Frederick Marryat: "And now he has sent out his three daughters to me—pawned them off upon me, laughing, I suppose, in his sleeve, as he did when he cheated me before." So the two phrases "palm off" and "pawn off" appeared in English within ten years of each other in the early 1800s. The birth of "pawn off" may have been illegitimate, but it's been around long enough to gain respectability.

Speaking of respectability, the verb "palm" has a past, too. In the nineteenth century it had underworld connotations. To conceal something in the palm of one's hand, like a bribe or the loot, was to "palm" it. Hence the terms "palm oil" (a bribe) and "palming," petty theft involving two people, one to distract the shop owner and the other to "palm" the merchandise (no doubt intending to pawn it afterward). In fact, the term "palm off" is used today by American lawyers to mean passing off a product as something it's not—say, selling a copy of an Hermès handbag as the real article.

A Perfect Storm

New England has given us plenty: Boston baked beans, Vermont maple syrup, the Red Sox, Robert Frost, L. L. Bean, and the image of a Maine lobsterman, his yellow slicker flapping in the wind as he braves a menacing nor'easter. The only problem with this stormy picture is that no self-respecting Penobscot Bay lobsterman would use the term "nor'easter." No, it's not, as many TV weather people have led us to believe, a quaint New England regionalism.

The word "nor'easter" is a contraction of "northeaster," a blustery storm with northeasterly winds. The storm has long been associated with New England, but the term "nor'easter" isn't native to the land of clam chowdah, according to many linguists and a great many coastal New Englanders. The locals, they say, have always pronounced the word by dropping the two *r*'s, not the *th*, making it sound something like "nawtheastah."

As for where "nor'easter" comes from, it all started in England, not New England. The earliest published reference to "nor'easter" in the *Oxford English Dictionary* is from an 1837 translation of an Aristophanes play, *The Knights:* "Slack your sheet! A strong nor'-easter's groaning." Somehow it doesn't sound Greek to me. The *OED* has even earlier citations for the abbreviations "nor" and "nor'east," which have been used to refer to compass points since Elizabethan times.

So how did "nor'easter" cross the Atlantic and end up in the mouth of that mythical Maine lobsterman? The linguist Mark Liberman, who grew up in southern New England, says the term "seems faker to me than the lederhosen at the Biergarten in Walt Disney World." He attributes the usage to overimaginative journalists who probably embraced "nor'easter" as a "literary affectation" (like "e'en" for "even"). "However," Liberman says, "as a linguist I have to admit that a nor'easter is what storms like this have become, in the English language at large, whether we like it or not."

When a regionalism is just too charming not to exist, I suppose it has to be invented.

In a Manor of Speaking

What would we do without Shakespeare? We couldn't "break the ice" or live a "charmed life," be "in a pickle" or feel "fancy free," reach a "foregone conclusion" or go on a "wild-goose chase," have "too much of a good thing" or "refuse to budge an inch" or, for that matter, know in our "heart of hearts" that we're "to the manner born." By now, those phrases are "household words" (another Shakespeare first), though one of them has undergone a "sea change" (ditto) since the original Hamlet spoke it around the end of the sixteenth century. Purists insist that "to the manner born" is the correct expression, but most people seem to prefer "to the manor born." Who's right? The simple answer is that there isn't a simple answer.

Since Shakespeare started all this, we'll let him set the scene. It's a cold and bitter night outside the castle at Elsinore. Hamlet and his friend Horatio can hear the sounds of drinking and revelry as Hamlet's uncle, the new king, carouses inside. "Is it a custom?" Horatio asks. "Ay," says Hamlet, adding that he's "native here and to the manner born," thus used to such goings-on. To Hamlet, the phrase "to the manner born" means accustomed to a behavior from birth. And that's the only way the expression was used for the next two and a half centuries.

In the mid-nineteenth century, though, writers began playfully replacing "manner" with "manor" for humorous effect, either as puns or as malapropisms in the mouths of fictional characters. The two words have nothing in common but their sound. "Manner," meaning a practice or custom or way of behaving, came into English around 1200. We got it from the Old French *maniere*, a way of handling something, and ultimately from the Latin *manus* ("hand"). As for "manor," a lord's estate, it came along in the late 1200s, also from Old French, where a *manoir* was a dwelling. The Latin source was *manere*, a verb meaning "remain." So we had two homonyms ripe for punning, and along came a punster. In 1847, a wag at *The Princeton Review* wrote: "He intended . . . to return to Scotland and reside on his estate there as 'though a native—and to the manor born.' " The author obviously knew his Shakespeare and was taking liberties for comic effect. Nothing wrong with that. Writers have been making puns with sound-alike words such as "manner" and "manor" since the earliest days of English.

It didn't take long for writers to turn the pun into a malapropism and put it into the mouths of their word-mangling characters. The British playwright James R. Planché, for example, has a tribal leader in *The Prince of Happy Land,* an 1851 comedy, saying: "My name is Tan-ti-vee, / A native chief, and to the manor born, / I trace my line from Nimrod, through French Horn!" Again, nothing wrong here (aside from the political incorrectness).

But the joke soon got out of hand. People began using "to the manor born" instead of "to the manner born," and giving the up-

dated expression a new meaning: born to wealth and privilege—
that is, with a silver spoon in one's mouth. Usage writers have
been rapping knuckles ever since. The crime—if we can call it
that—was aided and abetted by the British sitcom *To the Manor
Born,* whose title was intended as a pun. The "incorrect" version
is now the more popular of the two, and language guides are beginning to recognize both as legitimate with slightly different
meanings. *Merriam-Webster's Collegiate Dictionary* (11th ed.), for
example, includes both—one under its entry for "manner" and
the other under "manor"—without a frown. And *The Columbia
Guide to Standard American English* says both forms are acceptable. The older expression still means familiar with something
since birth. The upstart means privileged since birth.

Sticklers may grumble, but Shakespeare wouldn't have
minded. He knew that language changes. He changed a lot of it
himself.

Chapter 10

Brave New Words

The Good, the Bad, the Ugly

If my email is any indication, half the English-speaking world lies awake nights, grinding its teeth because the other half says "I could care less" when it means "I couldn't care less." If your enamel is starting to wear down, my advice is to care less. It's true that the original phrase was "I couldn't care less," which makes more sense. But since when do idiomatic expressions have to make sense?

"I couldn't care less"—meaning "I'm completely uninterested" or "I'm utterly indifferent"—first appeared in print in 1946, according to the *Oxford English Dictionary*. It was the title of a book by an Englishman, Anthony Phelps, about his experiences ferrying British aircraft during World War II. The expression has been used on both sides of the Atlantic ever since.

The shortened version, "I could care less," showed up twenty years later in the United States and has spread like kudzu, especially among the young. It has much the same meaning as the original, but with an ironic twist. The *OED*'s first published reference comes from an article in the *Seattle Post-Intelligencer* in

1966: "My husband is a lethargic, indecisive guy who drifts along from day to day. If a bill doesn't get paid he could care less."

The psychologist Steven Pinker has an interesting take on "I could care less," which he calls "an alleged atrocity" and a favorite target of language pundits. As he points out in his book *The Language Instinct,* the melodies and stresses in intonation between "I couldn't care less" and "I could care less" are completely different and convey a youthful sarcasm: "By making an assertion that is manifestly false or accompanied by ostentatiously mannered intonation, one deliberately implies its opposite."

Fret if you will—and lots of people do—but the abbreviated American idiom has never bothered me. It's obviously intended to be ironic (like saying "I should talk!" when you really mean "I shouldn't talk"). As I see it, the message is "Yeah, I guess if I tried really hard, I *could* care less."

Irony aside, many language lovers are truly bugged by such innovations. The more things change, the more they dig in their heels. In the 1920s, for example, Henry Fowler damned such newfangled words as "bureaucrat," "elevator," "femininity," "mentality," and "coastal." He even proposed a blacklist for some of them. But no one can freeze language in time, not even the most influential writer on English usage in the twentieth century. Of course Fowler, too, realized that language must grow, and eventually he would have grown with it. (If he were around today, he'd even have to accept "bicoastal," no doubt kvetching all the way.)

English simply won't stand still. To a fussbudget (circa 1904) or a stick-in-the-mud (1733), it must seem like a child with attention deficit disorder (1978). But English isn't sick, just in transit. Of course, we pay a price for all this restlessness. There are speed bumps on the road to change—myths arise because people don't realize or accept that English has moved on.

New words and new usages can leave us feeling discombobulated (1830s). When I was a teenager, to "hook up" with a friend was to get together. Today, as I mentioned earlier, that usage means to have casual sex. I learned this a few years ago when I innocently asked a friend's teenage daughter whether she'd hooked up with her boyfriend the night before.

As for "I could care less," go ahead and use it if you want, but be aware that many sticklers view it as an atrocity. If you're one of the sticklers, see your dentist about the tooth grinding. And try to worry about something that really matters, like the sugar content of a Twinkie.

Blind Data

I use "data" as a singular and I'm big enough to admit it. I've done so for years. But old habits die hard for language lovers who love their language the way it used to be. Perhaps we need a 12-step program to wean these diehards away from the belief that "data" can only be plural.

"Data" first appeared in English in the seventeenth century, but it didn't become a common word until a century or so ago. Since then, people have been arguing about its singularity. In its modern sense—information in the form of facts and figures—is "data" singular or plural? It was first used as a singular in 1902, and the practice soon became widespread, according to *Merriam-Webster's Dictionary of English Usage.* But battle lines formed.

English handbooks reared up in protest over the next couple of decades. Their reasoning? In Latin, *data* is plural and the singular is *datum.* But no less an authority than the journal *Science* joined the fray in 1927 on the opposite side, insisting that " 'data' in the sense of facts is a collective which is preferably treated as a singular." As *Science* pointed out, the term "datum" (plural: "datums") is a technical word used in surveying, while "data" means information. Even the revered *Webster's Second* of 1934, the dictionary that nobody with back problems should attempt to lift, endorsed the singular "data." As the usage authors Bergen Evans and Cornelia Evans noted dryly in the 1950s, "No one should think that he must treat *data* as a plural merely because Julius Caesar may have done so." The lesson? *Tempus fugit.*

In Caesar's day, *data* referred to things that were given, such as the givens in a scientific hypothesis. (It came from *dare,* the Latin verb for "give.") But we use "data" more broadly today to refer to factual information in general. In fact, the English word is closer to *indicium,* the Romans' word for "information," than it is to the Latin *data.* When a Latin word has a life of its own in English (think "audio" or "video") there's no reason to treat it as Caesar did.

Then why do so many people ignore the data on "data"? There's an old joke in journalism that when all else fails, you can always blame the media. And here, it seems, publishers of newspapers, magazines, books, and so on are largely to blame. For decades, the house style for most companies required treating "data" as a plural. That means generations of editors diligently changed "data *is*" to "data *are,*" and "*this* data" to "*these* data." I know, because I did it myself more times than I can remember. (*The New York Times* changed its house style to favor the singular "data" in 1999, after I'd left.)

The term "media," incidentally, can be either singular or plural. Any purists who claim it's only plural should take a look at an up-to-date dictionary. "Media" is singular when it refers to the world of mass communication as a whole ("The media is obsessed with celebrity trials"). It's plural for the people in this world ("The media are packed into the courtroom like sardines") or for the types of communication ("The media at the trial include radio, TV, and the blogosphere"). Who are the holdouts who insist that "media" is strictly plural? Ironically, many of them are members of the media who haven't heard the news.

If I have an agenda here, it's to show that words aren't written in stone. Many English nouns borrowed from Latin started out as plurals and changed to singulars. "Agenda" entered English in the 1700s as a plural noun meaning items on a list. By the late 1800s it was singular for the list itself. What's more, in the last few decades it's changed from a neutral noun ("What's on the agenda for tonight?") to a loaded one ("What's her agenda, anyway?").

Other Latin plurals that are now singular in English include "insignia," "opera," "candelabra," and "stamina." Indeed, "stamina" was used as a plural to refer to the qualities, strengths, or elements of a living thing well into the nineteenth century. And "erotica," a Greek plural, is almost always used today as a titillating singular.

A final, though less titillating, note brings us to the humble pea. The singular "piose" (from the Latin *pisum*) entered English in Anglo-Saxon days, eventually becoming "pease," as in this 1580 quotation: "As like as one pease is to an other." But people began mistaking "pease" for a plural, so a singular had to be invented. That's how "pea" burst from its pod in the 1600s. The old "pease" lives on, however, in a nursery rhyme many of us remember from childhood:

> *Pease porridge hot,*
> *Pease porridge cold,*
> *Pease porridge in the pot*
> *Nine days old.*

Some like it hot,
Some like it cold,
Some like it in the pot
Nine days old.

These days, pease porridge is known as split-pea soup, and *Some Like It Hot* as the funniest opus in Billy Wilder's opera.

Dead Certain

When we take a wrong turn in English, it's amazing how often the road leads to Rome. The word "decimate," for example, has taken enough twists and turns to scramble a global positioning system. And many sticklers seem to be stuck along the Appian Way.

"Decimate" comes to us from the Latin *decimus,* meaning a tenth, and *decimare,* to take a tenth. To the Romans, the verb meant to take a tax of one tenth. But it had a darker side too. Roman military commanders would sometimes "decimate" a mutinous or cowardly unit by taking every tenth man and executing him. This was called a *decimatio,* or "decimation." Occasionally only one in twenty were punished (a process called *vicesimatio*), or one in a hundred (*centesimatio*).

Livy, Plutarch, Tacitus, and other historians of the time all describe incidents leading to military decimations. From the bits and pieces of information available, it seems that a rebellious unit was divided into groups of ten, with each group forced to choose lots. The unlucky tenth man in each group was flogged or stoned to death, and as a final indignity the corpse might be decapitated. Afterward, the survivors were forced to sleep outside their encampment and to eat barley instead of their usual wheat. There's no evidence, though, that this kind of punishment was a frequent occurrence. And historians have suggested that commanders often rigged the lottery so only the ringleaders were actually killed.

When "decimation" first showed up in English, in 1549, it was used to mean a tithe or a tax of one tenth, according to the *Oxford English Dictionary*. It wasn't used to refer to the military punishment until 1580, but that was in a translation of Plutarch. Over the next three centuries, "decimation" and "decimate" were used in both senses—taxing and executing—though the taxation sense was more common. Most of the punishment usages were references to classical times, though the British did occasionally revive the ancient practice. The second earl of Essex, for example, used it in Ireland in 1599, apparently inspired by reading a translation of Tacitus. The *OED* quotes a seventeenth-century commentator as saying Essex "decimated certain troops that ran away, renewing a peece of the Roman Discipline." Essex himself was later beheaded for treason. What goes around comes around.

In the mid-nineteenth century, the word "decimate" executed a couple more turns in the road. It lost the sense of taxing or tithing, but it embraced another meaning that had been seen only rarely in earlier times: to destroy in part or cause great damage. Charlotte Brontë, for instance, wrote in a letter in 1848, "Typhus fever decimated the school periodically." We've used the word this way ever since.

But once again, the process of change left a myth in its wake. A lot of self-styled wordsmiths never got the word about "decimate." They stick stubbornly to what they think of as the literal meaning in Latin: to destroy one tenth. In fact, the literal meaning of *decimare* was merely to choose a tenth of something, whether a bunch of grapes or a bunch of mutineers. But no matter. That was then and this is now. In English, the sense of destroying in part is firmly established and has been for 150 years. War correspondents from the Civil War to the Crimean War to World War II and beyond have used "decimate" to refer to great destruction or loss of life, and today that's not only standard English, but also the most common meaning of the word.

Two caveats: Since the modern meaning of "decimate" is destroy in part, don't use it to mean destroy entirely. And although "decimate" has taken on a new life, it hasn't entirely shed the old. So don't use it with numbers, especially numbers other than ten (as in "the town was decimated by one third").

We Beg to Differ

Aristotle, a polymath if ever there was one, did it all. Mention any subject, and chances are that Aristotle got there first. He wrote about everything: biology, astronomy, music, drama, poetry, botany, physics, metaphysics, rhetoric, ethics, politics, aesthetics, mathematics, psychology, nutrition, and . . . well, you get the idea. More to the point, he wrote about logic, and therein lies a problem. If he hadn't used the expression "beg the question" for a common logical fallacy, I'd get a lot less mail grumbling about its misuse.

I was a philosophy major in college, so I have no excuse if I mess this up. Aristotle, in his *Prior Analytics* (350 BC), uses a Greek phrase, *en archei aiteisthai,* that roughly means "to assume at the beginning." (The Greek word for "assume," *aiteisthai,* has also been translated as "ask" or "beg.") In the twelfth century, Latinists translated the Greek as *petitio principii,* which means, more or less, "a petition at the beginning." The expression was apparently first seen in English in 1581 as "to begge the question." My old copy of Aristotle's works translates it as "to beg and assume the original question." No matter how you translate it, Aristotle is talking about an argument that doesn't hold water. The hole in the argument is taking for granted what you're trying to prove. For example, a mom might say that her son isn't a criminal, so he couldn't have committed a crime.

If English were as logical as, say, FORTRAN or COBOL, or even Esperanto, that would be the end of the story. But English speakers have treated "beg the question" illogically for more than a century and a half. They use it to mean avoiding, raising, or dismissing a question, as well as prompting a different one. And we're not talking about kindergarten dropouts. Henry Adams wrote in 1860 that "as long as there's no dodging or begging the question on our side, I'm not afraid."

To this day, though, purists can't let go of the expression's original meaning. Never mind that it's Greek to just about everybody else. Unless you're a debate coach or a philosophy major, you probably don't use "beg the question" the way Aristotle did. So what's the meaning of "beg the question" today? Frankly, it means so many things that for all practical purposes it doesn't mean anything at all. My advice? Let's give this expression a rest. As for those who still insist on the Aristotelian meaning, this is a lost cause. It's time for the purists to get a life—one in the twenty-first century.

Flame Wars

Now here's a burning question: Why do so many people give "inflammable" a bum rap? Some of them insist it means "not burnable" but is misused to mean "burnable." Others say it does indeed mean "burnable" but it's merely a puffed-up, redundant version of "flammable." Even my own state legislature has amended its statutes to change "inflammable" to "flammable." I say cool it.

For the record, "inflammable" does mean "burnable." And it's meant that since at least 1605, according to the *Oxford English Dictionary*. "Flammable," the new kid on the block, didn't appear in print until more than three hundred years later.

The cause of all the confusion is the "in" at the beginning of "inflammable." It turns out that the prefix *in-* can make a word negative (as in words like "incapable," "inflexible," "incompetent"), or it can add emphasis ("invaluable," "inflame," "intense"), or it can mean "within" ("incoming," "inbreeding," "infighting"). The *in-* of "inflammable" is of the emphatic type—it's called an intensive or an intensifier. The word "inflammable" comes from the Latin *inflammare,* meaning to inflame. The upstart "flammable" was coined in the early nineteenth century, but for decades it was rarely used. So how did "flammable" eventually catch fire?

We can thank the National Fire Protection Association for this one. In the 1920s it called for using "flammable" instead of "inflammable," which it considered confusing because of that *in-* at the beginning. Insurers and other fire-safety advocates soon joined the cause. In 1959, the British Standards Institution took up the torch: "In order to avoid any possible ambiguity, it is the Institution's policy to encourage the use of the terms 'flammable' and 'non-flammable' rather than 'inflammable' and 'non-inflammable.' "

Which word should a careful writer use today? Well, history may be on the side of "inflammable," but common sense wins here. If you want to be sure you're understood—say, the next time you see a smoker about to light up near a gas pump—go with "flammable."

Before we put prefixes behind us, here's something to think

about. Did you ever notice that a lot more of them are negative than positive? In fact, I can think of only one common prefix that's clearly positive: *pro-*. But the negatives go on and on: *anti-*, *counter-*, *de-*, *dis-*, *il-*, *im-*, *in-*, *ir-*, *mal-*, *mis-*, *non-*, *un-*, and so on. What does all this say about us English speakers? Maybe we need a more positive outlook on life. At any rate, there's a positive side to negative thinking. The abundance of negative prefixes in English gives us a lot of subtle way to express ourselves.

Take "irreligious" and "nonreligious": The first suggests a hostility to religion while the second means merely a lack of religion. Or "illiterate" and "nonliterate": The first means unable to read and write, but the second means without a written language. Or "misinformation" and "disinformation," which we all know, thanks to media hype and spin control.

In some cases, two negative versions of the same word competed for centuries before one of them won the popularity contest. "Inability" and "unability," for instance, were both common until the eighteenth century, when "inability" won out. Although "unability" is still occasionally seen, it's now largely a historical footnote, alongside another faded obscurity, "disresent," which in the mid-seventeenth century meant "resent" (as in "I disresent that remark!"). The "dis" made perfect sense because at that time "resent" meant, among other things, to approve of or appreciate. But "disresent" became extinct as "resent" lost its positive sense and came to mean what it does today.

It's survival of the fittest out there.

Isn't It Pedantic?

Quick, what's the plural of "octopus"? If you think "octopi" is classier than "octopuses," go stand in the corner. This is a misconception that dates back to the nineteenth century. (You might say it's got legs.)

Here's the story. The singular "octopus" comes from Greek and means eight-footed. The original plural, "octopodes," was Anglicized over the years to "octopuses." But in the mid-1800s some misguided Latinists (at it again!) tried to substitute the Latin plural ending *-pi* for the Greek *-podes*. It was an illegitimate idea that appealed to would-be pedants with weak classical educations. The traditional English plural is actually "octopuses," but the misbegotten "octopi" has been used by so many people for so long that it's now considered an acceptable alternative. If you want to be pedantic—and classically correct—opt for "octopodes." As for me, I'm a sucker for good old "octopuses."

Let's bid a farewell to arms—all eight of them—and look at a few more pompous plurals. We live in a postmodern world, but the Latinists are still among us, especially in academia. They insist on using plurals like "gymnasia," "syllabi," and "symposia," even though many dictionaries now recognize a preference for Anglicized plurals ("gymnasiums," "syllabuses," "symposiums"). There's pedantry off campus too, of course. I've seen real-estate ads offering "condominia" for sale—to ignorami, no doubt.

You don't have to throw Latin plurals around to be pretentious. You can be singularly pompous in Italian. Is that writing on the wall "a crude graffiti" or "a crude graffito"? (Hint: Would you refer to a piece of spaghetti as a "spaghetto"?)

Till Hell Freezes Over

"Till" is a four-letter word, but the only people who find it indecent are know-it-alls who think it ought to have three. Why?

"Till," the story goes, is the illegitimate child of "until." If it's to be written at all, it ought to be spelled "til"—or, even better, "'til." After all, it's an abbreviation.

Wrong on all counts. The popular belief that "till" comes from "until" turns history on its head. The real story is the other way around. "Until" is the child of "till." And the three-letter versions began life as mistakes. Here's how it all happened.

"Till" is an extremely old word, about as old—circa 800—as English words get. It originally meant just what you'd think. In about 1200, the prefix *un-* (an intensifier, not a negative) was added, creating an additional word, "untill." In the 1300s, some writers began dropping the final *l*, and by the early 1800s it disappeared completely, leaving us with "until." In modern usage, "till" and "until" are practically interchangeable ("until" is preferred at the beginning of a sentence).

So where do "til" and "'til" come in? Back in the 1700s, we find, some writers mistook "till" for an abbreviation and began using an apostrophe to show the omission: "'till." It was only a matter of time till they compounded the misconception by assuming the final *l* was a mistake. The result: "'til" and eventually plain "til."

What should we do today? Well, so many people have misused "til" and "'til" for so long that modern dictionaries now accept them (though often noting their illegitimate origins). But usage guides still consider them errors. Meanwhile, our old friend "till" is alive and well, and has no skeletons in its closet. It gets my vote.

A Hopeless Case?

I'm not hopeful about convincing all the fuddy-duddies out there, but here goes: It's hopeless to resist the evolution of "hopefully."

Usage experts used to insist, and many traditionalists still do, that there's only one correct way to use "hopefully"—as an adverb meaning "in a hopeful manner." ("Did my horse win?" Nathan asked *hopefully*.) It's a hanging offense, the sticklers say, to use it to mean "it is hoped" or "let us hope." ("*Hopefully* he won," Nathan said.) The word "hopefully," the argument goes, should modify a verb, not a whole sentence.

Oh yeah? Writers have been using adverbs to modify entire sentences for hundreds of years. In fact, the first complete English translation of the Bible, the Wycliffe version of about 1382, uses "plainly" (it was spelled "pleynly" then) as a sentence adverb. Here's the passage in modern English: "Plainly this is my infirmity, and I shall bear it."

Many other adverbs have been used in the same way by respected writers. Jane Austen in *Mansfield Park* (1814): "Luckily the strength of the piece did not depend upon him." Thomas Carlyle in *The French Revolution* (1837): "Happily human brains have such a talent of taking up simply what they can carry, and ignoring all the rest." Charles Darwin in an 1847 letter: "Oddly, I was never at all staggered by this theory until now, having read Mr. Milne's argument against it." Virginia Woolf in a 1939 diary entry: "Mercifully we have 50 miles of felt between ourselves and the den."

Words like "plainly," "luckily," "happily," "oddly," "curiously," "surely," "strictly," "seriously," "certainly," and more have been used as sentence adverbs for centuries without upsetting anybody. Yet, remarkably, people seem to have drawn the line at "hopefully." Why? Logically, there's no good reason. But the answer may lie in the relative newness of its appearance as a sentence adverb.

In fact, my old employer, *The New York Times Book Review*, appears to have introduced this usage in 1932, according to the

OED. Nobody seemed to mind at the time. Indeed, "hopefully" was used as a sentence adverb now and then over the next thirty years without calling much attention to itself. But in the early 1960s, the usage suddenly took off. Everybody and his cousin seemed to be using it.

There's something about a new usage—especially a popular one—that makes sticklers cranky, and "hopefully" really cranked them up. All hell broke loose in 1965, when the *Saturday Review, The New Yorker,* and *The New York Times* denounced this terrible new menace. (The *Times* had no doubt forgotten the word's parentage.) Thus began what the lexicographer R. W. Burchfield has called "one of the most bitterly contested of all the linguistic battles fought out in the last decades of the 20th century."

On one side were the traditionalists who condemned the practice. On the other side were nearly all the people who actually used the language. Over the years, most usage manuals and style guides have come to believe that it's illogical to condemn the use of "hopefully" as a sentence adverb, but they still warn writers against the practice because of all the naysayers out there. When I was at the *Times* in the 1980s and '90s, the stylebook entry on "hopefully" said it "means in a hopeful manner, and its use should be confined to that meaning." No wiggle room there. But the latest stylebook, which came out a couple of years after I'd left the paper, does plenty of wiggling. It acknowledges that style manuals, usage guides, and grammarians generally defend the new "hopefully," but advises that "writers and editors unwilling to irritate readers would be wise" to avoid the usage.

Dictionaries, which tell us how language *is* used as well as how it *should be* used, are in a tough position. Imagine being in the shoes of the editors at *The American Heritage Dictionary of the English Language* (4th ed.), whose lexicographers think the usage is justified, but whose own usage panel condemns the practice.

"It is not easy to explain why critics dislike this use of *hopefully*," the puzzled editors write, sounding like Alice at tea with the Mad Hatter and company.

This usage may have been the next new thing back in the sixties, but "hopefully" has long since earned its right to be a sentence adverb. It's so widely accepted because no other word does the job quite as well. I say go for it. Hopefully, the critics will come to their senses.

Moot Altering

People who don't know English quite as well as they think they do love to wring their hands over "moot." The traditional definition, they say, is "debatable" or "open for discussion," and they're dismayed when it's used to mean "irrelevant." My advice to the handwringers is to get over it. This usage isn't new and it isn't worth the fuss.

The "moot" question is more complicated than many people think. The word started life back in the eighth century as a noun for a "meeting" or "gathering." In King Alfred's day, it was often used for a judicial or legislative assembly. In the mid-sixteenth century, "moot" was used to describe a gathering of law students to argue a hypothetical case. Later in the century, it became an adjective meaning "debatable," "doubtful," or "proposed for discussion." A "moot" point, therefore, was uncertain or open to argument, and a "moot" court was a mock court.

But as early as 1807, the doubtful aspect of "moot" led people to interpret it as meaning "irrelevant," or "of no practical value." A "moot" point or a "moot" question, therefore, was merely academic. This usage took hold two hundred years ago because it made sense then, and it still makes sense today. Modern dictionaries define "moot" as either "debatable" or "irrelevant." In the United States, the predominant meaning is "irrelevant." In Britain, it's "debatable." Who's right? That depends on whether you're in Sioux Falls or Stoke-on-Trent.

Flaccid Test

Time for another pop quiz. How do you say "flaccid"? (1) FLASS-id. (2) FLAK-sid. Relax—there's no wrong answer. But FLASS-id, which used to be a blunder, is now the first pronunciation listed in most dictionaries. And before any traditionalists jump down my throat, here's a little history.

"Flaccid," adapted from the Latin word *flaccus* ("flabby"), was apparently first printed in a 1620 book by the physician Tobias Venner about the benefits of taking the waters at Bath. It meant then pretty much what it means today: limp, droopy, feeble. And yes, FLAK-sid was the one and only pronunciation for more than two hundred years. But people will talk. And a lot of talkers preferred FLASS-id, proper English or not. By the late nineteenth century, the authors of pronunciation guides were scolding miscreants for dropping their *k*'s.

Until well into the 1950s, dictionaries still listed a single correct pronunciation: FLAK-sid. Anyone ill-informed enough to say FLASS-id was an object of pity in the eyes of purists. But a generation later, this mistaken pronunciation had become so persistent that dictionaries started listing it as a legitimate variation, right behind FLAK-sid. Fast-forward again. Now, another generation later, FLASS-id is listed first. It's the rule rather than the exception, and someday the quaint old original may disappear completely. In the meantime, the case against FLASS-id is feeble.

Comp Time

Are you a controlling person? If so, you probably pick on people who pronounce "comptroller" the way it's spelled. Well, you've got a lot of history on your side, but the times they are a-changin'. Most dictionaries now list not only "con-TRO-ler" but also the once-illegitimate "COMP-tro-ler" and "comp-TRO-ler" as acceptable pronunciations. In fact, those last two are now preferred by a majority of the usage panel of *The American Heritage Dictionary of the English Language* (4th ed.).

But here's the catch. The word "comptroller" itself is an impostor. Although dictionaries now accept it, "comptroller" began life as an illegitimate spelling back in the fifteenth century. Like many misspellings, it entered English through the back door, with a little help from meddlesome scribes.

The first English version of the word, borrowed in the 1200s from a dialect of French, was "countreroullour," someone who kept a counter-roll—a duplicate set of financial records against which the original figures were checked. Over the next few centuries, the word appeared in various guises, such as "conter-roller," " counteroller," "countrollour, "controwler," and finally "controller." All those new and improved models had one thing in common: The first part of the word had something to do with a counter, or duplicate, set of records. The beginning was derived from the Latin *contra,* meaning opposite or against, as in a copy that you check an original against.

In those days, scribes loved to tinker with English spellings at every opportunity, and the tinkerers often screwed up. Here, some misinformed souls thought the first part of the word had to do with counting rather than countering. So they decided to emphasize the numerical angle by beginning the word with "compt," like the verb "count" in French (*compter*) or Latin (*computare*). Voilà! In 1486 a new spelling appeared: "comptroller." Some scholars believe the scribes were trying to Frenchify the word to make their bosses—the official auditors of the day—seem classier. Others think the intent was to make English more like Latin. Either way, the scriveners were mistaken.

To this day, the word "comptroller" reeks of officialdom. Think Comptroller General, Comptroller of the Currency, Comptroller of the Lord Chamberlain's Office. Although you can find "controllers" and "comptrollers" in both government and business, the fussier word seems more at home in the public sphere. Both words are legit. But if I had a choice, I'd go for "controller." Simpler is better. And I prefer the simpler pronunciations, too. Like people back in the fifteenth century, I pronounce "comptroller" like "controller."

Interfering scribes and other Latinist busybodies have a lot to answer for. They're responsible for many of the silent letters that confound us today and make scores of English spellings such a torture. Their intention, of course, was to make spellings reflect Latin roots.

"Subtle," for example, which was borrowed from the Old French word *sutil,* was originally spelled "sutil," "sutile," or "sotil." But fourteenth-century Latin scholars felt the word's spelling should reflect its source in classical history—the Latin *subtilis* ("finely woven")—and thus the silent *b* crept into the spelling. Centuries later, though, writers were still uncertain whether to *b* or not to *b.* The first editions of Milton's poems, for example, use the spelling "suttle," except for *Paradise Regained,* which has "subtle."

We're indebted to the Latinists for the *b*'s in "debt" and "doubt" as well. "Debt" in English was originally "det," but gained the *b* as a nod to the Latin *debitum*. "Doubt," originally "doute," was changed to reflect its Latin ancestor, *dubitare*. In the same way, "people" was saddled with an *o*. The word, spelled "peple" in the Middle Ages, picked up the *o* in the fourteenth century in imitation of the Latin *populus*. As a result of all this Latinification, words were changed left and right—whether they had classical roots or not. Some didn't, which is how "island" got its *s*. It came from the Old English "igland," which in turn came from old Germanic sources, not the Latin *insula*.

Well, no word is an island. The bell has tolled for those old spellings.

Same Old, Same Old

There's a word in English for almost everything. That little thingie at the end of a shoelace? An "aglet." The hairless space between your eyebrows? The "glabella." What you get when the sum is greater than the parts? "Synergy." You could live a couple of lifetimes without ever encountering the words "aglet" or "glabella." But I'll bet you're up to your eyebrows in "synergy." In fact, my Pet Peeves email folder is stuffed with complaints from readers about the overuse of this new kid on the block.

Well, overused it is. But new it isn't, unless you consider the seventeenth century new.

"Synergy," adapted from the Latin *synergia* ("working together"), was first used in print in 1660 by Peter Heylin, who was chaplain to King Charles I and a popular theological writer of the day. Heylin wrote of "such a Synergie, or cooperation, as makes men differ from a sensless stock, or liveless statua." He was referring to the belief that man's religious conversion requires the cooperation of human will and divine grace. The words "synergist" (first recorded in 1657) and "synergism" (1764) referred to the same religious belief.

"Synergy" had shed its clerical collar by the mid-nineteenth century, when it came into use as a medical word for the way things like body organs, mental processes, and remedies work together. By the 1950s it was being used, especially in the business world, to mean a group effort that's more effective than individuals working alone. In his book *Corporate Strategy* (1965), H. Igor Ansoff described "synergy" as "the '2 + 2 = 5' effect" because it results in "a combined performance that is greater than the sum of its parts."

A useful term, no doubt about it. That's probably why "synergy" is being used to death. But it's not the brash newcomer that critics make it out to be. And neither are some other words that true believers look down on as annoying new examples of psychobabble or bureaucratese. I'm talking about venerable old warhorses that have been revived and put back into harness. And this is the thanks they get!

For example, many wordies love to beat up on "doable" in the mistaken belief that it's some trendy new invention. Not so. "Doable" has been around for centuries. The *Oxford English Dictionary* cites published references that go back to the 1400s. A document from 1449 described the ideal law as one "which is doable and not oonli knoweable."

Others whine about the verb "vet," as in "Please vet this report before the meeting." It may sound like nouveau bureaucratic jargon, but it's been with us for more than a century. In the late 1800s, to "vet" your horse was to have it checked by a veterinarian. That led to a more general use of "vet" to mean evaluate or check. Rudyard Kipling is credited with being the first to use it this way. In "The Army of a Dream," a short story published in *The Morning Post* of London in 1904, a soldier comments on a group of naked recruits: " 'These are our crowd,' said Matthews. 'They've been vetted, an' we're putting 'em through their paces.' "

A lot of hot air has also been expended over "bloviate," which the word police regard as an ugly newcomer. But the word actually originated in mid-nineteenth century Ohio, when it meant what it means today—to blather on pompously. It's one of those humorous mock-Latin formations (like "absquatulate," "discombobulate," and others), and it blew in around the same time as "bloviator" and "blowhard."

In the 1920s "bloviate" became identified with President Warren G. Harding, a native of the state that gave us the word. Harding used it a lot—but apparently not in the way we use it now. To Harding, it meant "to loaf about and talk and enjoy oneself," according to a biographer, Francis Russell. So how did the long-winded word become so associated with Harding that some people mistakenly think he coined it? Well, by all accounts Harding was something of a bloviator himself. In fact, the crotchety H. L. Mencken, who has also been mistakenly credited with coining "bloviate," considered Harding's bloviations "the worst English that I have ever encountered." Mencken didn't mince words:

It reminds me of a string of wet sponges; it reminds me of tattered washing on the line; it reminds me of stale bean-soup, of college yells, of dogs barking idiotically through endless nights. It is so bad that a sort of grandeur creeps into it. It drags itself out of the dark abysm (I was about to write abscess!) of pish, and crawls insanely up the topmost pinnacle of posh. It is rumble and bumble. It is flap and doodle. It is balder and dash. But I grow lyrical.

Afterword: Morocco Bound

There's an old joke involving a language maven—sometimes Noah Webster, sometimes Samuel Johnson, sometimes an anonymous linguist or English teacher. In the version I like best, the maven is a linguist named Susan whose husband comes home to find her in bed with another man.

"Why, Susan!" he says. "I'm surprised!"

"No, dear," she answers. "You are astonished. I am surprised."

No matter which version of that joke you hear, it takes a language maven to get it these days. The words "surprised" and "astonished" used to be quite different from each other. In Webster's day, to be "surprised" primarily meant to be caught unawares or attacked unexpectedly, while to be "astonished" usually meant to be stunned or confounded. Today, though, "surprised" and "astonished" are often used interchangeably.

You may be surprised, if not astonished, to learn that language mavens can get as muddled as the next guy when English changes. We often resist using fine old words in new ways, and cling to traditional usages that are almost certainly lost causes. I know what you're thinking. You'd like to throw my own words back at me: English is a democracy. A single person, even a language maven, has only one vote. And the number of voters is growing every day as more and more people use English to do the world's work. Change is inevitable, and some good words will be lost. And so on and so forth. Yes, I know all that, but I don't always like it. I plead guilty to letting my hopes get the better of my common sense at times. Nevertheless, here's an appeal, hopeless though it may be, on behalf of a handful of the many fine old words on the endangered list. It's probably too late to save them, but I'm not quite ready to let them go.

A case in point is "bemused," a word that does not, contrary to popular opinion, mean "amused." Or rather, it shouldn't mean "amused," but so many people are misusing it that dictionaries are starting to go along with them. We are not amused.

For nearly three centuries, "bemused" has meant confused, muddled, or lost in thought, as in this 1735 couplet from Pope: "Is there a Parson, much bemus'd in beer, / A maudlin Poetess, a rhyming Peer?" An earlier noun, "muse," has meant a state of thoughtfulness since about 1500. And the verb "muse," meaning to be absorbed in thought, has been around since 1340. Both come from the Old French *muser* (to ponder or gape in wonder) and have nothing to do with the nine Muses of antiquity.

Interestingly, when "amused" first appeared in the 1600s, it meant to be in a muse—that is, absorbed, preoccupied, or distracted (not all that different from "bemused"). It wasn't until the next century that "amused" came to mean entertained, thanks again to our friend Pope. By the early 1800s, the two words had gone their separate ways. "Bemused" meant befuddled or lost in thought, while "amused" meant having fun.

And so things remained until the late twentieth century, when newspaper and magazine writers, broadcasters, and Internet pundits started using "bemused" to mean "amused." My guess is that writers were bored with "amused," and thought "bemused" would be more amusing.

The two leading American dictionaries are split on this new usage. *The American Heritage Dictionary of the English Language* (4th ed.) defines the verb "bemuse" in the traditional way: to confuse or cause to be engrossed in thought. But *Merriam-Webster's Collegiate Dictionary* (11th ed.) now includes a third meaning: to cause to have feelings of wry or tolerant amusement—a usage also endorsed in *Merriam-Webster's Dictionary of English Usage.* I can read the writing on the wall. Whether you side with the *AHD* or *M-W,* you can't deny that "bemused" is not what it was. It's rarely used in the old traditional way these days, and anyone using it that way is almost certain to be misunderstood.

I like "bemused" and I'm sorry to lose the old sense of the word, but one has to be practical. I'd still use it in the time-honored way if I were speaking to someone I knew would understand. But I can't bring myself to use it to mean "amused." I'd rather retire "bemused" for now, and hope that one day the old meaning will be revived. In the meantime, there are other ways to fill the gap—"puzzled," "bewildered," "confused," "lost in thought."

I wish I could say the same for "ironic," another word that I'm going to miss if the illiterati squeeze the life out of it. No other word means "ironic" but "ironic." There's simply no substitute. "Irony" is saying one thing while meaning another—often in a sly or sarcastic way. Noël Coward's wartime song "Don't Let's Be Beastly to the Germans" bubbles over with irony ("Let's be meek to them— / And turn the other cheek to them"). By the same token, a situation is "ironic" when the result is more or less the opposite of what was intended. A good example is O. Henry's story "The Gift of the Magi," where the young husband pawns his pocket watch to buy his wife a set of hair combs, while she sells her luxuriant hair to buy him a watch chain.

All in all, "ironic" is as sophisticated as a Coward lyric. But it may be just too sophisticated for its own good. Many writers and newscasters think it's merely a tony way of saying "coincidental" or "unusual" or "peculiar." A newspaper article, for instance, might say, "It's ironic that Mahatma Gandhi and Groucho Marx share the same birthday." Nope, not ironic—just coincidental. Or a newscaster might say, "It's ironic that the Radio Shack was broken into twice in one week." Nope, not ironic—just unusual. But if one of the stolen items is a GPS system that leads the police to the burglars, that's ironic.

Language does change, and no doubt "ironic" someday will too, since so many people routinely misuse it. But for now it's safe, at least officially, since dictionaries still object to the use of "irony" and "ironic" to refer to something that's merely improbable or coincidental. Meanwhile, can we please make a solemn pledge to use them correctly?

Another unique word that's losing its uniqueness is "unique" itself, which has traditionally meant "one of a kind." We got it in the early 1600s from the French, who got it from the Romans. In Latin, *unicus* means "one and only," and that's how "unique" was used in English for more than two hundred years. At first, "unique" was primarily used by scholars and others who were aware of its Latin roots. For them, "unique" was an absolute term (like "infinite" or "eternal" or "perfect"), so there were no degrees of uniqueness. Nothing could be very or almost or sort of "unique."

But in the 1800s, as the word became more popular, it began losing its uniqueness in everyday usage. Writers who didn't know or care about the word's history began using it for the merely "unusual" or "remarkable" or "uncommon." And like those wimpier adjectives, the watered-down "unique" was now often propped up with intensifiers—modifiers like "thoroughly," "absolutely," and "totally." Before long, we had all kinds of uniqueness, from "rather" to "somewhat" to "very" to "most" (and even to "uniquest").

For more than a hundred years, usage guides have consistently bemoaned the degradation of "unique" and berated "the illiterate" (Fowler's word) for emasculating it. Nevertheless, millions of people have ignored the gurus, and dictionaries are beginning to take note. *American Heritage,* for example, still rejects the use of "unique" with a modifier like "very" or "more" or "quite," but it accepts the informal use of the word to mean "unusual" or "extraordinary." *Merriam-Webster's Collegiate* goes further and accepts both the qualifiers and the more lenient definition as standard English.

So where does this leave us? I think there's a case to be made for using qualifiers with some absolute terms. Think of the expression "a more perfect union," from the Preamble to the Constitution. The Founders weren't talking about improving on perfection, but about striving toward perfection. So something that isn't perfect can still be more perfect than something else. But the essence of "unique" is its uniqueness. I'm a strict Constitutionalist on this. I won't qualify "unique," and I certainly won't use it to describe something that's merely unusual or remarkable, like a hole in one or a triple play. I know the horse is out of the barn here, but I wish it would come back home. In the original sense, there's just no other word like "unique." It would be an enormous loss.

Speaking of which, I also regret what's happened to "enormity." It's been so stretched out of shape that a very handy usage is being lost. Today, many people think an "enormity" is something that's enormous. But for the last 150 years or so, an "enormity" has been something horrendous, not something merely huge, while "enormous" (as well as the rarely used "enormousness") has referred to size alone. This is a valuable distinction, and it's a shame we're losing it.

What "enormity" and "enormous" have in common is a sense of abnormality (their Latin ancestor, *enormis,* means out of the norm). When the noun "enormity" first appeared in the late 1400s, it meant an abnormality in general or a violation of law or morality. The adjective "enormous," which first appeared in the early 1500s, was originally used to describe sinful behavior. By the late 1500s, both "enormity" and "enormous" referred to extreme wickedness, but "enormous" was also being used in the sense of huge. For many years, that's the way things stood. Then in the late 1700s "enormity" also came to mean hugeness. So both "enormity" and "enormous" were now being used for something either immensely bad or just plain immense. And they weren't through changing yet!

During the early decades of the 1800s, the two words took different paths: "enormity" lost its hugeness, while "enormous" lost its wickedness. In 1893, when the original *Oxford English Dictionary* was being compiled, the editors noted that the use of "enormity" to indicate size was "now regarded as incorrect," a judgment that still stands. Nearly every modern usage guide now defines "enormity" as extreme wickedness and "enormousness" as hugeness.

Careful writers have observed this distinction for a century and a half. Writers who don't, says *American Heritage,* "may find that their words have cast unintended aspersions or evoked unexpected laughter." You can see the point. Imagine, for instance, a critic writing about the artist Christo and remarking on the "enormity" of his works. Does that mean they're huge or they're awful—or both? If "enormity" can mean either hugeness or awfulness, then English is less precise. And that's awful, if you ask me.

But dissenting voices are making themselves heard, never mind the usage guides. More and more people are using "enormity" to refer to something that's overwhelming in size or importance. In fact, *Merriam-Webster's Collegiate* now accepts this wider use of "enormity," and other dictionaries can't be far behind. It may be that the "enormity" I know and love (in all its awfulness) is doomed. For the time being, though, it's still alive, it's still useful, and I still use it.

Someday the old meanings of "ironic" and "unique" and the rest will no doubt be lost forever, mere footnotes in the history of English. Perhaps in trying to keep them alive, I'm the one who's nurturing myths. My mind tells me we can't save them, but my heart won't let them go. Like Webster's dictionary, I'm morocco bound.

Notes

Introduction

xiv. **"crap"** See Chapter 6 for its etymology.

xv. **ferocious hunting dog** See Porter, David W., "Dogs That Won't Hunt and Old English Ghost Words," *Notes and Queries,* Vol. 45, No. 2 (June 1998), p. 168. Available at http://nq.oxfordjournals.org/content/vol45/issue2/index.dtl.

xv. **"call a spade a spade"** See Chapter 8 for the history of this expression.

xvi. **"nincompoop"** See the *Oxford English Dictionary* for Johnson's spurious etymology.

xvi. **"wife"** . . . **"fiery"** Their histories are from the *OED.*

xvi. **"flair"** See Gillet, Joseph E., "Flair," *American Speech,* Vol. 12, No. 4 (Dec. 1937), p. 248.

xvi. **there's no English equivalent of the French Academy (though the idea was floated a time or two)** See Read, Allen Walker, "Suggestions for an Academy in English in the Latter Half of the Eighteenth Century," *Modern Philology,* Vol. 36, No. 2 (Nov. 1938), pp. 145–56.

Chapter 1

3. **"The enjoyment of a common language"** This and the following quotations are from Churchill, Winston S., *The Second World War,* Vol. III, *The Grand Alliance* (Boston: Mariner Books, 1986), p. 609.

5. **"England and America are two countries"** . . . **"We have really every-**

thing in common" The Shaw and Wilde quotations are from Shapiro, Fred R., ed., *The Yale Book of Quotations* (New Haven and London: Yale University Press, 2006). Shapiro says Shaw's remark was attributed to him in the *Reader's Digest,* November 1942. Shapiro gives the source of the Wilde quotation as Part I of *The Canterville Ghost* (1887).

5. **"Why can't the English learn to speak?"** From Filmsite: http://www .filmsite.org/myfa.html.

5. **"The pronunciation of educated Americans"** See Kenyon, John S., "Some Notes on American R," *American Speech,* Vol. 1, No. 6 (March 1926), p. 339. Here Kenyon is quoting an article by William A. Read in the *Journal of English and Germanic Philology.* Elsewhere, Kenyon writes that American pronunciation is based on the seventeenth-century British standard. See Kenyon, *American Pronunciation,* 10th ed. (Ann Arbor, Mich.: George Wahr, 1966), pp. 13, 87–91.

6. **educated people in Britain began dropping their *r*'s** The American linguist Charles Hall Grandgent believed the *r*-dropping took place roughly between 1790 and 1820. See Grandgent, *Old and New: Sundry Papers* (Cambridge, Mass.: Harvard University Press, 1920), pp. 47–48. Available at http://books.google.com through Google Book Search.

6. **"The perception that the language was 'losing a letter' "** Crystal, David, *The Stories of English* (Woodstock and New York: Overlook Press, 2004), p. 467. Crystal recounts the Keats anecdote on the same page.

6. **Lord Byron blamed a critical article** See *Don Juan* (1823), Canto XI, stanza 60.

7. **The *a,* like the *r,* has ping-ponged in British pronunciation** For a history of the broad *a,* see Grandgent, *Old and New,* pp. 27–28. Also Kenyon, *American Pronunciation,* pp. 176–84.

7. **This is the *a* that went to America on the *Mayflower* in 1620** See Pyles, Thomas, and John Algeo, *The Origins and Development of the English Language,* 4th ed. (Fort Worth: Harcourt Brace Jovanovich, 1992), p. 213. The authors write: "There is a strong likelihood, for instance, that George III and Lord Cornwallis pronounced *after, ask, dance, glass, path,* and the like exactly the same as did George Washington and John Hancock—that is, as

the overwhelming majority of Americans do to this day. It was similar with the treatment of *r*. . . ."

7. **That's also about when literate Britons started pronouncing the *h* in "herb"** For an analysis of the historical fluctuation in the unstressed *h,* see Curme, George O., *A Grammar of the English Language,* Vol. I, *Parts of Speech* (Essex, Conn.: Verbatim, 1993), p. 61.

8. **Americans, on the other hand, pronounce all four syllables (SEC-ruh-teh-ree), as the British did until the eighteenth century** See Kenyon, *American Pronunciation,* pp. 87–90.

8. **"indistinct articulation"** See Algeo, John, ed., *The Cambridge History of the English Language,* Vol. 6, *English in North America* (Cambridge and New York: Cambridge University Press, 2001), p. 74.

8. **Americans "tend to invent all sorts of nouns and verbs and make words that shouldn't be"** See Nemy, Enid, "Chronicle," *The New York Times,* March 25, 1995.

9. **"fall" . . . "autumn"** See the citations for both in the *OED.*

11. **"clothed with the French livery"** This and Webster's other quotations on this page are from the Preface to his *Compendious Dictionary of the English Language* (Hartford and New Haven: Sidney's Press, 1806); retrievable from Wikisource: http://en.wikisource.org/wiki/ A_Compendious_Dictionary_of_the_English_Language.

11. **"it is in itself inaccurate"** This and Johnson's other quotations on this page are from *The Plan of an English Dictionary,* written to Lord Chesterfield in 1747; retrievable at http://andromeda.rutgers.edu/~jlynch/Texts/plan.html.

13. **"It is quite impossible"** See Mencken, H. L., *The American Language: An Inquiry into the Development of English in the United States* (New York: Knopf, 1937), p. 25.

13. **"the *Planters,* and even the *Native Negroes"*** See Read, Allen Walker, "British Recognition of American Speech in the Eighteenth Century," *American Speech,* Supplement 86 (2002; originally published in 1933), pp. 43–44. Hugh Jones's quotation is also cited in Paul K. Longmore's article " 'Good English Without Idiom or Tone': The Colonial Origins of

American Speech," *Journal of Interdisciplinary History,* Vol. 37, No. 4 (Spring 2007), pp. 514–15.

13–14. **"the propriety of Language here surprized me much"** Read, ibid., p. 44.

14. **William Eddis, a British customs official** For biographical information about Eddis, see Bain, Robert, Joseph M. Flora, and Louis D. Rubin, Jr., eds., *Southern Writers: A Biographical Dictionary* (Baton Rouge and London: Louisiana State University Press, 1980), p. 137. Also, Longmore, " 'Good English Without Idiom or Tone,' " p. 533.

14. **"totally at a loss"** Read, "British Recognition of American Speech," pp. 44–45.

14. **"Though the inhabitants of this Country"** See Read, ibid., p. 45. Also Longmore, " 'Good English Without Idiom or Tone,' " p. 537.

15. **the grammatical differences between us are so few** John S. Kenyon writes: "The *essential structure* of English is today what it was in King Alfred's day, before the Norman Conquest." *American Pronunciation,* p. 10.

15. **"There never has been any major linguistic difference"** See Culpeper, Jonathan, *History of English* (New York and London: Routledge, 2005), p. 77.

Chapter 2

18. **"You'd think we were splitting the atom"** The Oxford editor quoted is Frank R. Abate, then editor in chief of Oxford's dictionary programs in this country, in a 1998 interview with Patricia T. O'Conner.

18–19. **Margaret Mutch, a copy editor and proofreader** Mutch's position at *The Atlantic* was described in her obituary in *The Boston Globe,* Nov. 9, 1997.

19. **"When I split an infinitive, God damn it"** Shapiro, *The Yale Book of Quotations,* p. 142. A fuller version of the Chandler letter can be found in *The Notebooks of Raymond Chandler,* edited by Frank MacShane (New York: HarperPerennial, 2006), p. 29.

20. **"Lines to a Lady with an Unsplit Infinitive"** The lines quoted are from MacShane, ibid., p. 30. The entire poem appears on pp. 29–31.

21. **apocryphal as the preposition rule itself** For interesting analyses of this popular fiction, see Charnley, M. Bertens, "The Syntax of Deferred Prepo-

sitions," *American Speech,* Vol. 24, No. 1 (December 1949), pp. 268–77. Also, Bryant, Margaret M., "The End Preposition," *College English,* Vol. 8, No. 4 (January 1947), pp. 204–5.

21. **"grounded on impossibilities"** Dryden's remarks on Shakespeare and Jonson are from his essay "Defence of the Epilogue: Or, An Essay on the Dramatic Poetry of the Last Age." It is collected in *Essays of John Dryden,* Vol. I, selected and edited by W. P. Ker (Oxford: Clarendon Press, 1900), pp. 167 ff. Dryden's attitude toward Jonson's writing is also described in *Merriam-Webster's Dictionary of English Usage* (Springfield, Mass.: Merriam-Webster, 1994), p. 764.

21. **he went back over his own writings and relocated all the straggling prepositions** See Bately, Janet M., "Dryden's Revisions in the *Essay of Dramatic Poesy:* The Preposition at the End of the Sentence and the Expression of the Relative," *Review of English Studies,* New Series, Vol. 15, No. 59 (August 1964), pp. 126–69.

21. **a preposition didn't belong at the end of a sentence in formal writing** See Lowth, Robert, *A Short Introduction to English Grammar* (London: printed by J. Hughs for A. Millar and R. & J. Dodsley, 1762). Lowth writes of the final preposition: "This is an Idiom which our language is strongly inclined to; it prevails in common conversation, and suits very well with the familiar style in writing; but the placing of the Preposition before the Relative is more graceful, as well as more perspicuous; and agrees much better with the solemn and elevated style" (pp. 127–28). Lowth also defines prepositions as "so called because they are commonly *put before* the words to which they are applied" (p. 91).

22. **since Anglo-Saxon times** *Merriam-Webster's Dictionary of English Usage* notes that terminal prepositions were evidently a feature of Old English (p. 764).

23. **Benjamin G. Zimmer has traced the quotation** See Zimmer's posting to the Language Log on Nov. 27, 2005, "Churchill vs. Editorial Nonsense," http://itre.cis.upenn.edu/~myl/languagelog/archives/002670 .html.

23. **"It is said that Mr. Winston Churchill"** See Gowers, Sir Ernest, *Plain Words: Their ABC* (New York: Knopf, 1954), p. 207.

23. **Back in the days of vaudeville, the story goes** See *The Friars Club Encyclopedia of Jokes,* compiled by H. Aaron Cohl (New York: Black Dog & Leventhal, 1997), p. 180.

24. **"And then it started like a guilty thing"** *Hamlet,* Act I, scene 1.

24. **he speculates that well-intentioned English teachers** Arnold Zwicky's remarks about the initial "and" are from his posting to the Language Log, Nov. 1, 2006: http://itre.cis.upenn.edu/~myl/languagelog/archives/003723.html.

26. **"as it literally signifies *not one* or *no one*"** Murray, Lindley, *English Grammar, Adapted to the Different Classes of Learners* (York: Wilson, Spence & Mawman, 1795), p. 35. In an 1805 edition, Murray goes further and says that "none" originally "had no plural" (pp. 64–65). It's interesting to note that not even Robert Lowth, on whose work Murray modeled much of his *English Grammar,* objected to the plural "none." In *A Short Introduction to English Grammar* (1762), Lowth uses the phrases "none of them are" (p. 37) and "none of them have" (p. 38).

27. **"None are more ignorant"** Fielding, Henry, *The Adventures of Tom Jones,* Vol. 1 (New York: Bigelow, Brown), p. 321.

27. **"Yeah, yeah"** Arthur C. Danto told the Morgenbesser anecdote in an interview on Aug. 2, 2004, on NPR's *All Things Considered.* It was also related in Morgenbesser's obituary by Douglas Martin two days later in *The New York Times.*

28. **"Ther nas no man no-wher"** Chaucer, Geoffrey, *The Canterbury Tales,* from a 1903 edition published in New York by Thomas Y. Crowell (p. 4). Available at http://books.google.com through Google Book Search.

28. **"Two Negatives in English destroy one another"** Lowth, Robert, *A Short Introduction to English Grammar,* 2nd ed., revised (London: A. Millar and R. & J. Dodsley, 1763), p. 139. This passage does not appear in the first edition.

28. **"Nobody never went and hinted no such a thing"** Dickens, Charles, *David Copperfield* (New York: Oxford University Press, 1989), p. 20.

29. **"I do and I don't"** From Morgenbesser's obituary, by Douglas Martin, *The New York Times,* Aug. 4, 2004.

30. **"slow" is an adjective, "slowly" is an adverb, and never the twain**

shall meet For an interesting defense of "slow" and similar flat adverbs, see Wallace Rice's article "Go Slow. Proceed Slowly," *American Speech,* Vol. 2, No. 12 (Sept. 1927), pp. 489–91.

31. **that adjectives and adverbs should have different endings** See Lowth, *A Short Introduction to English Grammar* (1762), pp. 142–43.

32. **Writers have been shrinking English since Anglo-Saxon days** See Jack, George, "Negative Contraction in Old English Verse," *Review of English Studies,* New Series, Vol. 50, No. 198 (May 1999), pp. 133–54. See also: Moore, Samuel, and Thomas A. Knott, *The Elements of Old English: Elementary Grammar and Reference Grammar* (Ann Arbor, Mich.: George Wahr, 1919), pp. 55, 64, 74, 89.

32. **Addison, Swift, Pope, and others began raising questions** On the influence of Addison, Swift, and Pope, see Campbell, George, *The Philosophy of Rhetoric* (New York: Harper & Brothers, 1844), pp. 30, 34, 40–41, 176, 321, 354, 417. (Originally published in 1776.) Available at http://books.google.com through Google Book Search.

32–33. **"informal syntax and inelegant phraseology"** For a discussion of Johnson's free use of contractions and Boswell's later tampering, see Percy, Carol, "Bozzy, Piozzi, and the Authority of Intimacy: The Social Symbolism of Contractions and Colloquialisms in Contemporary Accounts of Dr. Samuel Johnson," *Historical Sociolinguistics and Sociohistorical Linguistics* (January 2002). Available at http://www.let.leidenuniv.nl/hsl_shl/bozzy,%20piozzi1.htm.

33. **fooling around with Lady Grosvenor** For a brief description of the adultery trial, see Brewer, John, *A Sentimental Murder: Love and Madness in the 18th Century* (New York: Farrar, Straus & Giroux, 2005), p. 163.

33. **the "vile contraction *don't* for *do not*"** See Percy, "Bozzy, Piozzi."

33. **opinion makers started coming to their senses** A grammar book published for American servicemen and -women in World War II singled out only one contraction for condemnation: "ain't." (However, it advised recruits to avoid "hisn," "hern," "ourn," "yourn," and "youse.") See Spangler, A. I., *English Grammar: A Self-Teaching Course,* published for the United States Armed Forces Institute (Macmillan, 1943), p. 99. And *Using Good English,* a textbook series used in many American schools in the 1950s and

'60s, treated contractions like "here's," "let's," "don't," "aren't," and so on as standard English, merely showing students how to use and spell them correctly. See *Using Good English 5* (River Forest, Ill.: Laidlaw, 1964), pp. 162–63, 224, 258, 262.

33. **"the handiest and most conspicuous device"** Flesch, Rudolf, *The Art of Readable Writing* (New York: Macmillan, 1949), p. 96.

33. **"If you would say it as a contraction"** Garner, Bryan A., *Securities Disclosure in Plain English* (CCH Inc., 1999), p. 22.

34. **traditionalists out there who haven't gotten the word** An example is Lovinger, Paul W., *The Penguin Dictionary of American English Usage and Style* (New York: Penguin Reference, 2000), pp. 80–81.

34. **"More doctors smoke Camels"** The quotations from cigarette ads come from "A Review of Health References in Cigarette Advertising, 1927–1964," a compendium prepared as a trial exhibit by the Brown & Williamson Tobacco Company (1964), containing ads for Brown & Williamson, Liggett & Meyers, and Philip Morris brands. Available at http://www.sourcewatch.org/index.php?title=A_Review_of_Health_References_in_Cigarette_Advertising_1927–1964.

The tobacco companies didn't entirely invent the doctors' claims. Some physicians really *did* say cigarettes were harmless, and they said so in medical journals. See Gardner, Martha N., and Allan M. Brandt, " 'The Doctors' Choice Is America's Choice': The Physician in US Cigarette Advertisements, 1930–1953," *American Journal of Public Health,* Vol. 96, No. 2 (February 2006), pp. 222–32. The authors write: "Through advertisements appearing in the pages of medical journals for the first time in the 1930s, tobacco companies worked to develop close, mutually beneficial relationships with physicians and their professional organizations. These advertisements became a ready source of income for numerous medical organizations and journals, including the *New England Journal of Medicine* and the *Journal of the American Medical Association (JAMA),* as well as many branches and bulletins of local medical associations."

35. **"It's a modern vulgarism"** Lederer, Richard, *A Man of My Words: Reflections on the English Language* (New York: St. Martin's, 2005), p. 251.

36. **"the obnoxious and ubiquitous couplet"** Kahn, E. J., "Comment," *The*

New Yorker, May 26, 1956, p. 23. The passage is quoted in *Merriam-Webster's Dictionary of English Usage,* p. 600.

36. **"We are overrun by them, like the Australians were"** Churchill, Winston S., *The Second World War,* Vol. II, *Their Finest Hour* (Boston: Mariner Books, 1986), p. 606.

36. **the bestselling brand in the country** See Gladwell, Malcolm, *The Tipping Point: How Little Things Can Make a Big Difference* (Boston: Back Bay Books, 2002), p. 25.

37. **"Do not use the colloquial *snuck*"** See Goldstein, Norm, ed., *The Associated Press Stylebook and Briefing on Media Law* (Cambridge, Mass.: Perseus Publishing, 2000), p. 232.

37. **an 1887 appearance in *The Lantern*** See the *OED.*

38. **"Not *dove* for the past tense"** See Goldstein, *The Associated Press Stylebook,* p. 76.

38. **"Dove as if he were a beaver"** As *Merriam-Webster's Dictionary of English Usage* points out (p. 369), Longfellow used "dove" when *The Song of Hiawatha* was published in 1855, and he was apparently the first to use it in print. But he changed it in later editions, "probably at the suggestion of critics." We checked an 1858 edition and found "dived."

38. **"By heaven, I'll make a ghost of him that lets me!"** *Hamlet,* Act I, scene 4.

39. **"the only proper Word to be used"** From *Observations Upon the English Language* (London: 1752). The anonymous author (possibly George Harris) is quoted in *Merriam-Webster's Dictionary of English Usage,* p. 895.

39. **Latinism may be responsible here, too** See Jespersen, Otto, *Essentials of English Grammar* (Tuscaloosa and London: University of Alabama Press, 1964), p. 359.

39. **"the apparently common, yet unfounded, notion that *that* may be used to refer only to things"** See *Merriam-Webster's Dictionary of English Usage,* p. 895.

40. **Shakespeare, for one, used "than" as a preposition** See *Julius Caesar,* Act I, scene 3: "A man no mightier than thyself or me." The prepositional usage by Milton can be found in Book II of *Paradise Lost* ("more detestable than him and thee"). The other citations are from Jespersen, *Essen-*

tials of English Grammar, p. 133 (for Goldsmith, Lamb, Thackeray, and Kipling); from the *OED* (for Scott); and from *Merriam-Webster's Dictionary of English Usage,* p. 892 (for Swift, whose quotation is from "To Stella, Visiting Me in Sickness").

40–41. **Lowth decreed that "than" should be treated as a conjunction** See Lowth, *A Short Introduction to English Grammar* (1762), pp. 143–44: "When the Qualities of different things are compared, the latter Noun is governed, not by the Conjunction *than . . .* but by the Verb . . . expressed or understood. As, 'Thou art wiser than *I* [am.]' 'You are not so tall as *I* [am.]' 'You think him handsomer than [you think] *me.*' In all other instances, if you complete the Sentence in like manner, by supplying the part which is understood, the Case of the latter Noun will be determined."

41. **the more sensible authorities are on their side** See Wilson, Kenneth G., *The Columbia Guide to Standard American English* (New York: Columbia University Press, 1993), p. 433: "*Than* is both a subordinating conjunction, as in *She is wiser than I am,* and a preposition, as in *She is wiser than me.*" Also, *The New Fowler's Modern English Usage,* 3rd edition, ed. by R. W. Burchfield (Oxford: Clarendon Press, 1996), pp. 769–70.

41. **"*Than* is both a preposition and a conjunction"** See *Merriam-Webster's Dictionary of English Usage,* p. 893.

43. **grammarians tried to stamp out the use of "wrote"** See Gustafsson, Larisa Oldireva, "Variation in Usage and Grammars: The Past Participle Forms of *Write* in English 1680–1790," *Historical Sociolinguistics and Sociohistorical Linguistics* (July 2002). She writes: "The prevalence of the participial *wrote,* as illustrated in Table 1, may explain the amount of criticism against this form in eighteenth-century grammars. According to Sundby et al. (1991:233–4), *wrote* is censured by 59 grammars out of the 187 sources which are quoted in this dictionary. In these grammars, the form is stigmatised as 'absurd,' 'corrupt,' 'inelegant,' 'improper,' 'ungrammatical,' 'bad,' 'vulgar,' 'colloquial,' a 'barbarism,' and a 'solecism.' "

Chapter 3

44. **"vulgar slang for 'penis' "** Rosten, Leo, *The Joys of Yiddish* (New York: Pocket Books, 1970), p. 303.

46. **"he thinks I'm a complete schmuck"** Groucho Marx's quotation comes from *Posterity: Letters of Great Americans to Their Children,* edited by Dorie McCullough Lawson (New York: Doubleday, 2004), p. 171.

47. **no such complaint had ever been filed** See Huber, Patrick, and David Anderson, " 'Butcherin' Up the English Language a Little Bit': Dizzy Dean, Baseball Broadcasting, and the 'School Marms' Uprising' of 1946," *Missouri Historical Review* 96 (April 2002), pp. 211–31.

48. **"I ain't sure but what I should feel something"** Trollope, Anthony, *The American Senator* (London: Penguin Books, 1993), p. 378.

48–49. **"ain't" was just one of the crowd** For histories of "ain't" and "aren't" and their pronunciations, see the following sources: Curme, *A Grammar of the English Language,* Vol. I, p. 248; Pyles and Algeo, *The Origins and Development of the English Language,* p. 203; Stevens, Martin, "The Derivation of 'Ain't,' " *American Speech,* Vol. 29, No. 3 (Oct. 1954), pp. 196–201; the *OED;* and *Merriam-Webster's Dictionary of English Usage,* pp. 60–64.

49. **"an error so illiterate that I blush to record it"** Partridge's lament (circa 1942) is quoted in *The New Fowler's Modern English Usage,* 3rd ed., edited by R. W. Burchfield (Oxford: Clarendon Press, 1996), p. 37. The eighth edition of Eric Partridge's *A Dictionary of Slang and Unconventional English* (New York: Macmillan, 1984), edited by Paul Beale after Partridge's death, merely calls it a "solecism" (p. 9).

51. **George Washington was particularly inventive** Information about presidential coinages comes from these sources: Metcalf, Allan A., *Presidential Voices: Speaking Styles from George Washington to George W. Bush* (Boston and New York: Houghton Mifflin, 2004), pp. 109–110; Abate, Frank, "On Language," *The New York Times Magazine,* Jan. 12, 2003; and the *OED.*

51. **"I am a friend to neology"** Jefferson's quotation is from Metcalf, ibid., p. 110.

52. **the word was spelled—and pronounced—"axe" in the fourteenth century** For a history of "ask/axe," as well as the quotations from Chaucer and Coverdale, see the *OED.*

55. **brought to you by the lexicographer Jesse Sheidlower** His article

"The Word We Love to Hate: Literally" appeared in *Slate,* Nov. 5, 2005: http://www.slate.com/id/2129105/.

56. **"Now I will try and write of something else"** Jane Austen's quotation, along with evidence for the antiquity of "try and" as well as its use by other authors, can be found in *Merriam-Webster's Dictionary of English Usage,* pp. 919–20.

56. **"Try *and* think, indeed! Try *to,* we can understand"** Moon, George Washington, *The Dean's English* (New York: A. Strahan & Co., 1865), p. 168. Available at http://books.google.com through Google Book Search.

56. **a "vulgarism"** See Ayres, Alfred, *The Verbalist* (New York: D. Appleton, 1887), pp. 14–15. Retrievable at http://www.gutenberg.org/files/22457/22457-h/22457-h.htm through Project Gutenberg.

56. **the "literary dignity" of the usage** Fowler, H. W., *A Dictionary of Modern English Usage* (Oxford: Clarendon Press, 1927), p. 666.

57. **The latest incarnation of "like"** Parts of this section are adapted from an article by O'Conner, Patricia T., "On Language," *The New York Times Magazine,* July 15, 2007.

58. **"Some of them can make do"** Trillin, Calvin, *Enough's Enough: And Other Rules of Life* (New York: Ticknor & Fields, 1990), pp. 96–97.

59. **"Ya wanna be dissed"** The *OED* credits the lyric, from the song "Spoonin' Rap," to *Rap: The Lyrics,* edited by Lawrence A. Stanley (New York: Penguin, 1992), p. 307.

60. **a pint of beer "chilling" by the fire** Dickens, Charles, *Sketches by Boz* (London: Penguin Classics, 1995), p. 513.

60. **"dis"** The verb is labeled informal in *The American Heritage Dictionary of the English Language* (4th ed.) and slang in *Merriam-Webster's Collegiate Dictionary* (11th ed.).

60. **"chill"** This is slang in both *American Heritage* and *Merriam-Webster's.*

60. **"cred"** The word is standard in *Merriam-Webster's.*

60. **"phat"** This is slang in both *American Heritage* and *Merriam-Webster's.*

60. **"bling"** Both "bling-bling" and the variant "bling" are standard in *Merriam-Webster's.*

60. **"gangsta"** This is standard in both *American Heritage* and *Merriam-Webster's.*

Chapter 4

62. **the first published references we have** Sam Clements, Bonnie Taylor-Blake, Stephen Goranson, and Joel S. Berson are among the word detectives who helped track down "the whole nine yards."

63. **"The word 'jeep' originated in the Popeye strip"** Florenz Eisman's quotation is from an email to the authors on Dec. 15, 2004.

64. **Wimpy fast-food chain** See *Brewer's Dictionary of Modern Phrase & Fable,* compiled by Adrian Room (New York: Cassell, 2002), p. 754.

64. **the Popeyes fried-chicken restaurants** See the restaurant chain's website: http://www.popeyes.com/story.php.

65. **"If I do, hang me in a bottle like a Cat"** *Much Ado About Nothing,* Act I, scene 1.

66. **"but not to swing a cat in, at least with entire security to the cat"** Twain, Mark, *The Innocents Abroad: Or, the New Pilgrim's Progress* (New York: Harper & Brothers, 1911), p. 13.

66. **appears to accept the Melton Mowbray angle** Partridge (Beale, ed.), *A Dictionary of Slang and Unconventional English,* p. 849.

67. **Barry Popik suggests it may have been Chicago** See Popik's website, *The Big Apple:* http://www.barrypopik.com/index.php/new_york_city/entry/paint_the_town_nyc_company/.

69. **no such ticket has ever been found** See Rawson, Hugh, *Devious Derivations: Popular Misconceptions—and More Than 1,000 True Origins of Common Words and Phrases* (Edison, N.J.: Castle Books, 2002), p. 163.

69. **"etymologies of this sort"** See Sheidlower, Jesse, ed., *The F-Word* (New York: Random House, 1995), p. xxiv. For more about the rarity of acronymic etymologies, see Eisiminger, Sterling, "Acronyms and Folk Etymology," *Journal of American Folklore,* Vol. 91, No. 359 (Jan.–March 1978), pp. 582–84.

69. **"I never write 'metropolis' for seven cents"** Twain, Mark, from "Spelling and Pictures," a speech delivered Sept. 18, 1906, at the annual dinner of the Associated Press at the Waldorf-Astoria Hotel in New York. Available at http://www.gutenberg.org/files/3188/3188-h/3188-h.htm.

70. **"The so-called experts in this line"** MacShane, Frank, ed., *The Selected*

Letters of Raymond Chandler (New York: Columbia University Press, 1981), p. 217.

74. **baking as a metaphor for gestation** See Rowland, Beryl, "The Oven in Popular Metaphor from Hosea to the Present Day," in *American Speech,* Vol. 45, No. 3/4 (Fall/Winter 1970). Rowland describes the expression "a bun in the oven" as "a colloquial use of an ancient folk metaphor" with roots in classical times. "The ancient gods such as Zeus were conceived as millers and their consorts as mills; the human race was the product they ground and baked, and on a terrestrial scale, man and woman performed similar functions."

76. **"A railing around the inside of the stockade"** From an inspection report filed on Aug. 5, 1864, and published in *The War of the Rebellion: A Compilation of the Official Records of the Union and Confederate Armies,* Series II, Vol. VII (Washington: Government Printing Office, 1899), p. 546. Available at http://books.google.com through Google Book Search.

76. **Wirtz, the commandant of the infamous camp, was tried and hanged** The Union general who presided over the military commission that tried Captain Wirtz happened to be an amateur artist, and was inspired by the testimony to make sketches for a painting based on one of the incidents described. His painting, *The Dead Line,* depicted a Union soldier being shot dead by a Confederate sentinel at Andersonville. The general, Lew Wallace, became better known later as the author of the bestselling sword-and-sandal epic *Ben Hur.*

Chapter 5

79. **"Prince Hamlet thought uncle a traitor"** The limerick, by Stanley J. Sharpless, is quoted in *The Penguin Book of Limericks,* edited by E. O. Parrott (New York: Penguin Books, 1986), p. 133.

80. **"When you are old and grey and full of sleep"** From *Selected Poems and Three Plays of William Butler Yeats,* 3rd ed., edited by M. L. Rosenthal (New York: Collier Books, 1986), p. 14.

81. **Army officers who didn't go to West Point** See Rawson, Hugh, *Wicked Words* (New York: Crown, 1989), p. 351.

82. **Dan Rather's alma mater changed its name** See Rather, Dan, with Mickey Herskowitz, *The Camera Never Blinks: Adventures of a TV Journalist* (New York: William Morrow, 1977), p. 26. The school is now known as Sam Houston State University.

83. **"Give thy cunte wisely"** We've updated the English in the *OED* citation to make it more readable.

83. **"Sitbithecunte"** Reaney, P. H., *The Origin of English Surnames* (London: Routledge & Kegan Paul, 1967); see the section on "Names of indecent or obscene connotation."

83. **"Gropecuntelane"** The street name is sometimes given as "Gropecunt Lane." The *OED*'s earliest citation for it is from about 1230, in Eilert Ekwall's *Street-Names of the City of London.* The source for its being a red-light district is Linnane, Fergus, *London—The Wicked City: A Thousand Years of Prostitution and Vice* (London: Robson Books, 2003), p. 3.

85. **The source most often quoted** Walker, Barbara G., *The Woman's Encyclopedia of Myths and Secrets* (San Francisco: Harper & Row, 1983), p. 197.

85. **a "Cunt Power" movement** See Yachnin, Jennifer, "Making a 4-Letter Word Respectable (to Some)," *Chronicle of Higher Education,* Jan. 5, 2001. Also: Muscio, Inga, *Cunt: A Declaration of Independence,* 2nd ed. (New York: Seal Press, 2002).

85. **the *Chicago Tribune* pulled an article** The story was reported by Brooks Barnes in *The Wall Street Journal,* online edition, Nov. 10, 2004: http://online.wsj.com/article_email/SB109890031518057350-jf4Njlad3n52ma4GIaayFm4.html.

86. **"By the time feminists were putting CUNT POWER! on buttons"** See Gloria Steinem's foreword to Eve Ensler's *The Vagina Monologues: The V-Day Edition* (New York: Villard, 2001), p. xiv.

86. **none of the apocryphal acronyms seem to have existed before the 1960s** See Sheidlower, *The F-Word,* p. xxiv.

87. **the underground rock group the Fugs** See "History of the Fugs," an online history by Ed Sanders, who founded the Fugs with Tuli Kupferberg in the East Village in the mid-1960s. The site is at http://www.thefugs.com/history2.html.

87. **"You're the man who doesn't know how to spell 'fuck' "** Roy Blount

Jr.'s foreword to *The F-Word* credits the remark to Dorothy Parker (p. ix). Hugh Rawson, in *Wicked Words,* attributes it to Tallulah Bankhead (p. 158). Mailer himself, in an interview with George Plimpton, said Bankhead's publicity agent made the story up. See Plimpton, George, *Truman Capote: In Which Various Friends, Enemies, Acquaintances and Detractors Recall His Turbulent Career* (New York: Anchor, 1998), p. 277.

88. **not only a good word but also a sacred one** See Walker, Barbara G., *The Woman's Encyclopedia,* pp. 109, 892.

89. **"son of a bitch"** Hester Piozzi's *Anecdotes of the Late Dr. Johnson* (1786) recounts a story illustrating how nasty Samuel Johnson could be: "He professed to love his mother. One day she called him a puppy. 'Pray,' says this dutiful and loving son, 'Do you know what they call a *puppy's* mother?' " The quotation is from Percy, "Bozzy, Piozzi."

89. **"the bitch-goddess SUCCESS"** See the *OED.*

90. **"Then, owls and bats, / Cowls and twats"** Browning, Robert, *The Major Works* (Oxford and New York: Oxford University Press, 2005). The excerpts from *Pippa Passes* are on pp. 65 and 98.

91. **the story between the lines** See Perrin, Noel, *Dr. Bowdler's Legacy: A History of Expurgated Books in England and America* (New York: Atheneum, 1969), pp. 215–17.

91. **"Browning constantly used words without regard to their proper meaning"** See Murray, K. M. Elisabeth, *Caught in the Web of Words: James A. H. Murray and the* Oxford English Dictionary (New Haven and London: Yale University Press, 1978), p. 235.

Chapter 6

94. **"crap" has been used to mean debris or discarded by-products since the 1400s** See the *OED.* For a dating of the noun meaning excrement, see the *OED* and *Random House Historical Dictionary of American Slang,* Vol. 1, A–G, edited by J. E. Lighter (New York: Random House, 1994), p. 508: "The earliest attested form clearly identical with current senses" is from 1846.

94. **"crapping" might have meant the same thing as far back as the 1600s**

The term "crapping ken," meaning an outdoor privy, was recorded in 1846 (see the *OED*). However, similar constructions ("croppinken," "croppin-ken," "croppen ken") had the same meaning—an outhouse—as early as 1673.

95. **before Crapper was born** Thomas Crapper was born in Yorkshire in 1836 and died in 1910. See the Thomas Crapper & Company website: http://www.thomas-crapper.com/.

95. **Crapper's business prospered** For a corporate history, see the above-mentioned website.

95. **the word was already in use in 1911** A 1911 reference to the noun "crapper" (for the room, not the fixture itself) can be found at http://www .folklore.ms/html/books_and_MSS/1910s/1911ca_my_lustful_adventures __ramrod/index.htm.

95. **The apparatus wasn't referred to as a "crapper" until 1932** See the *OED*.

96. **such an operation would cost the mother's life** For information about childbirth mortality in ancient times, see Sewell, Jane Eliot, "Cesarean Section—A Brief History," written for the American College of Obstetricians and Gynecologists for an exhibition on caesarean section at the National Library of Medicine, Bethesda, Maryland, in 1993. Available at http:// www.neonatology.org/pdf/cesarean.pdf.

96. **cut from his mother's womb (*a caeso matris utero*)** A 1610 translation of Pliny puts it more graphically. Pliny first describes Nero: the "late Emperour, who all the time of his reigne was a verie enemie to all mankind, was borne with his feet forward." He goes on: "But more fortunate are they a great deale, whose birth costeth their mothers life, and part from their mothers by meanes of incision: like as *Scipio Africanus* the former, who came into the world in that wise: and the first that ever was sur-named *Caesar*, so called because hee was ript out of his mothers bellie." See C. Plinius Secundus, *Historia Naturalis,* Book VII, available at http://penelope.uchicago.edu/Thayer/L/Roman/Texts/Pliny_the_Elder/ 7*.html.

97. **supposedly performed in 1500, by the patient's swineherd husband**

See Reiss, Herbert, "Abdominal Delivery in the 16th Century," *Journal of the Royal Society of Medicine,* Vol. 96/7 (July 2003), available at http://www.pubmedcentral.nih.gov/articlerender.fcgi?artid=539559.

97. **suggested the first Caesar was born with a full head of hair** For the Sextus Pompeius Festus etymology, see *Historia Augusta* (Cambridge, Mass.: Loeb Classical Library, 1921), p. 85 and editor's note 8. See also http://penelope.uchicago.edu/Thayer/E/Roman/Texts/Historia_Augusta/Aelius*.html.

97. **Julius bears no responsibility for Caesar salad** See Child, Julia, *From Julia Child's Kitchen* (New York: Gramercy Books, 1999), pp. 431–34. The famous cook describes a Caesar salad ordered by her parents when they took her to Cardini's Tijuana restaurant in 1925 or 1926.

98. **the source of the expression "his name is mud"** See the *OED;* Lighter, Vol. 2, p. 637; Partridge (Beale, ed.), *A Dictionary of Slang and Unconventional English,* pp. 776–77; and Rawson, *Devious Derivations,* p. 143.

99. **Flynn himself bragged** See Flynn, Errol, *My Wicked, Wicked Ways* (Cutchogue, N.Y.: Buccaneer Books, 1978), p. 290.

99. **"Your name is Flynn . . . you're in" . . . "your name is Flynn, meaning you're in"** These citations, which predate the rape charges against Flynn, were discovered by Barry Popik in the Peter Tamony Collection at the University of Missouri-Columbia.

101. **a Trivial Pursuit game card** See the Trivial Pursuit Genus Edition, with questions copyright 1981 by Horn Abbot Ltd., manufactured and distributed in the United States under license to Selchow & Righter Co.

102. **showed up in English for the first time in 1893** Michael Quinion's 1893 citation for "brassiere" can be found at his website, http://www.worldwidewords.org/qa/qa-bra5.htm.

102. **the French word for a baby's undershirt** See *Le Trésor de la Langue Française Informatisé,* available at http://atilf.atilf.fr/tlf.htm.

103. **"What's a mattah wit you, Charley Hoss?"** The *Washington Post* article discovered by Popik, dated Sept. 8, 1907, describes a baseball game played in the 1880s. See his 1998 posting to the American Dialect Society's Linguist List: http://www.americandialect.org/americandialectarchives/janxx98117.html.

104. **started using the phrase "charley horse" in 1886** As Popik also writes in the above-mentioned posting, he turned up an article in *Sporting Life* dated Sept. 15, 1886, headlined "JOE QUINN is troubled with 'Charley-horse.'" The philologist Sam Clements has found a slightly earlier reference (Aug. 29, 1886) from *The Constitution* in Atlanta that reads: "Sullivan, of Charleston, has the Charley Horse in his head." Clements reported his find in a 2003 posting to the Linguist List: http://listserv.linguistlist .org/cgi-bin/wa?A2=ind0308A&L=ADS-L&D=1&P=6724. To date, these are the earliest published references that have been found.

104. **Even doctors began skipping the medical jargon** "Treatment of *Charley Horse*" appeared in the *Journal of the American Medical Association* on Nov. 30, 1946, p. 821. The item is cited in "Mencken as Etymologist: Charley Horse and Lobster Trick," by H. B. Woolf, *American Speech,* Vol. 48, No. 3/4 (Autumn–Winter 1973), p. 229.

104. **Even slang lexicographers have described "flack" as a misspelling of "flak"** For example, see Partridge (Beale, ed.), *A Dictionary of Slang and Unconventional English,* p. 399.

104. **the now-obscure PR man who gave us "flack"** See Shapiro, Fred R., "The Etymology of *Flack,*" *American Speech,* Vol. 59, No. 1 (Spring 1984), pp. 95–96. Shapiro has traced "flack" back to a 1937 article in *The Oakland Tribune* that credits *Variety* with the coinage.

105. **The bowler was created in 1850** See Robinson, Fred Miller, *The Man in the Bowler Hat: His History and Iconography* (Chapel Hill: University of North Carolina Press, 1993), pp. 14–15.

107. **an editorial cartoon by Thomas Nast** The Tweed cartoon appeared in *Harper's Weekly* on Sept. 23, 1871. It can be seen at http://greatcaricatures .com/articles_galleries/nast/html/1871_0923_vultures.html.

107. **Tweed offered him a half-million dollars to skip town** The attempt to bribe Nast is described in Albert Bigelow Paine's book *Th. Nast: His Period and His Pictures* (New York: Macmillan, 1904), pp. 181–82. The book is available at http://books.google.com through Google Book Search.

107. **"His cutting political wit gave us the name based expression 'Nasty'"** The gallery link that gave this erroneous etymology (http:// www.cormiergallery.com:80/tn.html) is no longer available online.

107. **"nasty" first showed up in English** See the *OED*.

107. **As for Boss Tweed, he died in 1878** The first chapter of Kenneth D. Ackerman's book *Boss Tweed* describes Tweed's death in jail. The excerpt was printed in *The New York Times,* March 27, 2005, and is retrievable at http://www.nytimes.com/2005/03/27/books/chapters/0327-1st-ackerman.html?pagewanted=print&position=.

108. **"a combination of barroom and brothel"** Foote, Shelby, *The Civil War: A Narrative,* Vol. II, *Fredericksburg to Meridian* (New York: Random House, 1963), p. 234.

108. **a red-light district in Washington, "Hooker's Division"** There was such a district. See Leech, Margaret, *Reveille in Washington, 1860–1865* (New York and London: Harper & Brothers, 1941), pp. 264, 399. For more on prostitution in Civil War–era Washington, see Wiley, Bell Irvin, *The Life of Billy Yank: The Common Soldier of the Union* (Baton Rouge: Louisiana State University Press, 1979), pp. 253–54.

108. **"the general's surname entered the language"** Foote, *The Civil War,* p. 234.

108. **a witness had "called me a hooker"** Research by George Thompson, a librarian at New York University's Bobst Library, turned up the Sept. 25, 1835, citation for "hooker" in the *New York Transcript.*

108. **The word may ultimately come from the sixteenth century** See the *OED*.

Chapter 7

109. **not to mention making M. Allen a Commandeur des Arts et des Lettres** Woody Allen was made a Commandeur des Arts et des Lettres on March 31, 1989, by the French Culture Ministry. See "Dear Woody, Have We Got News for You," *The New York Times,* March 29, 1998: http://query.nytimes.com/gst/fullpage.html?res=9E01EFD7143BF93AA1 5750C0A96E958260.

111. **the poet Coleridge** For more about Coleridge's pen names, see "Samuel Taylor Coleridge's Names," part of the Samuel Taylor Coleridge Archive, created by Marjorie A. Tiefert and maintained at the Electronic Text

Center at the University of Virginia Library: http://etext.virginia.edu/
stc/Coleridge/descriptions/His_name.html.

111. **When a young lady refused his hand** Karsten Bier, in "The Question of
Identity in Coleridge's Major Poems," credits the Coleridge anecdote to
David Collings's paper "Resisting Identity, Contesting Biography:
Episodes in the Life of 'Silas Tomkyn Comberbache,' " *Wordsworth Circle,*
Vol. 28, No. 2 (Spring 1997). Collings's paper is available at http://
asp6new.alexanderstreet.com/romr/romr.browse.nonfiction.aspx?sortorder
=parent+title&pagesize=500&page=12.

111. **a Grammy-winning pop singer** Paula Abdul's awards are cited at
http://www.variety.com/profiles/people/main/106554/Paula+Abdul.html?
dataSet=1.

112. **fans of the popular TV show jumped all over her** For bloggers'
comments on Abdul's pronunciation, see http://www.breigh.com/wordpress/
archives/839 and http://www.afterellen.com/blog/carolinagrrrl/american-idol-
finals-beatles-night.

112. **"This is your niche"** Adbul's quotation, on March 11, 2008, is cited here:
http://www.tvsquad.com/2008/03/11/american-idol-top-12-perform/.

114. **"They will fly at the French" . . . "Brave Nelson's sea thunder"** See
Wright, Thomas, *Caricature History of the Georges* (London: John Camden
Hotten, 1868), pp. 329, 597. Wright quotes both the 1772 poem from
Westminster Magazine and the anti-French song. The book is available at
http://books.google.com through Google Book Search.

114. **made the rounds in 1803** The source of the date for the anti-French song
is Tidwell, James N., "Frogs and Frog-Eaters," *American Speech,* Vol. 23,
No. 3/4 (Oct.–Dec. 1948), pp. 214–16.

114. **another source for the epithet, the fleur-de-lis** Slang dictionaries that
mention the fleur-de-lis theory include Partridge (Beale, ed.), *A Dictionary
of Slang and Unconventional English,* p. 429 (though the editor notes that the
etymology is spurious), and *Brewer's Dictionary of Phrase and Fable,* Cente-
nary Ed., revised by Ivor H. Evans (New York and Evanston, Ill.: Harper &
Row, 1970), pp. 421, 440.

114. **he traced "marmalade" to Mary Queen of Scots** References to

the Michael Caine interview can be found at http://danowen
.blogspot.com/2007/12/parkinson-last-conversation.html and http://
www.dailywritingtips.com/a-sweet-story-about-marmalade/.

115. **a 1480 letter about a gift of oranges and marmalade** See Kingsford,
Charles L., *Kingsford's Stonor Letters and Papers 1290–1483,* edited by Chris-
tine Carpenter (Cambridge: Cambridge University Press, 1996), p. 361.
Available at http://books.google.com through Google Book Search.

115. **"cheese-eating surrender monkeys"** See the website for *The Simpsons:*
http://www.thesimpsons.com/bios/bios_school_willie.htm.

115. **the "Frenche pox"** See Duffin, Jacalyn, *History of Medicine: A Scandalously
Short Introduction* (Toronto: University of Toronto Press, 1999), p. 145.
Also: Quetel, Claude, *History of Syphilis* (Baltimore: Johns Hopkins Uni-
versity Press, 1990), p. 16.

116. **"useless protrusion of a single faculty"** The *OED* dates the quotation
from 1870, when Séguin's remarks were published. But a copy of his
speech (delivered Oct. 15, 1869) was preserved. See *Catalogue of the Library
of the State Charities Aid Association,* No. 20 (New York: State Charities Aid
Association, 1880), pamphlet No. 8, box P. The catalogue is available at
http://books.google.com through Google Book Search.

117. **"love affair"** The *OED*'s first citation for "love affair" is from a 1598 play
by George Chapman, *The Blinde Begger of Alexandria.* But Shakespeare,
who used the phrase in *The Two Gentlemen of Verona,* probably got there
first. Although the earliest edition of *Two Gentlemen* is from 1623, Shakespeare is believed to have written it in the early 1590s, and its title appears in a list of his plays that was published in 1598. See Karl Young's
Appendix B to the text of *The Two Gentlemen of Verona* in the Yale Shakespeare series (New Haven and London: Yale University Press, 1966),
p. 93.

118. **"*Pourquois* don't you *mettez* some *savon*"** Twain, Mark, *The Innocents
Abroad* (Hartford: American Publishing Co., 1869), p. 189.

Chapter 8

121. **"The auctioneer's block in Maryland"** See Douglass, Frederick, "A Simple Tale of American Slavery," an address delivered in Sheffield, England,

on Sept. 11, 1846, and printed in *The Sheffield Mercury* on Sept. 12, 1846. From *Frederick Douglass Papers, Series 1—Speeches, Debates, and Interviews*, Vol. I (New Haven: Yale University Press, 1979), p. 398.

121. **"auction block" and "auctioneer's block" were indeed products of the slave trade** Evidence in the *OED* also confirms that "auction block" originated in the slave trade. Here's one definition of "block" in the *OED*: "The stump on which a slave stood when being sold by auction." The *OED*'s citations for this use of "block" are more recent than Douglass's, and include this 1853 entry in *Chambers Journal*: "Boy mounts the block . . . the auctioneer kindly lends him a hand." Also cited is a brief quotation from an 1866 poem by William Cullen Bryant, "The Death of Slavery." Here's a fuller quotation from *The Complete Poems of William Cullen Bryant*, edited by H. C. Edwards (New York: Frederick A. Stokes Co., 1894), p. 319:

> *The slave-pen, through whose door*
> *Thy victims pass no more,*
> *Is there, and there shall the grim block remain*
> *At which the slave was sold.*

Many of the former slaves who were interviewed in the 1930s under the Federal Writer's Project of the Works Progress Administration used the expression "auction block" in recalling their experiences under slavery. (See the Library of Congress's website http://memory.loc.gov/ammem/snhtml/snhome.html.) And a popular Negro spiritual from the mid-nineteenth century, "Many Thousand Gone," sometimes referred to by its the opening stanza, "No more auction block for me," was collected in *The Jubilee Singers* by Gustavus D. Pike (Boston: Lee and Shepard, 1873), p. 186.

122. **the exemptions were called "grandfather clauses"** The first published reference in the *Oxford English Dictionary* is in the Jan. 22, 1900, *Congressional Record*: "The grandfather clause will not avail those citizens who . . . are unable to pay their poll tax." Dave Wilton, an independent language researcher, reported on the Linguist List forum in 2006 that he

had found an earlier citation in *The New York Times* of Aug. 3, 1899: "It provides, too, that the descendants of any one competent to vote in 1867 may vote now regardless of existing conditions. It is known as the 'grandfather's clause.' "

122. **lawmakers just as routinely use "grandfather clause"** It should be noted that the verb "grandfather," meaning to exempt from new regulations, is also derived from "grandfather clause." *Merriam-Webster's Collegiate Dictionary* (11th ed.) defines the verb as "to permit to continue under a grandfather clause." But the verb, which is often accompanied by the prepositions "in" or "out," doesn't appear to have been used in the racial sense. All five citations in an addition to the *OED* use the verb only in the modern way. Here's an example from the Kentucky Revised Statutes of 1953: "All certificates or permits grandfathered shall be subject to the same limitations and restrictions."

122. **"politically correct"** Justice Wilson's use of the expression is cited in Shapiro, *The Yale Book of Quotations*. The full paragraph of his opinion, which follows, comes from a transcript of *Chisholm v. State of Ga.,* 2 US 419 (1793): "In the United States, and in the several States, which compose the Union, we go not so far: but still we go one step farther than we ought to go in this unnatural and inverted order of things. The states, rather than the People, for whose sakes the States exist, are frequently the objects which attract and arrest our principal attention. This, I believe, has produced much of the confusion and perplexity, which have appeared in several proceedings and several publications on state-politics, and on the politics, too, of the United States. Sentiments and expressions of this inaccurate kind prevail in our common, even in our convivial, language. Is a toast asked? 'The United States,' instead of the 'People of the United States,' is the toast given. This is not politically correct. The toast is meant to present to view the first great object in the Union: It presents only the second: It presents only the artificial person, instead of the natural persons, who spoke it into existence. A State I cheerfully fully admit, is the noblest work of Man: But, Man himself, free and honest, is, I speak as to this world, the noblest work of God." See Wilson, James, *Collected Works of James Wilson,* Vol. I, edited by Kermit L. Hall and Mark David Hall, col-

lected by Maynard Garrison (Indianapolis: Liberty Fund, 2007), pp. 453–66. The text of the full opinion is at http://oll.libertyfund.org/ ?option=com_staticxt&staticfile=show.php%3Ftitle=2072&chapter= 156437&layout=html&Itemid=27.

122. "more politically correct" The quotations from Strachey, Bambara, and *The Nation* are from the *OED*. Their sources are Strachey, John, *Literature and Dialectical Materialism* (1934), p. 47; Bambara, Toni Cade, *Black Woman* (1970), p. 73; *The Nation,* June 6, 1987 (769/3).

123. "feminist scholarship at its best" Keniston, Kenneth, "Wife Beating and the Rule of Thumb," *The New York Times Book Review,* May 8, 1988. Keniston reviewed *Heroes of Their Own Lives: The Politics and History of Family Violence: Boston 1880–1960,* by Linda Gordon (New York: Viking, 1988).

124. "There is probably no truth whatever" See Kelly, Henry Ansgar, " 'Rule of Thumb' and the Folklaw of the Husband's Stick," *Journal of Legal Education,* Vol. 44, No. 3 (Sept. 1994), p. 341.

124. "who build by guess, and by rule of thumb" See Durham, James, *Heaven Upon Earth* (Edinburgh: printed by the heir of Andrew Anderson, 1685), p. 217. Available at Early English Books Online.

124. "by dint of practice" The 1785 quotation is from the *OED,* citing *A Classical Dictionary of the Vulgar Tongue.* The *OED* also cites part of this quotation from *A Complete Collection of Scotish Proverbs* (1721): "No Rule so good as *Rule of Thumb,* if it hit; spoken when a things falls out to be right, which we did at a venture" (p. 257).

124. to "give his wife moderate correction" Blackstone's full text, from *Commentaries on the Laws of England,* Book I, Chapter 15, is available at http://avalon.law.yale.edu/18th_century/blackstone_bk1ch15.asp. Blackstone is also quoted in Kelly, " 'Rule of Thumb,' " pp. 352–53.

125. the judge was ridiculed in the press and viciously caricatured See Kelly, ibid., pp. 349–51.

125. "a rule of thumb, so to speak" See Martin, Del, *Battered Wives* (Volcano, Calif.: Volcano Press, 1976), p. 31.

126. this myth was so entrenched For a longer treatment of the "rule of thumb" myth, see Sommers, Christina Hoff, *Who Stole Feminism? How*

Women Have Betrayed Women (New York: Simon & Schuster, 1994), pp. 203–8.

126. **"Under the Rule of Thumb"** See http://www.ncjrs.gov/App/ Publications/abstract.aspx?ID=82752.

126. **"The bridegroom's fig"** The text of Aristophanes' *Peace* is available on the Massachusetts Institute of Technology's Internet Classics Archive. The leader of the chorus makes the comment near the end of the play: http://classics.mit.edu:80/Aristophanes/peace.pl.txt.

127. **some suggestive wordplay about kneading** The text of Aristophanes' *The Clouds* is also available on MIT's archive. The references to kneading are in an exchange between Socrates and Strepsiades. See http:// classics.mit.edu:80/Aristophanes/clouds.html.

127. **The expression evidently first appears, minus the figs** Much of the information about the Greek passages mentioned here, as well as their attributions, was provided by a classical scholar, Professor Gerald Lalonde, of Grinnell College, who researched several of the authors' questions at the American School in Athens. He also provided original translations of certain Greek passages and current scholarship on the Menander fragment.

127. **he mistook the Greek word** Erasmus's mistake is further illuminated in Barker, William, *The Adages of Erasmus* (Toronto: University of Toronto Press, 2001): "Despite Erasmus' learned account, there is actually no classical proverb that says 'to call a spade a spade.' . . . Our proverb in English . . . is the direct result of Erasmus' retranslation." See pp. 170–71 and notes.

128. **"to calle a spade by any other name then a spade"** Udall's translation is taken from the *OED*. The entire passage: "Philippus aunswered, that the Macedonians wer feloes of no fyne witte in their termes but altogether grosse, clubbyshe [clownish], and rusticall, as they whiche had not the witte to calle a spade by any other name then a spade."

128. **"I have learned, plainly and boldly"** Knox's translation, from *Selected Writings of John Knox* (Dallas: Presbyterian Heritage Publications, 1995), is quoted in *For Kirk and Covenant: The Stalwart Courage of John Knox,* by Douglas Wilson (Nashville: Cumberland House, 2000), pp. 186–87.

128. **"I cannot say the crow is white"** The quotation is from the *OED*.

128. **"I am plaine"** The 1589 quotation, by the pseudonymous Martin Marprelate, is from the *OED*.

128–29. **"Jake is such a fool spade"** . . . **"Wonder where all the spades keep themselves"** The quotations from the Claude McKay and Wallace Thurman novels are in the *OED*.

129. **the color of the spades suit in a deck of cards** The suit named "spades" has little to do with actual spades. The name is from the Italian word *spada,* which means "sword" or "broadsword." In Italian the plural of *spada* is *spade* (pronounced SPAH-day).

129. **alive and well in modern Greece** Confirmation of the original expression's use in modern Greek comes from the press office of the Greek Embassy in Washington.

130. **"herstory"** According to the *OED,* the word first appeared in Robin Morgan's *Sisterhood Is Powerful: An Anthology of Writings from the Women's Liberation Movement* (New York: Random House, 1970), p. 604.

131. **The "his" in "history" is not the masculine pronoun** For the etymologies of "woman," "man," "girl," and "history," we relied principally on the *OED*.

132. **"girlie men"** See Battistella, Edwin, "Girly Men and Girly Girls," *American Speech,* Vol. 81/1 (Spring 2006), pp. 100 ff.

133. **"riot grrls"** The reference given, from the *OED,* is attributed to *Billboard,* March 28, 1992 (60/1): "The panelists festooned the wall with a bed sheet emblazoned with the legend 'Riot Grrls (sic).' " For more "grrrl" spellings, see "Among the New Words" in *American Speech,* Vol. 72/1 (Spring 1997), p. 89.

137. **"The use of female gendered pronouns"** The lawsuit was filed by Douglas Wallace on April 4, 2008, in Washoe County District Court in Nevada, docketed as case number CV08-00866—*Douglas Wallace vs. Ross Miller et al.* (D8).

137. **Anne Fisher, an eighteenth-century schoolmistress** See Tieken-Boon van Ostade, Ingrid, "Female Grammarians of the Eighteenth Century," *Historical Sociolinguistics and Sociohistorical Linguistics,* Aug. 28, 2000. All of Fisher's quotations are taken from this article, retrievable at http://www.let.leidenuniv.nl/hsl_shl/femgram.htm#N_1_.

137. **an advertisement for it appeared in 1745** The source for the advertisement, in the *Newcastle Journal* of June 29, 1745, is R. C. Alston, ed., in a "Note" to a facsimile reprint of *A New Grammar* by Anne Fisher (1750), which is No. 130 in *English Linguistics 1500–1800,* a collection of facsimile editions published by Scolar Press (Menston, England, 1968).

137. **making the grammar guide one of the most successful of its time** More information about Fisher is available in Rodríguez-Gil, María Esther, "Ann Fisher: First Female Grammarian," *Historical Sociolinguistics and Sociohistorical Linguistics* (Nov. 2002). This article can be found at http://www.let.leidenuniv.nl/hsl_shl/rodriguez-gil.htm. Also, see Rodríguez-Álvarez, Alicia, and María Esther Rodríguez-Gil, "John Entick's and Ann Fisher's Dictionaries: An Eighteenth-Century Case of (Cons)-Piracy?" *International Journal of Lexicography,* Vol. 19, No. 3 (Sept. 2006), pp. 287–319. It should be noted that while several scholars refer to Fisher as "Ann," her name appears as "Anne" on her books. See Mulvey, Christopher, "The Eighteenth Century English Project: Correcting the Language," available at http://www.englishproject.org/index2.php?option=com_content&do_pdf=1&id=74.

139. **a typical scene between Flywheel and his secretary** See Barson, Michael, ed., *Flywheel, Shyster, and Flywheel: The Marx Brothers' Lost Radio Show* (New York: Pantheon, 1988), pp. 65, 140.

140. **he'd heard an attorney use "shiseter" for an unscrupulous lawyer** Gerald L. Cohen's monograph *Origin of the Term 'Shyster'* (Frankfurt am Main, Bern: Verlag Peter Lang, 1982) is summarized in *The Merriam-Webster New Book of Word Histories* (Springfield, Mass.: Merriam-Webster, 1991), pp. 424–25.

141. **a quarter to three quarters of a million English words** The estimate comes from the Oxford University Press website www.askoxford.com.

141. **"And whoso fyndeth hym"** Chaucer's quotation is from "The Pardoner's Prologue."

142. **Great writers ... made great use of the sexless, numberless "they/them/their"** Evidence for the historical use of the singular "they," "them," and "their" comes from the *OED; Merriam-Webster's Dictionary of English Usage,* pp. 53, 901–3; Otto Jespersen's *Essentials of English Grammar*

(Tuscaloosa: University of Alabama Press, 1994), p. 193; and Patricia Lorimer Lundberg's review of the book *Grammar and Gender* by Dennis E. Baron, in *American Speech,* Vol. 63, No. 2 (Summer 1988), p. 174.

142. **"Can any one, on their entrance into the world"** Murray, Lindley, *English Grammar: Adapted to the Different Classes of Learners* (York: Wilson, Spence and Mawman, 1795), p. 96.

142. **Noah Webster defined "they," "them," and "their" as strictly plural** Webster, Noah: *An American Dictionary of the English Language* (New York: S. Converse, 1828).

142. **"sets the literary man's teeth on edge"** Fowler, *Modern English Usage,* p. 392. See also p. 648.

142. **"*they* is unfit to represent a singular antecedent"** Follett, Wilson, *Modern American Usage: A Guide,* revised by Erik Wensberg (New York: Hill & Wang, 1998), p. 33.

143. **"The process now seems irreversible"** Burchfield, ed., *The New Fowler's,* p. 779.

144. **"thon," a sexless third-person pronoun** Converse is credited as the inventor in *"Thon*—That's the Forewho," by an author identified as Quidnunc, *American Speech,* Vol. 48, No. 3/4 (Autumn–Winter 1973), pp. 300–302. Quidnunc gives the date as 1858, but Dennis E. Baron (see following note) argues that 1884 is more likely.

145. **"the creation of an epicene or bisexual pronoun"** Baron, Dennis E., "The Epicene Pronoun: The Word That Failed," *American Speech,* Vol. 56, No. 2 (Summer 1981), pp. 83–97.

145. **"No, thonx"** Ogden Nash's poem "The Bronx? No, thonx!" (1931) is cited by Shapiro, *The Yale Book of Quotations,* p. 546.

145. **Supposedly it's an acronym** See Eisiminger, Sterling, "Acronyms and Folk Etymology," p. 582.

145. **a derogatory term for an Italian** The *OED*'s first citation for "wop" is from 1912, but *Merriam-Webster's Collegiate Dictionary* (11th ed.) dates it from 1908.

145. **immigration documents . . . weren't even required of newcomers until 1918** Marian L. Smith, senior historian for the Department of Homeland Security's United States Citizenship and Immigration Ser-

vices, provided the following information in an email to the authors on June 18, 2008: "The US required all arriving aliens to present a passport beginning in 1918. Passports are issued/created by the immigrant's own country and given to the individual to carry or present. The Immigration Act of 1921 required that the passport contain a 'visa stamp' from a US official abroad. The Immigration Act of 1924 required all arriving immigrants to present a visa document issued by a US Embassy or consulate abroad. The document was prepared by US officials and issued to the immigrant to carry to the US. It was taken up by a US Immigrant Inspector at the port of entry and filed away by the government."

Further information on the documents required of immigrants can be found at the website *U.S. Immigration Legislation Online:* http://tucnak .fsv.cuni.cz/~calda/Documents/1920s/ImmigAct1924.html. Also see Ngai, Mae M., "The Strange Career of the Illegal Alien: Immigration Restriction and Deportation Policy in the United States, 1921–1965," *Law and History Review,* Vol. 21, No. 1 (Spring 2003), paragraph 17: http:// www.historycooperative.org:80/journals/lhr/21.1/ngai.html.

145. **the symbols didn't include WOP** For more about the symbols used at Ellis Island, see Kendall, Constance Lynn, "The Worlds We Deliver: Confronting the Consequences of Believing in Literacy," a 2005 PhD dissertation retrievable at http://www.ohiolink.edu/etd/send-pdf .cgi?miami1117215518 (see p. 98).

146. **"The derogatory term 'wop,' an acronym for 'With Out Papers'"** Bennett, Tony, with Will Friedwald, *The Good Life: The Autobiography of Tony Bennett* (New York: Pocket Books, 1998). In Chapter 1 of the book, Bennett describes his maternal grandparents' immigration in 1899.

146. **It's almost impossible to kill a myth** See Manjoo, Farhad, "Rumor's Reasons," *The New York Times Magazine,* March 16, 2008.

146. **"Boas's small example"** See Martin, Laura, "Eskimo Words for Snow: A Case Study in the Genesis and Decay of an Anthropological Example," *American Anthropologist, New Series,* Vol. 88, No. 2 (June 1986), pp. 418–23.

147. **about a dozen words for snow "counting generously"** Pinker, Steven, *The Language Instinct* (New York: William Morrow, 1994), pp. 64–65.

148. **We have only a few surviving examples of the quilts that slaves**

sewed for their own use See Benberry, Cuesta, *Always There: The African-American Presence in American Quilts* (Louisville: Kentucky Quilt Project, 1992), p. 27. Benberry, an African-American folklorist and quilt historian, writes: "As the majority of extant slave quilts are in the possession of the slave owners' descendants, various scholars have assumed that all of those quilts were originally made for the owners' households by slave seamstresses. Searches have been ongoing for quilts created by slaves for their own use, but few have been located."

148. **numerous schoolchildren have been taught** See, for example, "Campus Journal; Retracing Freedom's Route to Oberlin," *The New York Times,* April 14, 1993.

148. **And this isn't just a kid thing** Mainstream adult articles include "How Slaves Read Between the Threads," *The New York Times,* Feb. 18, 1999; "Lessons in Sewing a Map to Freedom," *The New York Times,* Feb. 17, 2006; "Comforter of slaves bound for freedom—Two women unraveled the code on quilts," *USA Today,* Jan. 19, 1999; and "Did Quilts Hold Codes to the Underground Railroad?" *National Geographic,* Feb. 5, 2004.

148. **National Security Agency's museum of codes** For information about the quilt "codes" exhibited at the National Security Agency's Cryptologic Museum, see http://www.nsa.gov/about/cryptologic_heritage/museum/virtual_tour/museum_tour_text.shtml.

148. **quilts "with the color black"** Fry, Gladys-Marie, *Stitched from the Soul: Slave Quilts from the Antebellum South* (New York: Dutton Studio Books in association with the Museum of American Folk Art, 1990), pp. 52, 65.

148. **nothing to support the claim** Leigh Fellner in emails to the authors in April 2008.

148. **a new and expanded version of the quilt story** See Tobin, Jacqueline L., and Raymond G. Dobard, *Hidden in Plain View: The Secret Story of Quilts and the Underground Railroad* (New York: Anchor Books, 2000). Williams died on May 19, 1998 (p. 167). The quotations cited are found on pp. 70, 71, 83, 84, and 112.

148. **The book was featured on *Oprah*** Dr. Dobard appeared on *The Oprah Winfrey Show* in November 1998, and his segment was rebroadcast on Jan. 18, 1999.

149. **most of the ten quilt patterns weren't even around until the late nineteenth or early twentieth centuries** Barbara Brackman, a quilt historian and the author of *The Encyclopedia of Pieced Quilt Patterns,* says, "The Double Wedding Ring, Sunbonnet Sue and most of the other quilt patterns supposedly used as code did not exist before the Civil War." See her website, http://www.barbarabrackman.com/factsheet.pdf. See also Fellner, Leigh, *Betsy Ross Redux: The Underground Railroad "Quilt Code,"* available at http:// ugrrquilt.hartcottagequilts.com/. Additional information comes from emails between Fellner, a quilt historian, and the authors in April 2008.

149. **Giles R. Wright** The historian's arguments were reported in *The New York Times,* Jan. 23, 2007.

149. **nurtured by a host of children's books** Children's books that retail the "code" myth include Hopkinson, Deborah, *Sweet Clara and the Freedom Quilt* (New York: Knopf, 1993); Stroud, Bettye, *The Patchwork Path: A Quilt Map to Freedom* (New York: Candlewick, 2005); and Hopkinson, Deborah, *Under the Quilt of Night* (New York: Atheneum Books for Young Readers, 2002).

150. **"a myth, bordering on a hoax"** David Blight's quotations come from *The New York Times,* Jan. 23, 2007, and the *Yale Daily News,* Feb. 1, 2007.

150. **"It's like Washington chopping down the cherry tree"** Marsha MacDowell's quotation is from *The New York Times,* Jan. 23, 2007.

150. **according to three bestselling authors** The "he said/she said" figures cited by the self-help gurus are catalogued in "Sex on the Brain," an article by Mark Liberman, a linguist and professor of phonetics at the University of Pennsylvania, published in *The Boston Globe* Sept. 24, 2006.

151. **Two social psychologists** See Leaper, Campbell, and Melanie M. Ayres, "A Meta-Analytic Review of Gender Variations in Adults' Language Use: Talkativeness, Affiliative Speech, and Assertive Speech," *Personality and Social Psychology Review,* Vol. 11, No. 4 (November 2007), pp. 328–63.

151. **another study published the same year** See Mehl, Matthias R., et al., "Are Women Really More Talkative Than Men?" in *Science,* Vol. 317, No. 5834 (July 6, 2007), p. 82.

152. **a Frenchman was still a frog and a German a Hun** Typical examples from British newspapers: "Hun-believable! I'd play for NOTHING;

BORIS BECKER EXCLUSIVE," a headline in the *Sunday Mirror,* June 23, 1996. And "Frogs need a good kicking," a headline on an editorial in the *Daily Star,* March 2, 1998.

152. **the Golliwogg, a black rag-doll character** The character was introduced in *The Adventure of Two Dutch Dolls and a "Golliwogg"* (London: Longmans, Green & Co., 1895), the first of Florence Kate Upton's books. The prolific children's-book writer Enid Blyton also wrote books featuring golliwogs, including *The Three Golliwogs* (1944).

152. **A golliwog named Golly was featured on the Robertson & Sons jam and marmalade jars** See Bowcott, Owen, "Time runs out for Robertson's golly," *The Guardian,* Aug. 23, 2001. Also " 'Controversial' golly to be shelved," a BBC news report from Aug. 23, 2001, retrievable at http://news.bbc.co.uk/2/hi/business/1505411.stm.

152. **a mid-twentieth-century revival of blackface minstrel shows** According to the Victoria Palace Theatre in London, *The Black and White Minstrel Show* ran for 4,344 performances. The information is retrievable at https://www.victoriapalacetheatre.co.uk/online/past_shows.asp as well as at the website of the Museum of Broadcast Communications in Chicago, in an article by Sarita Malik retrievable at http://www.museum.tv/archives/etv/B/htmlB/blackandwhim/blackandwhim.htm.

Chapter 9

154. **malapropism** Mrs. Malaprop's deathless lines in Sheridan's *The Rivals* come from Act III, scene 3 ("allegory"); Act IV, scene 2 ("affluence"); Act I, scene 2 ("illegible"); and Act III, scene 3 ("reprehend").

154. **a "different fettle of kitsch"** See Rosenblatt, Roger, "Oops! How's That Again?" *Time,* March 30, 1981.

154. **"I'd rather have a bottle in front of me"** Tom Waits's quip, originally quoted in *Creem* magazine in March 1978, is cited in Shapiro, *The Yale Book of Quotations,* p. 794. It's one of many witticisms often misattributed to Dorothy Parker (see note to p. 87).

154. **"terriers and bariffs"** George W. Bush joked about this blunder on March 29, 2001, in an address to the Radio-Television Correspondents Association

annual dinner in Washington. See Bruni, Frank, "Word for Word," *The New York Times,* April 1, 2001.

155. **"And laid him on the green"** From the Francis J. Child Ballads, listed as Child Ballad #181 ("The Bonny Earl o' Moray"). It is retrievable at http://www.contemplator.com/child/index.html.

155. **many a Jimi Hendrix audience** See Shapiro, Harry, and Caesar Glebbeek, *Jimi Hendrix: Electric Gypsy* (New York: St. Martin's Griffin, 1995), p. 148. Also, Kramer, Edward E., and John McDermott, *Hendrix: Setting the Record Straight* (New York: Grand Central Publishing, 1992), p. 72.

155. **"eggcorn"** Mark Liberman discussed the etymology of the term he helped invent in a posting to the Language Log: http://itre.cis.upenn.edu/~myl/languagelog/archives/000018.html.

156. **When the word "dungeon" entered English** The etymology comes from the *OED.*

156. **"and on thy blade and dudgeon gouts of blood"** Macbeth's speech is from Act II, scene 1.

157. **the longest hiccup attack on record** See "Guinness Medical Record Breakers," a feature of BBC News: http://news.bbc.co.uk/2/shared/spl/hi/pop_ups/05/health_guinness_medical_record_breakers/html/2.stm.

159. **widely misspelled in France as** *dilemne* Citations for the French misspelling *dilemne* are retrievable at these sites: http://www.languefrancaise.net/forum/viewtopic.php?pid=45064 and http://le-celibat-ne-passera-pas-par-moi.skynetblogs.be/post/4130862/le-dilemme—grand-sondage-virtuel.

159. **Senator Charles Schumer of New York** From "Best of the Web Today" in *The Wall Street Journal,* online edition, by James Taranto, Oct. 24, 2005. Retrievable at http://www.opinionjournal.com/best/?id=110007449.

159. **An 1840 political cartoon** The Martin Van Buren cartoon is available at the Library of Congress's searchable *Prints & Photographs Online Catalog:* http://lcweb2.loc.gov/pp/pphome.html.

163. **We got both words from French fencing terms** See the *OED.*

163. **"a Foyle . . . hath two Parts"** Lord Herbert's remark on fencing is quoted in the *OED* under the entry for "feeble." The longer version of his quota-

tion, in context, can be found in *The Life of Edward Lord Herbert of Cherbury: Written by Himself* (London: J. Dodsley, 1792), p. 46. Retrievable at http://books.google.com through Google Book Search.

167. **"Thy Neck is like a Tower of Ivory"** Woodford, Samuel, *A Paraphrase Upon the Canticles* (1679), from a digitized transcript by Chadwyck-Healey (Cambridge, 1992), page 45. Available at http://xtf.lib.virginia .edu/xtf/view?docId=chadwyck_ep/uvaGenText/tei/chep_2.0274.xml.

167. **"We called you the Ivory Tower group"** The Mary McCarthy citation is from the *OED*.

167. **"our eastern ivy colleges"** The 1933 citation for this quotation in the *New York Herald Tribune,* as well as the 1935 citations for the first uses of "Ivy League," are cited in Shapiro, ed., *The Yale Book of Quotations.*

168. **"The 'Ivy League' is something which does not exist"** See the *OED*.

168. **an "Ivy Group" agreement** The Ivy League history is from http:// www.ivysport.com/history.php.

169. **"Have you not tried in some instances to palm off "** Charles Lamb's remark, from his essay "Distant Correspondents," is in *The Works of Charles Lamb* (New York: Derby & Jackson, 1856), p. 124.

169. **"And now he has sent out his three daughters"** See Marryat, Frederick, *Newton Forster or the Merchant Service* (1832), reissued by Kessinger Publishing (Whitefish, Mont., 2005), p. 286.

170. **the term "nor'easter" isn't native to the land of clam chowdah** See Freeman, Jan, "Nor' by Nor'east?" *The Boston Globe,* Dec. 21, 2003, retrievable at http://www.boston.com/news/globe/ideas/articles/2003/12/21/ guys_and_dolls/. Also, "How 'Nor'easter' Became Standard, Even Though We Don't Talk That Way," *The Boston Globe,* Feb. 17, 2008, retrievable at http://www.boston.com/bostonglobe/ideas/articles/2008/02 /17/stormy_weather/.

170. **"Slack your sheet! A strong nor'-easter's groaning"** The translator of this passage from Aristophanes, Benjamin Dann Walsh, was born in England, where the translation was published. He emigrated to the United States the following year. His biography, from *Appleton's Cyclopedia,* is available at http://www.famousamericans.net/benjamindannwalsh/.

171. **"seems faker to me than the lederhosen at the Biergarten in Walt**

Disney World" Mark Liberman's postings to the Language Log about "nor'easter" are retrievable at http://itre.cis.upenn.edu/~myl/languagelog/archives/001824.html and at http://158.130.17.5/~myl/languagelog/archives/000386.html.

171–72. "native here and to the manner born" *Hamlet,* Act I, scene 4.

172. "manner" . . . "manor" The etymologies are from the *OED.*

172. "He intended . . . to return to Scotland" From the *OED.*

172. "A native chief, and to the manor born" From *The Extravaganzas of J. R. Planché, Esq.,* Vol. IV, edited by Thomas Francis Dillon Croker and Stephen Tucker (London: Samuel French, 1879), p. 195. The book is available at http://books.google.com through Google Book Search.

Chapter 10

175. "an alleged atrocity" See Pinker, *The Language Instinct,* p. 377.

175. intended to be ironic (like saying "I should talk!") For the analogy of "I could care less" with "I should talk," with its "underlying semantic negation," we're indebted to a contributor (identified only as C.C.D.) to the journal *American Speech,* Vol. 54, No. 2 (Summer 1979), p. 159.

176. "data" For its history as a singular, see *Merriam-Webster's Dictionary of English Usage,* pp. 317–18.

176. " 'data' in the sense of facts is a collective" From *Science,* July 1, 1927, and quoted in *Merriam-Webster's Dictionary of English Usage,* p. 318.

177. "No one should think that he must treat *data* as a plural" *A Dictionary of Contemporary American Usage,* by Bergen Evans and Cornelia Evans (New York: Random House, 1957), p. 126.

179. To the Romans, the verb meant For the meanings of *decimare* (in the senses of both taxing and discipline), see Ayto, John, *Dictionary of Word Origins* (New York: Arcade Publishing, 1993), pp. 159–60.

179. *decimatio . . . vicesimatio . . . centesimatio* The terms for military punishments in ancient times are from *Dictionary of Greek and Roman Antiquities,* edited by Sir William Smith (Boston: C. Little & J. Brown, 1870), p. 387.

180. inspired by reading a translation of Tacitus See Shapiro, James, *A Year*

in the Life of William Shakespeare: 1599 (New York: HarperCollins, 2005), p. 261.

180. **"Typhus fever decimated the school"** The quotation from Brontë's letter, published in Elizabeth Gaskell's *The Life of Charlotte Brontë,* is quoted in the *OED.*

181. **War correspondents from the Civil War** See *Merriam-Webster's Dictionary of English Usage,* p. 320.

181. **If he hadn't used the expression "beg the question"** See McKeon, Richard, ed., *The Basic Works of Aristotle* (New York: Random House, 1966), p. 93. The discussion of *en archei aiteisthai* ("to assume at the beginning") comes from *Prior Analytics,* II, 16, translated by A. J. Jenkinson.

182. **"as long as there's no dodging or begging the question"** Henry Adams is quoted in *Merriam-Webster's Dictionary of English Usage,* p. 172.

183. **Even my own state legislature** See Section 29-310 of Chapter 541 of the Connecticut General Statutes, describing the duties of the State Fire Marshal.

183. **So how did "flammable" eventually catch fire?** For a history of "the publicity campaign undertaken to urge wider adoption of *flammable,*" see *Merriam-Webster's Dictionary of English Usage,* p. 450.

183. **"In order to avoid any possible ambiguity"** The British Standards Institution is quoted in the *OED.*

186. **began using an apostrophe to show the omission** The *OED*'s seventeenth-century citation for "'till," printed with the apostrophe, comes from Robert Greville, 2nd Baron Brooke: "They desire they may have leave (as Probationers) to exercise, or keepe Acts, before the Church; 'till the Church shall approve of them." The quotation is found in *A Discourse Opening the Nature of that Episcopacie Which Is Exercised in England* (1641).

187. **"Plainly this is my infirmity"** We've taken the liberty of putting the *OED*'s citation from the Wycliffe Bible (under the entry for "plainly") into modern English to make it readable.

187. **"Luckily the strength of the piece"** Jane Austen's use of a sentence adverb in *Mansfield Park* is cited in *Merriam-Webster's Dictionary of English Usage,* p. 837.

187. **"Happily human brains have such a talent"** Carlyle is quoted in the *OED*.

187. **"Oddly, I was never at all staggered"** See Darwin, Charles, *More Letters of Charles Darwin: A Record of His Work in a Series of Hitherto Unpublished Letters,* Vol. II, edited by Francis Darwin and A. C. Seward (Adamant Media, 2003), p. 178.

187. **"Mercifully we have 50 miles of felt between ourselves and the den"** See Woolf, Virginia, *A Writer's Diary,* edited by Leonard Woolf (San Diego: Harvest/HBJ, 2003), p. 284.

188. **the *Saturday Review, The New Yorker,* and *The New York Times* denounced this terrible new menace** See *Merriam-Webster's Dictionary of English Usage,* p. 837.

188. **"one of the most bitterly contested of all the linguistic battles"** See Burchfield, ed., *The New Fowler's,* p. 702.

188. **Over the years, most usage manuals and style guides** See, for example, Bernstein, Theodore M., *Miss Thistlebottom's Hobgoblins: The Careful Writer's Guide to the Taboos, Bugbears and Outmoded Rules of English Usage* (New York: Noonday Press/Farrar, Straus & Giroux, 1973), p. 51.

188. **it "means in a hopeful manner, and its use should be confined to that meaning"** See *The New York Times Manual of Style and Usage: A Desk Book of Guidelines for Writers and Editors,* revised and edited by Lewis Jordan (New York: Times Books, 1977), p. 95.

188. **"writers and editors unwilling to irritate readers would be wise"** to avoid the usage See *The New York Times Manual of Style and Usage: Revised and Expanded Edition,* by Allan M. Siegal and William G. Connolly (New York: Times Books/Random House, 1999), p. 161.

189. **The word started life back in the eighth century** For the etymology of "moot," see the *OED*.

190. **apparently first printed in a 1620 book** For the etymology of "flaccid," see the *OED*.

191. **The first English version of the word** See the *OED* for the history of "comptroller."

192. **"suttle" . . . "subtle"** For Milton's spellings of the word, see the *OED*.

193. **"such a Synergie, or cooperation"** Peter Heylin's quotation is from the *OED*.

194. **"the '2 + 2 = 5' effect"** Ansoff's quotation is cited in the *OED*.

195. **Kipling is credited with being the first** Kipling's "The Army of a Dream" was first published in installments in *The Morning Post* of London, June 15–18, 1904. It appeared later that year in a story collection, *Traffics and Discoveries,* published by Macmillan in London.

195. **"to loaf about and talk and enjoy oneself"** Harding's definition of "bloviate" is from Russell, Francis, *The Shadow of Blooming Grove: Warren G. Harding in His Times* (New York: McGraw-Hill, 1968), p. 52. See also: Merriam-Webster's "Word of the Day," June 23, 2003.

195. **"the worst English that I have ever encountered"** Mencken, H. L., *On Politics: A Carnival of Buncombe* (Baltimore: Johns Hopkins University Press, 1996), pp. 42–43.

Afterword

198. **"Is there a Parson, much bemus'd in beer"** Pope's poem is cited in *Merriam-Webster's Dictionary of English Usage,* p. 176.

198. **"muse" . . . "amused"** For their first appearances in print, see the *OED*.

199. **"Let's be meek to them— / And turn the other cheek to them"** See Morley, Sheridan, *Coward* (London: Haus Publishing, 2004), p. 80.

200. **We got it in the early 1600s from the French** The etymology of "unique" is from the *OED* and *Merriam-Webster's Dictionary of English Usage,* pp. 927–28.

201. **"the illiterate"** See Fowler, *Modern English Usage,* p. 679.

202. **the noun "enormity" first appeared in the late 1400s** See the *OED*.

202. **"now regarded as incorrect"** The reference to the *OED* editors' treatment of the word in 1893 comes from *Merriam-Webster's Dictionary of English Usage,* p. 398.

Bibliography

Standard and Etymological Dictionaries

The source we used more than any other was the *Oxford English Dictionary Online,* a subscription service offered by Oxford University Press. The *OED Online* is updated quarterly, and subscription information is available at http://dictionary.oed.com/subscribe/. We also consulted these sources:

The American Heritage Dictionary of the English Language, 4th ed. (Boston and New York: Houghton Mifflin, 2000).

The American Heritage Dictionary of Indo-European Roots, 2nd ed., revised and edited by Calvert Watkins (Boston and New York: Houghton Mifflin, 2000).

Cassell's Dictionary of Slang, 2nd ed., by Jonathon Green (London: Weidenfeld & Nicolson, 2005).

Chambers Dictionary of Etymology, edited by Robert K. Barnhart (New York: Chambers, 2006).

The Columbia Guide to Standard American English, by Kenneth G. Wilson (New York: Columbia University Press, 1993).

A Dictionary of Slang and Unconventional English, 8th ed., by Eric Partridge, edited by Paul Beale (New York: Macmillan, 1984).

Dictionary of Word Origins, by John Ayto (New York: Arcade, 1993).

Merriam-Webster's Collegiate Dictionary, 11th ed. (Springfield, Mass.: Merriam-Webster, 2007).

Merriam-Webster's Dictionary of English Usage (Springfield, Mass.: Merriam-

Webster, 1994). Also, *Merriam-Webster's Concise Dictionary of English Usage* (Springfield, Mass.: Merriam-Webster, 2002).

Random House Historical Dictionary of American Slang, Vol. I, A–G (1994), Vol. II, H–O (1997), edited by J. E. Lighter (New York: Random House).

Random House Webster's College Dictionary (New York: Random House, 1991).

Other Sources

Crystal, David, *The Fight for English: How Language Pundits Ate, Shot, and Left* (New York: Oxford University Press, 2006).

———, *The Stories of English* (Woodstock and New York: Overlook Press, 2004).

Curme, George O., *A Grammar of the English Language,* Vol. I, *Parts of Speech,* Vol. II, *Syntax* (Essex, Conn.: Verbatim, 1993).

Evans, Bergen, and Cornelia Evans, *A Dictionary of Contemporary American Usage* (New York: Random House, 1957).

Fowler, H. W., *A Dictionary of Modern English Usage* (Oxford: Clarendon Press, 1927). Also, 2nd ed., revised by Sir Ernest Gowers (Oxford: Clarendon Press, 1965). Also, 3rd ed., edited by R. W. Burchfield and published as *The New Fowler's Modern English Usage* (Oxford: Clarendon Press, 1996).

Garner, Bryan A., *Garner's Modern American Usage* (New York: Oxford University Press, 2003).

Greenbaum, Sidney, *The Oxford English Grammar* (New York: Oxford University Press, 1996).

Huddleston, Rodney, and Geoffrey J. Pullum, *The Cambridge Grammar of the English Language* (Cambridge: Cambridge University Press, 2005).

Jespersen, Otto, *Essentials of English Grammar* (Tuscaloosa and London: University of Alabama Press, 1994).

Kenyon, John Samuel, *American Pronunciation,* 10th ed. (Ann Arbor, Mich.: George Wahr, 1966).

Mencken, H. L., *The American Language: An Inquiry into the Development of English in the United States* (New York: Knopf, 1937).

Morris, William, and Mary Morris, *Harper Dictionary of Contemporary Usage* (New York: Harper & Row, 1975).

Pinker, Steven, *The Language Instinct* (New York: Morrow, 1994).

Pyles, Thomas, and John Algeo, *The Origins and Development of the English Language,* 4th ed. (Fort Worth: Harcourt Brace Jovanovich, 1993).

Rawson, Hugh. *Devious Derivations: Popular Misconceptions—and More Than 1,000 True Origins of Common Words and Phrases* (Edison, N.J.: Castle Books, 2002).

———, *Wicked Words* (New York: Crown, 1989).

Shapiro, Fred R., ed., *The Yale Book of Quotations* (New Haven and London: Yale University Press, 2006).

ACKNOWLEDGMENTS

The world would stand still if it weren't for librarians. We're grateful to one in particular, Fred R. Shapiro of the Yale Law School, not only for answering emails but for producing *The Yale Book of Quotations,* an invaluable resource. We also owe a debt of gratitude to the entire staff of the New York Public Library; to Gloria Urban and her crew in Vineland, New Jersey; to Valerie G. Annis and her colleagues in Roxbury, Connecticut; to Jeffrey T. Phillips in Chestertown, Maryland; to Carolyn Warren of the microfilm department at the St. Louis Public Library; and to the librarians at the Hackley School in Tarrytown, New York, and the Taft School in Woodbury, Connecticut.

Professor Gerald Lalonde of Grinnell College was tireless in answering questions about classical Greek and devoted hours of his time at the American School in Athens to tracking down and translating obscure references. Officials at the Greek Embassy in Washington were helpful in explaining modern Greek. For fielding queries about French (or not-so-French) idioms, we're grateful to Marc Naimark in Paris, to Denis Niez in Connecticut, and to Arnaud Constans and Charlotte Ranelli at the French Consulate in New York.

Isabel Cymerman, a genealogist in New York and Connecticut, was invaluable in providing historical background about procedures at Ellis Island and the paper trail created by the immigration process. She also led us to another significant source, Marian Smith, senior historian for the United States Citizenship and Immigration Services in Washington (formerly the INS). Many thanks to both of you.

William Hamilton suggested we check out the mythological origins of the expression "rule of thumb" and led us to several scholarly sources. Florenz Eisman tipped us off to the origins of "jeep." Leigh Fellner, a quilt historian, kindly provided information about quilting patterns, fabrics, and techniques, as well as about the misinformation and dubious scholarship that have linked slave quilts with secret codes.

The linguists Geoffrey J. Pullum, Arnold Zwicky, and Jennifer Dailey-O'Cain provided interesting insights into the use of the quotative "like" when Pat wrote about it for *The New York Times Magazine,* and Calvin Trillin later shared with us his delightful essay on the subject. (As a result we're like, "Hey, thanks!") Tim Gray at *Variety* offered helpful advice about show-biz slang in general and "flack" in particular. Wes Pedersen, the publicists' publicist, formerly of the Public Affairs Council in Washington, was also helpful with "flack." Michael Barson, an author and a connoisseur of the Marx Brothers, shared some Groucho lore. Michael Sniffen's knowledge of St. Louis baseball history came in handy when he kindly reviewed our account of Dizzy Dean and "ain't." (He pointed out that the Browns and the Cardinals couldn't have been crosstown rivals in the forties because they occupied the same stadium.)

Leonard Lopate, his staff at WNYC, and scores of radio listeners came up with ideas, suggestions, and questions about many of the topics we've addressed here. We're also indebted to Rob Franciosi and JoEllyn Clarey for advice about research, and to many other friends for help, for support, and for simply putting up with us.

All true language sleuths are indebted to the research of Barry Popik, Gerald L. Cohen, Mark Liberman, Sam Clements, Michael Quinion, Benjamin G. Zimmer, and Hugh Rawson. To the lexicographers and authors whose works are mentioned in the notes and bibliography, thanks to one and all, and apologies to anyone we've overlooked.

Dan Green, to whom we've dedicated this book, suggested dozens of improvements in its organization and content, and we couldn't have a better agent. He also gave the book a boost by placing it with two particularly gifted and sensitive editors, Daniel Menaker and Judy Sternlight, who have been a joy to work with. We owe thanks to many others at Random House as well, particularly Millicent Bennett, Jennifer Huwer, Lea Beresford, Vincent La Scala, and Holly Webber, whose gracious help has been the icing on the cake.

INDEX

PATRICIA T. O'CONNER, a former editor at *The New York Times Book Review,* has written for many magazines and newspapers and is a well-known commentator online and on the air. She is the author of four books on language and writing: the bestselling *Woe Is I* and *Words Fail Me,* as well as *Woe Is I Jr.* and, with Stewart Kellerman, *You Send Me.*

STEWART KELLERMAN has been an editor at *The New York Times* and a foreign correspondent for United Press International in Asia, Latin America, and the Middle East. He reported on the Vietnam and Arab-Israeli wars for UPI, and has written frequently on literary topics for the *Times.* He co-authored *You Send Me,* a book about writing in the Internet age, and he runs the authors' popular website and blog.

Check out their website: Grammarphobia.com.